Studies in Empirical Economics

Robin Boadway · Baldev Raj
Editors

Advances in Public Economics

With 4 Figures
and 42 Tables

Physica-Verlag
A Springer-Verlag Company

First published in "Empirical Economics"
Volume 24, Issue 4, 1999

ISBN 3-7908-1283-8 Physica-Verlag Heidelberg, New York

Cataloging-in-Publication Data applied for
Die Deutsche Bibliothek – CIP-Einheitsaufnahme
Advances in public economics: with 42 tables / Robin Boadway; Baldev Raj (eds.).
– Heidelberg; New York: Physica-Verl., 2000
  (Studies in empirical economics)
  ISBN 3-7908-1283-8

Physica-Verlag is a company in the specialist publishing group BertelsmannSpringer.
© Physica-Verlag Heidelberg 2000
Printed in Germany

Cover design: Erich Kirchner, Heidelberg

SPIN 10759279   88/2202-5 4 3 2 1 0 – Printed on acid-free paper

Preface

This book is a collection of eight papers that were published in a special symposium issue of Empirical Economics during 1999. These papers cover several areas of interest in contemporary public economics, including tax incidence, underground economy, welfare system, fiscal federalism, public infrastructure and the growth of government. The contributions utilize a variety of quantitative tools of analysis, including applied econometrics, applied general equilibrium modeling analysis, technical efficiency analysis and institutional analysis. The introductory essay in the book summarizes the contributions of applied public economics papers in this book and places them in a broader context of modern public finance economic theory. The objective of the book is to make these essays available in a convenient form to scholars and students engaged in research on public policy topics as well as to instructors of courses in public economics, both undergraduate and graduate. A brief motivation for the book is given below.

The study of public economics has experienced a number of dramatic changes during the past two decades. These changes have revolutionized, in a fundamental way, the subject of public economics. This is due largely to several major developments in economic theory, including the roles of information theory and game theory along with its derivative theories, such as design of institutions as well as inter-temporal analysis. These economic theory developments have altered in a fundamental way the way economists and policy analysts perceive the role of government. Also these developments have called into question the ability of governments to carry out some of its traditional tasks, particularly the efficient design of redistribution and tax systems. The theoretical research in public economics has contributed to the development of new instruments and approaches to tackle problems of economic policy in a more effective manner. Given that the evaluation of policy options requires a sound understanding of both the nature and magnitude of economic, behavioural and institutional constraints that are faced by governments, there is a need for empirical analysis of underlying policy questions and issues.

This collection of essays on empirical finance indicates that empirical assessment is possible using a rich and diverse set of empirical approaches. The various papers exemplify some of the various techniques that can be used by applied researchers for shedding light on the questions of interest in applied public finance and its applications.

The editors are grateful to the contributing authors for their contributions, and to the reviewers of the papers in Empirical Economics for their timely and insightful comments. The names of the authors are listed in the table of contents and the names of reviewers, along with their affiliations, are listed in section 4 of the introductory essay. Also, the editors extend special thanks to Werner A. Mueller (Executive Economics Editor, Physica-Verlag) and Scott Carson (Dean of the School of Business and Economics, Wilfrid Laurier University) for their encouragement and support for this project.

Robin Boadway
Baldev Raj

Contents

V   Optimality of the public capital stock

I Introduction and overview

Contemporary public economics

Robin Boadway[1], Baldev Raj[2]*

[1]Department of Economics, Queen's University, Kingston, ON K7L 3N6
(e-mail: boadwayr@qed.econ.queensu.ca)
[2]Department of Economics, Wilfrid Laurier University, Waterloo,
ON N2L 3C5, (e-mail: braj@wlu.ca)

Abstract. This chapter provides an overview of reasons for and nature of dramatic changes that have taken place in public economics in the past few decades. It gives a brief account of innovations in public economics that have taken place in large part due to developments in economic theory. It is argued that ideas and tools of information theory and game theory have significantly altered the theory and practice of public economics. Developments in the public choice theory and inter temporal analysis also had far reaching impact on way in which economists think about public economics issues and design public policy. These theoretical developments in turn have implications for empirical analysis. The subsequent eight chapters in this book reflect some of these implications. They cover topics such as the targeting of income transfers to the disabled, the control of tax evasion, the efficiency of government, the tendency of the political process to be benevolent towards the electorate, and the role of government in fostering economic growth.

* This project is supported in part by Physica-Verlag Heidelberg, Germany, Queen's University Kingston, Canada, CIRANO, and C.R.D.E., Montreal, Quebec, Canada, and Wilfrid Lauier University, Waterloo, Ontario, Canada.

1. Background and motivation

Like most other fields of economics, public finance, or *public economics* as it is now called, has undergone dramatic changes in the past two decades. Major developments in economic theory, such as the role of information in economic analysis,[1] the almost universal use of simple game theory, the incorporation of institutional constraints into economic models[2] and the role of inter-temporal analysis, have revolutionized economic reasoning. The application of these innovations to public economics has changed the way we view the role of government. On the one hand, the constraints of information and institutions have called into question the ability of the government to carry out some of its traditional tasks. Such tasks include the provision of public services, redistributing income, providing social security, regulating the use of common resources, and finding remedies for negative externalities of air pollution. On the other, it has led to new, sometimes non-standard, instruments and approaches for dealing with the problem of economic policy. These instruments include the use of quantity and price controls and in-kind transfers for redistributive purposes as adjuncts to the standard tax-transfer system, or the use of principal-agent analysis to guide the design of regulatory systems in areas such as government contracting, environmental policy and the management of natural resources.[3]

In the design of a public policy, policymakers face a further problem besides that of imperfect information. They inevitably have to balance two objectives: efficiency and equity. Economic policy debates concerning, say, the tax-transfer system often tend to be dominated by discussions about fairness of the system, although economists tend to focus on the efficiency aspects primarily. The two goals of efficiency and equity generally conflict and economics alone may not provide unambiguous guidance in finding a best way to balance these conflicting objections. The issues involve public economics as well as political philosophy. One way to resolve the conflict between these goals is to let the political process determine the weights for each goal. In the meantime, economic analysis can be useful in terms of informing the political process as to the most efficient ways of achieving given re-distributive goals. Put more technically, much of modern public economic analysis is concerned with designing policies so as to expand the second-best utility possibilities

---

[1] The relevance of information to economic theory as well as to is summarized in Dixit and Besley (1997) in their testimonial to the awarding of the Nobel Memorial Prize in Economics to James Mirrlees. The implications for public economics are discussed in Boadway (1997).

[2] A recent summary of the issues involved in taking organizational considerations into account may be found in Tirole (1994). The classic work on bureaucracy is by Niskanen (1994). There is also a large literature on public choice, which focuses on the constraints imposed on governments by the political process. The standard reference work on this is Mueller (1994). See also Inman (1985). Surveys of the more recent literature may be found in Dixit (1996) and Persson and Tabellini (1999).

[3] The classic reference on the application of principal-agent analysis to public policy issues is Laffont and Tirole (1993). For an application to environmental externalities, see Laffont and Tirole (1996).

frontier out as far as possible. This leaves it to the political process to determine the preferred point along that frontier.

While these innovations in economic theory have directly affected analytical approaches to public economic issues, they also feed back to the empirical investigation of these issues. It is the purpose of this book to present a series of empirical studies that are representative of the current empirical approaches to public finance and that reflect current analytical approaches. This introductory overview is intended to place these empirical applications in context by summarizing some of the issues in modern public economic theory.

2. Innovations in public economics

Modern public economics owes much to the rich synthesis formulated by Musgrave's (1959) classic. His trichotomy between the efficiency, distribution and stabilization functions of government still applies. Modern theory has enhanced our understanding of how governments may pursue these functions, as well as how the three functions are intertwined. Four strands of theoretical innovations in particular have been very influential in informing public economics research – the economics of information, game theory, institutional economics, and inter-temporal economics. Consider these briefly in turn.

Imperfect information

Information, or the absence of it, is particularly important for government policy. Indeed, the lack of perfect information is now viewed as being the major constraint facing governments in the design and implementation of policies for improving market outcomes.[4] Governments are neither perfectly well informed about the needs, preferences and activities of its citizens; nor can they monitor and therefore control the performance of their own agencies. The implications of this are profound. Besides limiting severely the ability of the government to implement first-best policies, it also accounts for the widespread use of policy instruments that traditional economics would have dismissed out of hand.

Take redistribution policy as an example. Despite the emphasis traditionally placed on the tax-transfer system, much important redistribution takes place outside the progressive income tax-transfer system. Instead, substantial reliance is placed on non-standard policy instruments such as in-kind transfers (e.g., education, welfare services, public housing, etc.), price controls (e.g., minimum wages, rent controls, etc.) or mandates (e.g., compulsory saving for retirement, mandatory education, etc.). Moreover, even when cash transfers are the policy of choice, they are often delivered outside the income tax system by welfare agencies that employ social workers to monitor welfare recipients for need and eligibility. The reason for this state of affairs is that governments are not well informed about exactly who is deserving of transfers. Income alone (which itself cannot be perfectly observed) is not a good indicator of need since it is partly under the control of potential recipients.

---

[4] The role of information limitations for government policy with special emphasis on its implications for redistributive policy is outlined in Boadway (1997).

There is a growing literature that supports the use of these non-traditional instruments as ways of helping the government sort out the needy from the non-needy.[5] In-kind transfers and quantity controls allow government to target needy households more effectively than straight income transfers. For example, those who take up government provided services often self-select according to need. Minimum wage laws can assist governments in identifying those with limited productive capacities. The existence of this myriad of ways that governments actually accomplish redistributive objectives naturally lends itself to the empirical study of effects of such policies on market outcomes and income distribution.[6]

Imperfect information also accounts for the vast array of social insurance programs that are delivered publicly rather than by private insurers. Examples include health and disability insurance and unemployment insurance. The delivery of redistribution is typically through public agencies whose task is precisely to uncover information about recipients that can be used to determine eligibility and target transfers to those in need. This has led economists to focus research on the effectiveness of alternative policy instruments as well as mechanisms for delivering public services, including those for the needy. Information uncertainty impinges on the design of public service delivery in two main ways. One the one hand, target groups for public services must sometimes be identified for eligibility rather than relying on voluntary take-up. Thus, eligibility for welfare and unemployment insurance is determined by monitoring applicants for need, disability, employment status, and job search activities. Only by engaging in costly monitoring can the services be delivered cost-effectively.[7] Second, the need to monitor places those who do the monitoring in a privileged position. The information they obtain is private to them and those being monitored. This raises a classic agency problem between the government and those delivering the public services and agency problem that can be addressed by the application of modern contract theory.[8] One response to these problems of information in the delivery of services is to decentralize the responsibility to lower levels of government. Indeed, much of the impetus for the current drive for decentralization worldwide is a result of the recognition of information problems.

In a parallel fashion, the inability of governments to perfectly observe the activities inside firms precludes it from using simple Pigouvian tax-subsidy policies to control externalities. Instead, quantity controls, accompanied by more or less elaborate policing activities, provide a second-best, but more efficient form of policy in a world of imperfect information. Similar comments can be applied to competition or anti-trust policies, to product and labour mar-

---

[5] Examples include Besley and Coate (1992) for the case of workfare, Marceau and Boadway (1994) for the minimum wage and Boadway and Cuff (1999), and Boadway and Marchand (1995) and Blomquist and Christiansen (1995) for in-kind transfers. The general case for these non-standard instruments was first pointed out in Nichols and Zeckhauser (1982). For a recent survey, see Boadway and Keen (1999).

[6] For a recent collection of studies of the distributive effects of public spending programs, see van de Walle and Nead (1995).

[7] For an analysis of the effects of monitoring on the effectiveness of transfers, see Boadway and Cuff (1999).

[8] For an analysis of this, see Boadway, Marceau and Sato (1999).

ket safety regulation, to innovation policy, and to the enforcement of laws, including the reporting of one's income.[9] All these policy areas are plagued by incomplete information being available to government.

Game theory

The contribution of game theory has at the same time highlighted the importance of strategic aspects of government behaviour, and of the relationships of governments to each other as well as to agents in the economy. Consider first the relationship of government to its citizens. In modeling government behaviour, it is important to know whether governments have first-mover advantage over agents in the economy or not, that is, whether they can commit to their policies before agents in the economy make their decisions. For example, if decisions of households or firms are of a longer-term nature than government policy decisions, policies can often do more harm than good. This is the well known problem of *time inconsistency* whereby well-meaning governments end up taking actions after irreversible decisions of firms or households have been made which exploit the fact of irreversibility.[10] For example, consider the problem of saving and capital accumulation. Capital investment is a long-term decision. Once in place, it becomes fixed and a ready object for taxation. Well-meaning governments that would prefer not to impose a high tax rate on capital before investment decisions have been undertaken will not be so reluctant once capital has been accumulated. Anticipating this in advance, firms will be precluded from investing, leading to sub-optimal outcomes. The problem of time inconsistency and the adverse effect it has on decisions of a long term nature leads many economists to argue in favour of constraining the size of government by constitutional means or by subjecting it to forms of competition. Its relevance is further enhanced by the growing recognition of the importance of policies for long-run economic growth.

The problem of time inconsistency can also explain some forms of government intervention in social insurance and redistribution. Mandatory saving for retirement, education or insurance purchases can reduce dependence on government and help overcome the so-called Samaritan's Dilemma problem whereby the anticipation of government assistance in the event of adversity reduces the incentive to avoid the adversity occurring. It is widely accepted that individuals, especially those at the lower end of the income scale, systematically save too little for their own retirement. A plausible explanation for this is that they are super-rational: they recognize that the government will provide for them in retirement. One sensible policy response for the Samaritan's Dilemma is to mandate individual saving for retirement, a feature of most industrialized economies.[11]

Simple game theory has also been at the heart of the growing literature on inter-governmental fiscal competition. The essence of this literature is that, as

---

[9] For an overview of various issues relating to recent issues of antitrust enforcement of the US antitrust system and analysis of trend s, see Lin, Raj, Sanford and Slotttje (1999).

[10] A useful summary of the problems that time inconsistency raises for public economics may be found in Persson and Tabellini (1990).

[11] An analysis of this phenomenon may be found in Coate (1995) for the case of public insurance.

in oligopoly situations, decision-makers – here governments – are 'large', so strategic considerations become important in analyzing their decisions and their interactions. Thus, lower-level governments in a federation (or economic union) are typically modeled as engaging in a non-cooperative game in policies. The solution to this non-cooperative game is a Nash equilibrium in which government decisions are non-optimal. For example, if tax bases are mobile among jurisdictions, governments will compete for the tax base and set their tax rates too low. Or, if there is a central government as well, lower-level governments will neglect the effect that their tax policies have on the central government's tax base, leading to excessive tax rates. This literature is rich in empirical implications, which have only just begun to be investigated [12]

Public choice

In recent years public economists have been turning their attention to constraints on public policy imposed by the political process. Public choice theory emphasizes the fact that governments in democracies must get elected.[13] On the one hand, the need to win votes may induce governments to enact policies that cater to the wishes of the electorate. Indeed, the logic of maximizing votes leads some economists to argue that the outcome of public choice must be Pareto efficient policies: otherwise, more votes could be won by Pareto improvements in policies.[14] On the other, efficiency may fail because of imperfect information. That is, electorates may not be perfectly well informed about the government, so that there is no assurance that governments are acting entirely in the interests of the citizens they are supposed to serve. Public policy failures can also occur because of self-serving activities of the interest groups as part of the political process or because of inadequate incentives in the public service or a combination of the two. [15]

An important consideration is whether those in the political process are benevolent public servants who go into public life to further the good of society, or whether they are self-serving individualists whose objective is solely personal welfare and gratification. Much of the public choice literature is premised on the latter assumption, a lineage that goes back to the seminal works of Downs (1957) and Buchanan and Tullock (1962).[16] But more recent work on

---

[12] The interactions between governments at the same level or at different levels, which give rise to fiscal externalities between governments, have been nicely summarized in Dahlby (1996). For an example of an empirical analysis of the fiscal interaction between governments, see Besley and Rosen (1998).

[13] A comprehensive survey of public choice theory may be found in Mueller (1989).

[14] An example of this approach may be found in Hettich and Winer (1999).

[15] The evaluation of public policy in the presence of public policy failures is important not only in public economics but also in labour economics. Some recent contributions on this and other empirical topics on income inequality, poverty and welfare economics can be found in Slottje and Raj (1997).

[16] In these earlier works, politicians were largely passive vote-maximizers. More recent work has stressed the possibility that those who choose to be politicians must self-select, and that self-interest, along with electability, is the basis for the self-selection. These are the so-called citizen candidate models formulated by Osborne and Sliwinski (1996) and Besley and Coate (1997).

political economy allows for politicians to care not only about votes, but also about an ideology.[17]

The literature on public choice is very much an evolving field. There appears to be no consensus about the precise nature of the political process – that is the extent to which politicians are either self-serving or benevolent or motivated to maximize votes as opposed to ideology or subject to the influence of pressure groups. Similarly, it is unclear whether they are either passive or provide leadership in formulating policies. It is very much an empirical issue. It has implications not only for the constraints that policy makers face but also for the design of institutions. For example, if politicians really have Leviathan tendencies, various institutional and constitutional constraints (e.g., decentralization of powers) can be contemplated that limit the ability of politicians to exercise their powers.

Inter-temporal economics

Economic policy issues are inherently dynamic and that has long been recognized. But in recent years, dynamic issues have been given new impetus by two new developments in inter-temporal analysis. The first is the advent of *endogenous growth theory*, which postulates among other things that the growth process is characterized by inherent externalities.[18] Investments of various sorts – in real capital, in R&D, in human capital and in public sector infrastructure – have effects that spread beyond those engaging in the investment. Capital and R&D investment leads to innovation that increases the rate of growth and whose fruits are not fully appropriated by investors. Human capital investment increases skills and learning that are transmitted to others. And infrastructure investment cause higher productivity in the private sector.[19] These externalities lend themselves both to policy intervention and to attempts to estimate empirically the strength of such effects.

The second area is the development of the *overlapping generations* (OLG) *model* of growth, whose focus was on the consequences of policies for different age cohorts. The OLG model has proven especially useful in public economics as a devise for evaluating the key policy issues of the 1990's – the tax treatment of capital income, debt policy and public pensions. The advent of powerful computing capacity has enabled sophisticated OLG models to be used to simulate realistic policy options.[20] And, out of this has sprung the concept of *generational accounting*, which is a device for assigning benefits and costs of long-run policies to various age cohorts.[21] This has the potential to inform the policy process in a much more satisfactory way than standard annual budgets.

---

[17] See, for example, Dixit and Londregan (1998) and Roemer (1999).

[18] The new growth theory, which is to some an extent a rediscovery of some of the results of the 1960's growth literature, was initiated by Lucas (1988) and Romer (1986). A comprehensive summary can be found in Aghion and Howitt (1998).

[19] For recent contributions on the role of infrastructure for economic development in relation to transportation, see Gillen and Walter II (1996).

[20] One of the first comprehensive approaches to simulating policy options using OLG models may be found in Auerbach and Kotlikoff (1987).

[21] For a full discussion of generational accounting, see Kotlikoff (1992).

As mentioned in Section 1, all these innovations have led us to re-evaluate the role of government in the economy. Given that the asymmetric information problems plague the public sector just like the private one and that processes of public choice may be far from perfect, considerable agnosticism has developed about the ability of the public sector to improve significantly on the efficiency with which the private sector allocates resources. At the same time, the problems of information have also led to a fruitful search for more efficient ways to deliver policies as compared to those that came out of the old welfare economics. Moreover, arguments for major institutional changes in the ways in which public services were delivered have been solidified. These include suggestions for more decentralized provision of public services, a universal call for de-regulation and privatization, and more reliance on contracting out to the private sector or public-private partnerships. These sorts of policy initiatives have been the hallmarks of the late twentieth century, and all owe a great deal to advances in public economic reasoning.

This book is concerned with the consequences for empirical analysis of the new public economics. Many of these aspects of the new public economics are reflected in the papers in this monograph. The papers include the importance of the targeting of income transfers to the disabled, the control of tax evasion, which is explicitly an information problem, the efficiency of government, the tendency or otherwise of the political process to be benevolent towards the electorate, and the role of government in fostering economic growth. Let us now turn to the empirical relevance of the new approaches to public economics.

3.   Some contemporary empirical public finance issues

Understanding the importance of the economic behavioral and institutional constraints facing government is critical for evaluating policy options. This is ultimately an empirical issue. The purpose of this monograph on empirical public finance has been to indicate the richness and diversity of empirical approaches that have been used to shed light on the problems of applied public finance and its applications. We have included eight papers in this book besides the section on introduction and overview, which address a variety of problems in empirical public finance in a variety of countries and reflect the breadth of approaches that are used. These papers are grouped into four themes: (i) Economics of Public Programs; (ii) Tax Leakages and Efficiency; (iii) Do Governments Act in the Interest of their Constituents?; (iv) Optimality of the Public Capital Stock and Adequacy of Public Capital. A brief overview of the papers on these four themes is provided below:

4. Overview of papers

4.1 Economics of public programs

Much of what governments actually do is redistributive in nature, ranging from the tax-transfer system to social insurance schemes to the provision of public services. Many major social programs introduced in the early postwar period were universal in nature. As such, they were both very expensive and were not very effective at reaching those most in need. In recent years, encouraged by theoretical advances in redistributive theory in the wake of the optimal income tax literature, the emphasis has been on replacing universal programs with those that target transfers to those most in need. The paper by Robert Haveman, Karen Holden, Barbara Wolfe, Paul Smith and Kathryn Wilson provides some well-documented evidence of the importance of targeting. They show how successful, or unsuccessful, Social Security Disability Insurance has been at meeting the needs of workers with disabilities in the United States. They argue convincingly that disabled men, especially those who were disabled early in life, are much less well-off than their nondisabled counterparts.

The extent of redistribution is also the topic of the paper by Keshab Bhattarai and John Whalley. Their interest is in estimates of the incidence of the tax system, most of which rely on some form of general equilibrium (GE) analysis. Detailed analyses of this form are much more readily available nowadays with the advances in computer technology and the improvement in data sources. The results of these analyses depend very much on the specifics of the GE models used. Until now, most GE models have assumed that labour services are homogeneous. This, combined with a full employment assumption, effectively means that the demand for labour is perfectly elastic, so that incidence depends only on the supply side. Bhattarai and Whalley show that when different classes of labour are imperfect substitutes so that demand elasticities become finite, incidence estimates can change significantly.

4.2 Tax leakages and efficiency

Taxes can have many effects besides redistributive ones. As tax rates have become higher and higher, a major concern has been the extent to which households and firms are driven into the underground economy to avoid/evade taxes. One of the problems with determining the size of the underground economy is that it is by definition not included in reported statistics. David Giles uses an innovative latent variable method of estimating the size and determinants of the underground economy and applies it to New Zealand. The method relies on the demand for money depending separately on the sizes of the legitimate and underground economies, with the latter in turn depending on a number of variables including tax ones. This enables him not only to estimate the size of the underground economy, but also how this is affected by taxes, and how much is lost in uncollected tax revenues as a result of the underground economy.

There are other leakages from the tax system besides underground economy activities. Governments can be more or less efficient at collecting taxes, and their efficiency can be affected by incentives facing them. Raghbendra Jha, M.S. Mohanty, Somnath Chatterjee and Puneet Chitkara draw on techniques of estimating production frontiers to estimate the efficiency of tax collection among the diverse states of India. They show how tax efficiency varies across states and how it is affected by the extent to which they rely on grants from the central government. Their evidence suggests that tax efficiency could be improved by putting more emphasis on tax effort as a determinant of the size of grants.

4.3 Do governments act in the interest of their constituents?

A more general question about tax collections concerns the determinants of the amount of taxes that governments choose to collect. Do governments act in the interests of their constituents, or are they driven by other motives, including the their own self interests? The answer to this question is important for determining both the extent to which governments should be relied on to deliver policies, and whether explicit constraints should be imposed on them. Steven Sheffrin considers the issue of whether structural changes in the tax system can affect the growth of government in and of themselves. For example, some have argued that the more efficient and broad-based the tax system, the easier it is for governments to extract revenues, and the more revenues will they extract. He compares methods for determining the connection between tax structures and the growth of government and concludes that time series analysis by itself will not be sufficient to determine the causal link. Institutional considerations are bound to be important as well.

Takero Doi, on the other hand, presents evidence that policy makers in Japan do take account of the interests of the median voter when selecting levels of provision of local public goods. Japanese prefectures do provide the services preferred by the median voter despite the fact that the prefectures themselves have limited discretion compared with the central government. He shows that the desires of the local residents are effectively transmitted by the election of governors of prefectures. In particular, re-election is more likely the closer is the level of public goods to that desired by the median voter.

4.4 Optimality of public capital stocks and adequacy of public capital

In a paper on a related issue, Jiro Nemoto, Kimiyoshi Kamada and Makoto Kawamura analyze the extent to which public capital stocks conform to their optimal level. Optimality in this context entails rates of return on public capital which equal the appropriate weighted-average discount rate. The authors show that, despite the worldwide rhetoric about the size of governments being excessive, public capital stocks in Japan were sub-optimal in the two decades following 1960. They did, however, moved closer to the optimal size over the period.

Raymond Batina updates earlier estimates of the affect of public capital, such as infrastructure investment, using revised public capital data, an array of proxies for labour and private capital and, dynamic least squares estimation on economic growth and development.[22] The main conclusion of the paper is that public capital has some impact, but significantly less than provided in an earlier study by Aschauer (1989). As mentioned earlier, these papers provide a wide sampling of the kind of empirical public finance that should shed light on important public policy design issues. We are grateful to our contributors for allowing us to include them in this symposium.

5. Acknowledgments

We are not only grateful to the contributors to this special issue for allowing us to include their papers in the symposium but also to the reviewers of the papers. We also wish to express sincere appreciation to the referees for their invaluable input to the editorial process. Their help with the review process is greatly appreciated. The names of the referees and their affiliations are listed below in alphabetical order:

J.T. Araujo, World Bank --EDIMP
C.M. Beach, Queen's University, Canada
D.K. Bhattacharyya, University of Leicester, England
T. Bogart, Case Western University, USA
D.F. Burgess, University of Western Ontario, Canada
R.V. Burkhauser, Syracuse University, USA
B. Dahlby, University of Alberta, Canada
J.E. Dinardo, University of California, Irvine, USA
B. Frey, University of Zurich, Switzerland
J.R. Hines Jr., University of Michigan, USA
S.C. Kumbhakar, University of Texas at Austin, USA
C.A. Knox Lovell, University of Georgia, USA
A. Munnell, Boston College, USA
A.L. Robb, McMaster University, Canada
G.C. Ruggeri, University of New Brunswick, Canada
G. Saxonhouse, University of Michigan, USA
D.J. Smyth, Middlesex University Business School, UK
W.F. Stine, Clarion University, PA, USA
E. Toder, Cabin John, Maryland USA
G. Turnbull, Louisiana State University, USA
F. Vaillancourt, University of Montreal, Canada
M. Veall, McMaster University, Canada
W. Veloce, Brock University, Canada
J.-F. Wen, Wilfrid Laurier University, Canada
D.E. Wildasin, Vanderbilt University, USA
T. Wirjanto, University of Waterloo, Canada
G.W. Yohe, Wesleyan University, USA

---

[22] A comprehensive discussion of other empirical issues relating to the old and new economic growth theories may be found in Durlauf, Helliwell and Raj (1996).

We further express appreciation to Werner A. Müller from Physica-Verlag, the co-editors of Empirical Economics, and Dr. Scott Carson, School of Business and Economics, Wilfrid Laurier University, Waterloo, Ontario, Canada for their support. Ms Carolyn Holden provided the editorial and secretarial assistance for the project. We remain indebted to the authors, referees, funding agencies and the support staff without whose help this project could not have been completed.

6. Conclusion

In this essay a brief review of the nature of and reasons is provided for some of the dramatic changes that have taken place in public economics during the late twentieth century in the new public economics. These changes are the direct result of many significant changes that have taken place in economic theory in the areas of information theory and game theory on the one hand, and in the public choice theory and inter temporal theory on the other hand. The impact of these theoretical developments has been far reaching on both the theoretical modeling and practice of new public economics. Furthermore, all sorts of new policy initiatives have taken place, and they form the hallmark of these new approaches. These developments owe a great deal to the advances in public economic reasoning.

These developments have also implications for empirical analyses of public economics issues. Some of these aspects of new public economics are reflected in the subsequent eight chapters in this book. The chapter provides a summary account of the issues and answer to questions in the contemporary empirical public economics. These contributions are grouped into four parts in this book: economics of public programs, tax efficiency and leakage, the extent to which Governments act in the interest of their constituents, and optimality and adequacy of public capital stock.

References

Aghion P, Howitt P (1998) Endogenous growth theory. MIT Press, Cambridge, Mass.

Aschauer DA (1989) Is public expenditure productive? Journal of Monetary Economics 23: 177-200

Auerbach AJ, Kotlikoff LJ (1987) Dynamic fiscal policy. Cambridge University Press, Cambridge, U.K.

Besley T, Coate S (1992) Workfare versus welfare: incentive arguments for work requirements in poverty-alleviation programs. American Economic Review 82: 249-261

Besley T, Coate S (1997) An economic model of representative democracy. Quarterly Journal of Economics 112: 85-114

Besley T, Rosen H (1998) vertical externalities in tax setting: evidence from gasoline and cigarettes. Journal of Public Economics 70: 383-398

Blomquist S, Christiansen V (1995) Public provision of private goods as a redistributive device in an optimum income tax model. Scandinavian Journal of Economics 97: 547-567

Boadway R (1997) Public economics and the theory of public policy. Canadian Journal of Economics 30: 753-772

Boadway R, Cuff K (1999) Monitoring job search as an instrument for targeting transfers. International Tax and Public Finance (forthcoming)

Boadway R, Keen M (1999) Redistribution. In: Atkinson A B Bourguignon F (eds), Handbook of income distribution. Amsterdam, North-Holland (forthcoming)

Boadway R, Marchand M (1995) The use of public expenditures for redistributive purposes. Oxford Economic Papers 47: 45-59

Boadway R, Marceau N, Sato M (1999) Agency and the design of welfare systems. Journal of Public Economics 73: 1-30

Buchanan JM, Tullock G (1962) The calculus of consent. The University of Michigan Press, Ann Arbor, Michigan

Coate S (1995) Altruism, the samaritan's dilemma, and government transfer policy. American Economic Review 85: 46-57

Dahlby B (1996) Fiscal externalities and the design of intergovernmental grants. International Tax and Public Finance 3: 397-411

Dixit AK (1996) The making of economic policy. MIT Press, Cambridge, Mass.

Dixit AK, Besley T (1997) 'James Mirrlees' Contributions to the theory of information and incentives. Scandinavian Journal of Economics 99: 207-235

Dixit AK, Londregan J (1998) Ideology, tactics, and efficiency in redistributive politics. Quarterly Journal of Economics 113: 497-529

Downs A (1957) An economic theory of democracy. Harper and Row, New York

Durlauf S, Helliwell JF, Raj B (eds) (1996) Long-run economic growth. Special issue of Empirical Economics 21(1)

Gillen DW, Walter WG II (eds) (1996) Special issue on transport infrastructure investment and economic development. The Logistic and Transport Review 32(1)

Hettich W, Winer S (1999) Democratic choice and taxation: A theoretical and empirical analysis. Cambridge University Press, New York

Inman RP (1985) Markets, government and the new political economy. In: Auerbach A, Feldstein MS (eds) Handbook of public economics vol. 2, Amsterdam, North-Holland, pp 647-777

Kotlikoff LJ (1992) Generational accounting. The Free Press, New York

Laffont JJ, Tirole J (1993) A theory of incentives in procurement and regulation. MIT Press, Cambridge, Mass.

Laffont JJ, Tirole J (1996) Pollution permits and compliance strategies. Journal of Public Economics 62: 85-125

Lin P, Raj B, Sanford M, Slottje D (1999) The US antitrust system and recent trends in antitrust enforcement. Journal of Economic Surveys (forthcoming)

Lucas RE Jr (1988) On the mechanics of economic development. Journal of Monetary Economics 22: 3-42

Marceau N, Boadway RW (1994) Minimum wage legislation and unemployment insurance as instruments for redistribution. Scandinavian Journal of Economics 96: 67-81

Mueller D (1989) Public choice II. Cambridge University Press, Cambridge, U.K.

Musgrave RA (1959) The theory of public finance. McGraw-Hill, New York

Nichols AL, Zeckhauser RJ (1982) Targeting transfers through restrictions on recipients. American Economic Review 72: 372-377

Niskanen WA (1994) Bureaucracy and public economics. Edward Elgar, Aldershot, U.K.

Osborne MJ, Slivinski A (1996) A model of political competition with citizen-candidates. Quarterly Journal of Economics 111: 65-96

Persson T, Tabellini G (1990) Macroeconomic policy, credibility and politics. Harwood
   Academic Publishers, Chur, Switzerland
Persson T, Tabellini G (1999) Public economics and political economy. Handbook of public
   economics (forthcoming)
Roemer JE (1999) The democratic political economy of progressive income taxation.
   Econometrica 67: 1-19
Romer PM (1986) Increasing returns and long-run growth. Journal of Political Economy
   94: 1002-1037
Slottje DJ, Raj B (eds) (1997) Symposium on income, inequality, poverty, and economic
   welfare. Empirical Economics 22(1)
Tirole J (1994) The internal organization of government. Oxford Economic Papers 46: 1-
   29.
van de Walle D, Nead K (1995) Public spending and the poor: theory and evidence. Johns
   Hopkins University Press, Baltimore

II Economics of public programs

III Dynamics of public programs

The changing economic status of U.S. disabled men: Trends and their determinants, 1982–1991*

Robert Haveman[1], Karen Holden[2], Barbara Wolfe[3], Paul Smith[4], Kathryn Wilson[5]

[1] Department of Economics and La Follette Institute of Public Affairs, University of Wisconsin-Madison, 1180 Observatory Drive, Madison, WI 53706, USA (e-mail: haveman@lafollette.wisc.edu)
[2] La Follette Institute of Public Affairs and Department of Consumer Science, University of Wisconsin-Madison, 1180 Observatory Drive, Madison, WI 53706, USA (e-mail: holden@lafollette.wisc.edu)
[3] Department of Economics and Preventive Medicine, University of Wisconsin-Madison, 1180 Observatory Drive, Madison, WI 53706, USA (e-mail: wolfe@lafollette.wisc.edu)
[4] Office of Tax Analysis, U.S. Department of the Treasur, 1500 Pennsylvania Ave., NW, Washington, D.C. 20220, USA
[5] Department of Economics, Kent State University, 126 Lowry Hall, Kent Campus, Kent, Ohio 44242-0001, USA (e-mail: kwilson@bsa3.kent.edu)

First version received: May 1998/final version received: July 1999

Abstract. We track the level of economic well-being of the population of men who began receiving Social Security Disability Insurance benefits in 1980–81 from the time just after they became beneficiaries (in 1982) to 1991. We present measures of the economic well-being of disabled individuals and their nondisabled peers as indicators of the relative economic position of these two groups. These measures also provide an intertemporal comparison of well-being and hardship as disabled persons and their nondisabled peers age and retire. We first show several economic well-being indicators for new male recipients of disability benefits in 1982 and 1991. We then compare their economic position to that of a matched group of *non*disabled males with sufficient work histories to have been disability-insured. Because labor market changes over this decade have led to a relative deterioration in the position of younger and less-educated workers, we compare men with disabilities to those without disabilities and distinguish different age and educational levels within the groups. We conclude by assessing the antipoverty effectiveness of Social Security income support for both younger and older male SSDI recipients.

JEL classifications: H55, I12, I30

Key words: Disability, economic status, social security, poverty

---

* This research was partially supported by a grant from the Social Security Administration. Conclusions represent those of the authors alone and not of the funding agency. The authors gratefully acknowledge the help of John Wolf and Dawn Duren and the suggestions of two anonymous reviewers.

The past two decades have seen major changes in the work patterns of men in the United States, including increases in the pace of early retirement (Quinn, Burkhauser, and Myers 1990), the incidence of joblessness (especially among young workers with low educational attainment), and wage rate inequality among workers (Danziger and Gottschalk, 1995). Moreover, the earnings gap between younger and older workers has increased dramatically, as has that between low-skilled and high-skilled workers (Levy and Murnane, 1992). These changed labor market patterns have long-term consequences for men with work-limiting disabilities.

Labor market opportunities for workers with disabilities determine the advantage of continuing market work relative to receiving public transfer benefits.[1] In making this choice, disabled workers implicitly or explicitly assess their future trajectory of labor market opportunities and compare this with the trajectory of income flows should they receive disability benefits. This latter assessment also depends on expected labor market opportunities since Social Security disability benefits in the United States are tied both to the number of years worked and to earnings during working years. Hence, the decision to continue to work made at any wage will alter the trajectory of Social Security disability benefits received in the future.[2] Moreover, this work-continuation/benefit-recipiency decision faced by men with disabilities requires assessments of both options based on uncertain information about labor markets and public policy changes.

This work-continuation/benefit-recipiency assessment may differ substantially between younger and older workers with disabilities. For young workers with impairments, early receipt of U.S. Social Security Disability Insurance (SSDI) benefits means that they forgo any sharing in the standard earnings gain pattern over the life cycle, which gain will be experienced by most of their nondisabled peers.[3] On the other hand, for those young impaired workers with low schooling levels and few skills, SSDI benefits and the accompanying Medicare coverage may yield higher net income than does labor market work, in spite of the sacrifice of life-cycle earnings increases. Hence, for younger workers with health limitations, the decision to apply for SSDI benefits is likely to be taken by those with the poorest labor market prospects.

For older disabled workers, on the other hand, SSDI benefits may be a bridge to early retirement (Haveman, Warlick, and Wolfe, 1988; Berkowitz, 1997). Disabled workers who apply for and receive benefits before age 65 are not assessed an early retirement penalty, and the earnings averaging period is

---

[1] Although many individuals with disabilities have labor market opportunities, we recognize that many persons with severely limiting conditions will not. For a fuller discussion of the labor market choice of men with disabilities, see Haveman and Wolfe (1984), Leonard (1986), Bound (1989), and Haveman, de Jong, and Wolfe, (1991). In addition, both Bound and Burkhauser (forthcoming) and Haveman and Wolfe (forthcoming) survey the recent literature on the consequences of SSDI and other public transfer programs on the behavior and well-being of people with disabilities.

[2] This is also true for most employer-provided disability benefits as well, but is not true of Supplemental Security Income (SSI) benefits paid to low-income persons who are aged, blind, and disabled. The benefit amount in SSI is a fixed family-size-conditioned amount available to those who are eligible, having passed an income and assets means test.

[3] This is so because SSDI benefits are restricted to severely disabled workers; eligibility for benefits is forgone if earnings exceed a very low earnings limit ($500 per month).

truncated at their date of disablement.[4] In addition, SSDI may bring eligibility for Medicare at a younger age than 65, the age at which retired-worker beneficiaries become eligible for Medicare. Thus, older workers able to meet the Social Security disability criteria—which are somewhat relaxed at ages 50 and 55 (Ycas, 1996)—may assess early SSDI application as a better option than (1) later application for SSDI benefits or (2) delaying receipt (and, presumably, continuing to work) until becoming eligible for retired-worker benefits.

The differences in the nature of the work-continuation/benefit-recipiency choice between younger and older workers point to the importance of distinguishing younger and older SSDI recipients in assessing the relative economic status of the disabled. Because the trajectories of economic status of SSDI recipients compared to like-aged individuals without disabilities are likely to be quite different for younger and older cohorts, this distinction must also be made in assessing the effectiveness of SSDI benefits in maintaining the relative well-being of disabled workers over time.

In this paper, we track the level of economic well-being of the population of men who began receiving SSDI benefits in 1980–81 from the time just after they became beneficiaries (in 1982) to 1991, nearly a decade later. We present measures of the economic well-being of disabled individuals and their nondisabled peers as indicators of the relative economic position of these two groups. These measures also provide an intertemporal comparison of well-being and hardship as disabled persons and their nondisabled peers age and retire. We first show several economic well-being indicators for this group of new male recipients of disability benefits in 1982 and 1991.[5] Then, we compare their economic position to that of a matched group of *non*disabled males with sufficient work histories to have been disability-insured, that is, eligible for SSDI benefits had they been unable to engage in substantial gainful employment.[6]

---

[4] Application for SSDI between ages 62 and 64 eliminates the early retirement reduction that would otherwise be imposed for receipt of retired-worker benefits. Application before age 62 reduces the years over which covered earnings would otherwise be averaged. Social Security benefits are based on Average Indexed Monthly Earnings (AIME), which is equal to total indexed covered earnings averaged over the number of years between 1956 or age 25 (whichever is later) and age 62 or the year prior to disability. A worker who left covered work at age 55 would have an AIME calculated over a period that included 7 years of zero earnings and a benefit that was reduced by 20 percent. If the worker was able to qualify for disability at age 55, the averaging period would be reduced by those 7 years and no actuarial reduction would be imposed.

[5] The years 1982 and 1991 are chosen for analysis as information from one of the primary data sets used, the Social Security New Beneficiary Survey, contains information for only these years. In this survey, respondents were interviewed in 1982 and provided information for that year. These respondents were reinterviewed in 1991. (See the Appendix for more information on the data sets.) While macroeconomic conditions differed between these two years, our analysis compares the situation of disabled respondents with that of their nondisabled counterparts at the same two points in time. To the extent that the recession conditions in the early year could reduce earnings and income for the nondisabled comparison group relative to the disabled population, comparisons of changes in relative economic position across time should be interpreted with some caution.

[6] Eligibility for SSDI depends on (1) meeting the definition of disability: the inability to engage in substantial gainful activity by reason of "physical or mental impairment" that is expected to last at least a year or result in death, *and* (2) being eligible for Social Security (having at least 20 quarters of coverage or if younger than 31, having quarters equal to 50 percent of those since age 21). Once eligible, after a waiting period of 2 years, a person is eligible to receive Medicare coverage. For simplicity we use the term "population with disabilities" or "men with disabilities" in this analysis. However, the reader should keep in mind that we are limiting our discussion to those who meet both of these eligibility criteria and applied to receive benefits.

Because labor market changes over this decade have led to a relative deterioration in the position of younger and less-educated workers, we compare men with disabilities to those without disabilities and distinguish different age and educational levels within the groups. In studying these comparative trends in well-being, we focus on the prevalence of poverty and its correlates. We conclude by assessing the antipoverty effectiveness of Social Security income support for both younger and older men who became SSDI recipients in 1980–81.

I. Data and procedures

The 1982 U.S. Social Security Administration's New Beneficiary Survey (NBS) provides a reliable basis for studying the level and trend of economic well-being of U.S. men and women with severe disabilities.[7] However, because our primary sample consists of men who are SSDI beneficiaries at the time we first observe them, we cannot examine the economic forces associated with the onset of their work-limiting health condition, or the factors that led to their choosing SSDI beneficiary status over continued labor force participation. By employing another, longitudinal data set with information comparable to that included in the NBS—the Michigan Panel Study of Income Dynamics (PSID) —we are able to compare the economic status of SSDI beneficiaries over time with that of a sample of men without disabilities. These comparisons reveal the long-term differences in economic well-being between comparable groups of men with and without severe work-limiting disabilities, and hence the well-being consequences of the occurrence of such health conditions.

Consider first our NBS data on disabled men. The NBS surveyed a sample of individuals who first received U.S. Social Security benefits between June 1980 and June 1981 (Ycas, 1992). Surviving respondents and surviving spouses were resurveyed in 1991; 66.7 percent of the 1982 male disabled respondents were still alive in 1991, and 88.1 percent of them were reinterviewed.[8]

New male SSDI beneficiaries who were 20–65 when first interviewed in

---

[7] Because the male disabled population that qualifies for SSDI benefits is a subset—and by some estimates a minority—of the male working-age population with functional limitations, our results apply only to men with sufficient work histories to meet SSDI eligibility and whose work limitations are sufficiently severe to apply for and be approved for SSDI cash benefits. By limiting our analysis to the severely disabled SSDI recipients, we are excluding other men with substantial work limitations, such as those who only receive SSI and who are likely to have lower levels of economic well-being because SSDI benefits are not available to them.

[8] Those men who attrite from the sample are very similar to those who remain. There are no statistically significant differences in the means of the income variables for either an older or a younger disabled sample between those who continue in the sample until 1991 and those who attrite. For older men, those who attrite have lower poverty rates (13.5 percent versus 15.1 percent for those who remain), but the difference in average income is less than $40. For the younger sample, poverty rates are the same, but mean income for attritors is about $800 more than for those who continue in the sample, suggesting that the difference in income is at the higher income levels. A probit estimation of the likelihood of attriting supports the claim that those who attrite are similar to those who remain. Although the attritors have slightly higher education levels, the coefficient estimates on the income variables are not statistically significant. For further analysis of mortality in the NBS, see McCoy, Iams, and Armstrong (1994), who show that disabled men had generally stable death rates over this period, with probability of death not influenced by socioeconomic status among the disabled.

1982 and who were reinterviewed in 1991 constitute our primary sample.[9] To construct the nondisabled male comparison group, we use the PSID, from which we selected a sample of nondisabled men who in 1980 had a sufficient work history to gain SSDI benefits should they have experienced a serious work-limiting disability. Like the sample of SSDI recipients, these nondisabled men were aged 20–65 in 1982, the year corresponding to the NBS interview. We selected our nondisabled sample in 1980 since it was in that year that the NBS sample was first identified as sufficiently disabled to be eligible for SSDI benefits. The comparison sample consists of the 1991 survivors of this group.

We matched our samples of disabled and nondisabled men by calculating weights derived from the distribution of the NBS disabled male sample across cells defined by race, age, education, and marital status. When these weights are applied to the 1982 PSID nondisabled sample, these two groups of men have identical distributions of these labor market and demographic characteristics.[10] Our sample consists of 2,110 disabled men and 2,621 matched nondisabled men. The Appendix briefly describes the NBS and PSID data used in the analysis, and presents a detailed description of the selection and matching process.[11]

II. Male recipients of disability income transfers: A profile

Table 1 presents descriptive statistics for our (surviving) sample of disabled men in 1982 (after they first received SSDI benefits) and in 1991.[12] The average age of the men was 51.0 years, and they averaged only 10 years of schooling. About 17 percent of them were nonwhite, and just under three-fourths of this disabled group were married. They were not a well-to-do

---

[9] In a related paper (Haveman, Holden, Wolfe, Smith, and Wilson, forthcoming), we study levels and trends in relative well-being of women SSDI recipients. For earlier studies of the economic well-being of persons with disabilities, see Burkhauser, Haveman, and Wolfe (1993), Haveman and Wolfe (1990), Grad (1989), and Weaver (1997). The latter two studies focus on the economic well-being of recipients of various forms of Social Security benefits. See also Bound and Burkhauser (forthcoming) and Haveman and Wolfe (forthcoming).

[10] The matching cell weights applied to the PSID nondisabled comparison group in effect redistributes them across the relevant cells such that equal percentages of disabled (NBS) and nondisabled (PSID) men are included in each cell. Hence, the well-being patterns calculated for the population of nondisabled males reflects economic position for a sample of nondisabled males with the same 1982 labor market and demographic characteristics as the SSDI recipients.

[11] Although an SSDI beneficiary must be under age 64 at the time of application (in 1980–81 for this sample), by the 1982 interview some had reached age 65. Although the Social Security Administration administratively redefines disabled beneficiaries at age 65 as retired-workers, there is no change in benefit amount. Analytically, we continue these disabled in SSDI status.

[12] It should be noted that our analysis deals with 1982 SSDI beneficiaries who survived until 1991. If we, instead, had analyzed all of the 1982 beneficiaries (as opposed to those who survived until 1991), we would have found similar levels of well-being for the 1982 group, and similar levels of 1982 SSDI replacement benefits. This is so because the 1982 beneficiaries who did not survive until 1991 tend to not be different in terms of income compared to those who survived. Attritors and survivors do differ with regard to education: for each additional year of education, the chances of attrition increases by .9 percentage points among disabled workers. See Antonovics et al, 1999.

Table 1. Newly entitled male recipients of social security disability insurance benefits: 1982–1991

	All Men	1982		1991	
		< 55	55+	< 55	55+
Demographic characteristics					
Mean age (years)	51.0	41.0	60.0	49.5	68.5
Mean education (years)	9.9	10.5	9.4	10.5	9.4
% nonwhite	17.4%	20.0%	15.1%	20.0%	15.1%
% married	73.8%	63.1%	83.4%	61.2%	76.1%
Mean family size	2.4	2.6	2.1	2.1	1.9
% in South	39.2%	40.0%	38.5%	n.a	n.a
% in West	15.7%	16.2%	15.3%	n.a	n.a
% in Northeast	17.6%	15.9%	19.1%	n.a	n.a
Family income characteristics					
Mean total family income	$21,724	$19,430	$23,767	$19,157	$21,291
Mean income-to-needs ratio	2.13	1.84	2.39	1.98	2.26
% poor	20.9%	29.6%	13.2%	24.2%	9.9%
Families with transfer/pension income	95.7%	92.7%	98.4%	86.8%	99.7%
Families with earnings	36.4%	39.3%	33.8%	39.7%	17.8%
Disabled individuals with earnings	6.6%	10.2%	3.5%	14.5%	4.2%
Men with spouse earnings	31.8%	32.0%	31.6%	30.8%	15.1%
Families with asset income	50.8%	38.9%	61.3%	47.8%	63.9%
Mean family transfers plus pension					
income	$12,808	$10,540	$14,829	$9,602	$15,666
Mean family earnings	$5,449	$6,214	$4,767	$7,251	$2,218
Mean personal income	$13,374	$12,001	$14,597	$12,409	$13,271
Mean spouse income	$5,602	$5,273	$5,895	$5,555	$5,210
Mean asset income	$2,340	$1,497	$3,091	$1,142	$2,717

Notes: 1982 data are only for individuals still in the sample in 1991. Figures in 1994 dollars.

group; mean family income in 1982 (in 1994 dollars) was about $21,700.[13] In a year when 14 percent of all U.S. families were poor, 21 percent of the families of these male SSDI recipients lived in poverty.[14] The average ratio of their family income to the family-size-specific official U.S. poverty line was 2.1.[15] Only about 36 percent of the families of these disabled men reported any earnings by either the disabled male or his wife. Annual earned income (either the disabled man's own earned income or that of his wife, if married) averaged about $5,500 and accounted for one-quarter of total family income.

---

[13] The 1982 income of the male SSDI recipients is the extrapolation to 1 year of 3 months of income recorded after they began receiving SSDI benefits. Because the NBS collected income data consistently for only the disabled individual, his spouse (if married), and children under 18, we define the sum of the incomes of these individuals to be family income. Similarly, the sum of these individuals equals the size of the family of the disabled man.

[14] This reflects the official U.S. poverty measure, which compares the annual cash income of a family with a family-size-conditioned needs threshold (or poverty line). Those families with income below the relevant poverty line are classified as poor. Other indicators of poverty are also commonly applied in the U.S. context, including a comparison of a family's income with 1.5 times the relevant poverty line.

[15] This ratio is known in the literature as either the "family income-to-needs ratio," or the "welfare ratio"; we use the former term.

Not surprisingly for these male SSDI recipients, family transfer income (including Social Security benefits and retirement pensions) accounted for about 60 percent of family income, or an average of about $12,800. Finally, while half of the families of these men received income from assets, the average amount was small, accounting for 11 percent of their total income. On average, the disabled men contributed (from all income sources, including SSDI benefits) about 62 percent of aggregate income of their families. The low labor force participation of their wives (only about one-third of these wives recorded any earnings) contributes to the relatively low level of economic well-being of their families.

The mean characteristics of the entire sample of SSDI recipients mask the quite different characteristics of the younger (aged less than 55 in 1982) and older (aged 55 years or more in 1982) disabled men. Columns 2 and 3 present the mean characteristics of these two age groups. Almost 30 percent of the younger group is poor, compared to 13 percent of the older disabled men; the average income-to-needs ratio of the older group is 30 percent higher than that of the younger group. The relatively advantaged position of the older group is due largely to a substantially higher level of transfer income ($14,829 versus $10,540), which itself is attributable to a longer working career and, hence, higher predisability earnings. Asset income is also somewhat higher for the older group. Interestingly, the percentage of families with earnings (including those of the spouse) is only slightly lower among the older group. On average, the income of spouses is about the same in the two age groups, although far fewer of the younger cohort are married (see below).

The patterns of change in well-being over the subsequent decade also differed between the younger and older groups, as shown in columns 4 and 5. The average family income of the younger group of disabled men remained fairly constant, while that of the older group declined slightly (by about 10 percent). The decline in their average family size (by 0.2 and 0.5 of a person for the older group and younger group, respectively) offset family income changes; as a result the average family income-to-needs ratio increased over time for the younger group and declined by 5 percent for older men. In spite of the convergence over time, average family income of the younger group was only about 90 percent of that of the older group, and the percentage of the younger disabled group in poverty remained more than double that of the older group at the end of the period.

Transfer income received by both younger and older disabled men (82 percent of which is SSDI benefits) provided a fairly constant base of income support over the period, declining by 9 percent among the younger group and increasing by 6 percent among older disabled men. For the older group, the decline over time in both own earnings and the percentage with spouse earnings is consistent with their aging into retirement years. A few among the younger group increased their labor force involvement, but only a small number had left the SSDI rolls permanently by 1991 (Hennessey, 1997; Ycas, 1996).[16] By 1991, the poverty rate had fallen from its 1982 level for both groups of disabled males, to less than 10 percent among older men and to 24 percent among younger men.

---

[16] Less than 1 percent of older disabled men left SSDI and began working. While the labor force involvement of the younger disabled sample is larger than that of the older, only 6 percent of the younger sample left SSDI and began working.

III. How do disabled men fare relative to their nondisabled counterparts?

To understand how the relative economic position of these two cohorts of disabled men changed over time and the role of SSDI in maintaining their relative economic well-being, it is necessary to compare them to a group of nondisabled men with identical labor market and demographic characteristics. Table 2 presents mean characteristics of the disabled SSDI recipients compared to those of the nondisabled sample, matched to achieve identical distributions of age, marital status, education, and race.

Disability status—and the consequent withdrawal from the labor force by both the younger and older groups of SSDI recipients—had a substantial effect on the economic well-being of the families of these men. However, among the disabled, the families of the older cohort fared much better than those of the younger cohort, both absolutely and relative to the families of comparable men without disabilities.[17]

Consider the younger cohorts of disabled and nondisabled men. For both 1982 and 1991, the level of household income and the income-to-needs ratio of the younger disabled men were about 45 percent of those of their nondisabled counterparts. In 1982, 56 percent of the younger disabled men lived in families that were poor or near poor (defined as an income-to-needs ratio of below 1.5), compared to only 17 percent of the families of the younger nondisabled men. Although mean income of the group fell somewhat from 1982 to 1991, the near-poor rate for the young disabled group decreased from 56 percent to 47 percent over the subsequent decade. Although the near-poor rate for the young nondisabled group rose over the decade (to 26 percent), in 1991 the risk of near poverty was still nearly twice as large for the younger disabled group as it was for their nondisabled peers. Hence, relative to their nondisabled counterparts, the younger cohort of disabled men remained at a serious economic disadvantage over this period.

In 1982, the older SSDI recipients had family incomes and income-to-needs ratios equal to about two-thirds of those of their nondisabled counterparts. Over the next decade, as the older group of nondisabled men experienced reduced incomes associated with retiring from the labor force, the economic conditions of these two groups converged. In 1991 mean income and the income-to-needs ratio of the families of the disabled stood at about 80 percent of those of the nondisabled men. Between 1982 and 1991 both the income and the average income-to-needs ratio of the nondisabled fell, while the conditions of the disabled were more stable. In 1992 about 30 percent of the families of both of these older groups were either poor or near poor.

Table 2 also indicates the relative role of income transfers (in particular, Social Security—including SSDI) in maintaining family income of both the younger and older cohorts. In 1982, Social Security income was the major source of family income for both cohorts of disabled men, accounting for

---

[17] It should be noted that a more comprehensive measure of economic well-being would dampen the income differences among the four comparison groups to some extent. Public in-kind transfers (e.g., food stamps and Medicaid) tend to be income-conditioned, with larger benefits accruing to lower-income groups. In addition, much of the transfer income received through the Social Security program is not subject to taxation.

Table 2. Disabled and matched SSDI-eligible nondisabled men: Changes in economic status, 1982 to 1991

	Age < 55 in 1982		Age 55+ in 1982	
	1982	1991	1982	1991
Family income				
Disabled	$19,430	$19,157	$23,767	$21,291
SSDI-eligible nondisabled	$42,053	$44,476	$38,200	$26,380
Disabled as % of nondisabled	46%	43%	62%	81%
Income-to-needs ratio				
Disabled	1.84	1.98	2.39	2.26
SSDI-eligible nondisabled	4.16	4.42	3.95	2.78
Disabled as % of nondisabled	44%	45%	61%	81%
% in poverty				
Disabled	30%	24%	13%	10%
SSDI-eligible nondisabled	10%	10%	9%	15%
Disabled as % of nondisabled	316%	240%	141%	68%
% below 1.5 × poverty				
Disabled	56%	47%	31%	30%
SSDI-eligible nondisabled	17%	26%	17%	31%
Disabled as % of nondisabled	329%	181%	182%	97%
Social Security as % of family income				
Disabled	56%	55%	57%	66%
SSDI-eligible nondisabled	3%	13%	18%	53%
Disabled as % of nondisabled	1639%	420%	317%	125%
Transfers as % of family income				
Disabled	64%	61%	63%	69%
SSDI-eligible nondisabled	9%	17%	20%	55%
Disabled as % of nondisabled	719%	361%	317%	125%
Pensions as % of family income				
Disabled	5%	5%	13%	13%
SSDI-eligible nondisabled	2%	7%	10%	17%
Disabled as % of nondisabled	278%	69%	126%	76%
Earnings as % of family income				
Disabled	22%	24%	15%	7%
SSDI-eligible nondisabled	79%	63%	50%	8%
Disabled as % of nondisabled	28%	38%	30%	86%
Spouses' income as % of total – all individuals				
Disabled	20%	20%	19%	21%
SSDI-eligible nondisabled	10%	19%	16%	12%
Disabled as % of nondisabled	200%	107%	116%	169%
Spouses' income as % of total – married couples only				
Disabled	31%	32%	23%	28%
SSDI-eligible nondisabled	19%	25%	19%	16%
Disabled as % of nondisabled	160%	129%	124%	181%
% married (matching variable)				
Disabled	63%	61%	83%	76%
SSDI-eligible nondisabled	64%	72%	81%	76%
Disabled as % of nondisabled	98%	84%	103%	101%

Table 2 (continued)

	Age < 55 in 1982		Age 55+ in 1982	
	1982	1991	1982	1991
Family size				
Disabled	2.6	2.1	2.1	1.9
SSDI-eligible nondisabled	3.1	2.7	2.5	2.1
Disabled as % of nondisabled	84%	78%	84%	90%

Notes: 1982 data are only for individuals still in the sample in 1991. Figures in 1994 dollars

nearly 60 percent of total family income. By comparison, earned income is the largest income component of the families of the nondisabled men. Earned income accounted for 80 percent of family income for the younger nondisabled cohort, and for 50 percent for the older cohort (many of whom were early Social Security retired-worker beneficiaries). However, by 1991, although transfer income for the younger cohort of nondisabled men was slightly higher than it was in 1982, earnings continued to account for nearly two-thirds of total family income. In part this is due to an increase in the percentage of nondisabled men who were married and who, as a result, benefitted from the contribution of spouse earnings to family income. In contrast, by 1991 transfer income as a percentage of family income had risen for the older nondisabled cohort and approached that of their disabled peers. By 1991, earned income of the families of the older nondisabled men had decreased to about 8 percent of total family income.

Retirement among the older nondisabled group resulted in a sharply reduced share of total family income accounted for by earnings as well as an increase in the share accounted for by pensions and Social Security. Similar but far more modest changes are recorded for the older disabled group. As a result, the economic status of the older cohort of disabled men converged toward that of their nondisabled peers. By 1991 the percentage near poor was about 30 percent for both groups, and the mean income and mean income-to-needs ratio were only 20 percent lower among the disabled than among the nondisabled. Because of the reduction in the earned income of the nondisabled older group, the disabled-nondisabled income gap among older men fell from about $14,000 to $5,000. While the income-to-needs ratio of the disabled older men remained at about 2.3, that for the families of their nondisabled peers fell by 30 percent, from 4.0 to 2.8.

Among the younger nondisabled, the percentage married increased (with a consequent increase in the share of total family income contributed by the spouse), and, as some among this group retired, earnings fell as a percentage of family income and the share of family income accounted for by Social Security rose. The net effect on the relative economic status of the younger disabled was small. Although some convergence in percentage poor between the two groups is observed, mean income and income-to-needs ratio for this younger disabled group remained well below one-half of the mean level for the nondisabled. Hence, even though SSDI benefits offset some of the lost earnings of this younger group of disabled men, their economic position remained weak relative to that of the younger nondisabled group. This low level of income of the younger disabled group suggests difficulty in saving for later years, and hence little prospect for increased living standards over time.

To summarize:

- At the beginning of our observation period (1982), both the younger and older cohorts of disabled men had substantially lower levels of economic well-being than their nondisabled counterparts, and the younger cohort was substantially worse off than the older nondisabled recipients.
- The disparity between disabled and nondisabled men fell substantially over time for the older cohorts, while that disparity remained stable over time for the younger cohorts.
- These patterns are accounted for by
  a) the rapid decrease in the earnings of the older cohort of men without disabilities as they and their spouses retired and withdrew from the labor force, substituting a lower level of transfer (largely, Social Security retirement) income for lost earnings, and
  b) the increase in marriage rates and early retirement income for the families of younger nondisabled men.
- Because the increase in transfer income did not fully offset the earnings loss of the older nondisabled group, they recorded a decline in overall income and a doubling of the rate of poverty and near poverty.
- Although the nondisabled older men remained economically better off than their disabled counterparts in 1991, the difference in well-being between these two groups diminished substantially over the 1982–1991 period. This convergence reflects the oft-recognized tendency of older people to trade off income for leisure, a behavior that accounts for the standard hump-shaped age-income profile.
- The persistent lower income of the disabled younger cohort compared to both their nondisabled peers and the disabled older cohort suggests that the younger disabled cohort will enter their retirement years with substantially lower incomes than (1) those who entered the Social Security rolls as older disabled workers and (2) their nondisabled peers.

IV. Predictors of poverty status among disabled and nondisabled men

Our discussion in Section III revealed that SSDI recipients who enter the rolls at older ages (55 or more) have quite different characteristics than those who enter SSDI recipiency when they are younger. Moreover, both the younger and older disabled groups have important differences from their respective nondisabled cohorts. As we have shown, the younger group of SSDI recipients experienced low levels of well-being by every indicator, relative to people who entered the SSDI rolls when they were older and to younger nondisabled people with the same characteristics.

While the many differences in personal and family characteristics among the young-old and disabled-nondisabled groups are likely to be associated with the differences in well-being across the groups, cross-tabulation comparisons such as those reported in Section III do not enable us to determine the independent relationship to relative well-being of any single factor. In Table 3, we present results from a bivariate probit estimation of the correlates of poverty status designed to identify the independent relationship of various

Table 3. Bivariate probit of being below the near-poor threshold, disabled and matched SSDI-eligible nondisabled men
Coefficient (standard error)

Variable	1982		1991	
	Base	× Disabled	Base	× Disabled
Constant	−1.920* (0.218)		−1.323* (0.165)	
Disabled	1.552* (0.286)		0.559* (0.241)	
Age in 1982				
<35	0.688* (0.170)	0.160 (0.228)	0.014 (0.133)	0.532* (0.197)
35–51	0.339* (0.152)	−0.103 (0.200)	−0.297* (0.122)	0.418* (0.176)
55–58	0.137 (0.168)	−0.057 (0.212)	0.357* (0.122)	−0.426* (0.181)
59–61	0.681* (0.165)	−0.781* (.213)	0.458* (0.132)	−0.746* (0.189)
62–65	0.497* (0.160)	−0.744* (0.210)	0.495* (0.123)	−0.791* (0.184)
Married	−0.024 (0.772)	−0.484* (0.124)		
Single in 1982/Single in 1991			0.398* (0.132)	0.164 (0.119)
Single in 1982/Married in 1991			−0.122 (0.078)	0.369** (0.191)
Married in 1982/Single in 1991			−0.128 (0.117)	0.157 (0.153)
Children <18 Living at Home	0.217* (.030)	0.167* (0.046)	0.152* (0.032)	−0.007 (0.044)
White	−0.620* (0.077)	0.199** (0.119)	−0.527* (0.076)	−0.009 (0.115)
< High School Education	1.226* (0.142)	−0.324** (0.180)	0.758* (0.100)	0.272** (0.148)
Some High School Education	1.070* (0.146)	−0.721* (0.187)	0.757* (0.103)	−0.230 (0.155)
High School Graduate	0.601* (0.142)	−0.369* (0.177)	0.236* (0.106)	−0.068 (0.154)
South	0.112 (0.083)	0.133 (0.116)	0.506* (0.073)	−0.171 (0.110)
Northeast	−0.359* (0.109)	0.076 (0.150)	−0.043 (.0965)	−0.439* (0.141)
West	−0.366* (0.127)	0.451* (0.163)	−0.198* (.099)	0.209 (0.144)
Rho	0.612* (0.022)			

Table 3 (continued)

Variable	1982		1991	
	Base	× Disabled	Base	× Disabled
Mean dependent	.258		.275	
Log likelihood −4057				
N = 4731 (disabled: 2110; nondisabled: 2621)				

Notes: Near-poor threshold is 1.5 times poverty threshold. Nondisabled sample is weighted with matching weights.
*Significantly different from 0 at the 5% level.
**Significantly different from 0 at the 10% level.

sociodemographic characteristics to this outcome.[18] We estimate the model over the entire sample of disabled and nondisabled men, with the discrete dependent variables indicating being in poverty or near poverty in 1982 and in 1991.[19] The sample of nondisabled males is weighted with the matching weights described in the Appendix.[20] In columns 1 and 3, the coefficients and standard errors of the characteristics of independent variables are shown for the two years. Columns 2 and 4 show coefficients and standard errors on each correlate when it is interacted with being disabled. The algebraic sum of the

---

[18] Unobserved factors are likely to be correlated with a household's poverty status in both 1982 and 1991; that is, knowledge of poverty status in 1982 conveys information about the probability of poverty status in 1991. A bivariate probit model allows for correlation in the error terms of the two probit estimates, reflecting this likely persistence of unmeasured characteristics within the group over time. The large positive and significant rho value indicates the strong persistence of these characteristics over time. Note that the coefficients estimated in bivariate probit models cannot be interpreted as "marginal effects." The signs on the coefficients indicate the direction of the relationship, and the t-statistics indicate the statistical significance of the estimated relationship.

[19] In this analysis, we use the broader poverty measure—family income less than 1.5 times the family-specific poverty line—for two reasons. First, the U.S. Social Security program is designed to provide higher benefits (relative to prebeneficiary income) for individuals with below-average prebeneficiary income. This redistributive goal is better captured by a more inclusive low-income standard than the more restrictive official U.S. poverty measure. Second, the near-poverty standard applied to the matched nondisabled population yields a weighted poverty measure equal to between 0.4 and 0.5 of median income for this group, hence increasing the comparability with the relative poverty indicator of 0.5 of median income used by many OECD countries. The absolute poverty or near-poverty indicator is the standard measure used in the U.S. context for assessing the targeting of public transfer benefits.

[20] The weighted observations capture the joint probability that an observation is included in a particular gender-race-age-education-marital status category. These demographic variables are included in the estimation, where the coefficients reflect the effect of these factors, but not the joint probabilities. Estimation with weighted observations is necessary for reliable simulations of impact, when some variables are held constant at their mean values. We also estimated the bivariate probit with unweighted observations. The results of this estimation (and the simulations based on it) are available from the authors. Very few changes of import are recorded in the coefficients and significance levels, and simulations based on the unweighted probit are very similar to those reported in Table 4 (below). (Of the 9 simulated probabilities for the entire sample, 3 deviated from those shown by more than .01, and all of these deviated by less than .02. None of the simulated probabilities for the disabled deviated by more than .01. Most of the differences are recorded for the nondisabled population, where 3 of the probabilities deviated by from .02–.03, and 3 deviated by from .01–.02.)

coefficients in columns 1 and 2 (for 1982) and columns 3 and 4 (for 1991) indicates the effect of the variables on the disabled population.[21]

Overall relationships (columns 1 and 3)

The Disabled variable in column 1 indicates that men entering the SSDI rolls in 1982 had a significantly higher probability of being poor or near poor than did men with the same matched characteristics but without disabilities.[22] Compared to the excluded group of 52- to 54-year-olds, being aged less than 51—and particularly less than 35—is associated with a higher probability of being poor in 1982 for both the disabled and nondisabled groups. For the pooled disabled and nondisabled groups, being white and living in the Northeast or West (relative to the Midwest) decrease the risk of being poor or near poor. Conversely, having no postsecondary schooling[23] and having children under age 18 living in the family increase the chance of being poor or near poor.

Column 3 shows the independent effect of the same set of variables on the probability of being poor or near poor in 1991. The Disabled variable is again positive and significant, but it has a substantially lower coefficient relative to its standard error than in the 1982 analysis. This is consistent with the results, shown above, indicating a convergence between the economic status of the disabled and nondisabled populations as the nondisabled substitute lower Social Security retirement benefits for higher earnings as they retire.[24] By 1991, being less than 35 years old in 1982 (less than 44 years in 1991) has no different effect on the chances of being poor or near poor than being 52–54 in 1982 (61–63 in 1991) (the omitted category). In 1991, however, men older than the omitted category have a higher probability of being poor or near poor.[25] The 1991 specification also measures the effect of *changes* in marital status over the 1982–1991 period on the probability of being poor or near poor in 1991. Compared with those who are married in both years (the omitted category), being single over the entire period has a positive and sta-

---

[21] While the results are displayed in this column format for ease in exposition, all of the variables for all four columns are included in the same bivariate probit estimation. We also estimated separate bivariate probit models for the disabled and nondisabled. Those results are consistent with the estimates discussed above based on the fully interacted model. A log-likelihood test of whether there is a statistically significant difference in the models for the disabled versus the nondisabled is significant at the 1 percent level (twice the log-likelihood difference was 284.2, which is distributed chi-square with 30 degrees of freedom). This result supports the need to run the model either separately or with the full interactions, as we do here. The separate estimates are available from the authors.

[22] This is not surprising, of course, given that when observed in 1982 the disabled were out of the workforce while the nondisabled, because they had to be currently insured for SSDI benefits to be included in the sample, were largely employed. However, this variable captures the effect of disability, allowing the other variables to capture differences among the disabled and between them and the nondisabled that are due to factors other than the influence of disability alone.

[23] The More than High School category is the omitted category in this estimate.

[24] Note that in Table 2 we showed that poverty rates for the younger disabled and nondisabled converged, even though other measures of economic status did not.

[25] This pattern is consistent with Table 2 and is expected, because men in the omitted category have a far lower prevalence of retirees who rely on social insurance transfers for income than do men aged 64 or more in 1991.

tistically significant effect on the probability of being poor or near poor, while either becoming married or becoming single has no statistically significant effect on the poverty outcome. The effects of the other variables (race, children, schooling, and region) on the probability of being poor or near poor are generally consistent with the 1982 estimates.

Relationships for the disabled (columns 2 and 4)

The model estimates reported in columns 2 and 4 of Table 3 allow Disabled to have both a direct relationship to the probability of being poor or near poor and an indirect "effect" through the relationship of disability status and the other independent variables. For both years, the indirect effect of disability status is to diminish the effects of older age on the risk of poverty.[26] Similarly, the effects on the probability of being poor or near poor of being white, having no postsecondary education, and living in the West are diminished for the disabled relative to the nondisabled for 1982. In contrast, having children less than 18 living in the household in 1982 increases the chances of being poor for the disabled relative to the nondisabled.[27] For 1991, the significant effect of being a young disabled person on the risk of poverty complements our earlier finding regarding the persistent adverse effect on relative well-being of becoming disabled when young.

By 1991, the positive and significant relationship between the presence of minor children in the household and poverty risk among the disabled had disappeared, probably because there were fewer children under 18 (and therefore included in our family poverty thresholds) remaining in these homes. However, the relationship of low schooling among the disabled to the higher probability of being poor or near poor observed in 1982 was reinforced in 1991, perhaps reflecting the lower probability that these individuals were able to supplement low income with market earnings. Finally, becoming married between 1982 and 1991 increased the chances of being near poor for the disabled relative to the nondisabled. This may reflect differences in the nature of marriage opportunities for the disabled relative to the nondisabled, and the fact that becoming married to a spouse younger than age 62 (even if she had her own dependent children) would not qualify the family for additional SSDI benefits.

Simulation results

We now use the bivariate probit coefficients of Table 3 in a simulation exercise designed to reveal the difficult-to-interpret quantitative magnitude of assumed

---

[26] The pattern of coefficients on the age dummy variables indicates a distinct inverted-u-shaped age-income profile for the nondisabled population in both 1982 and 1991. The pattern for our population of disabled new 1982 beneficiaries has no discernible peak, implying persistently rising incomes over the life cycle. We thank an anonymous referee for this insight.

[27] The marriage estimate may be because spouses caring for dependent children may be eligible for a Social Security benefit. That additional children increase rather than reduce poverty risk among the disabled, despite benefits paid to minor children of disabled beneficiaries, may reflect the maximum constraint on family SSDI benefits.

Table 4. Simulated probability of being below the near-poor threshold in both 1982 and 1991

		Entire Sample	Disabled	Nondisabled
Base probability		.1804	.2841	.1129
i)	Those single in 1982 gain a spouse	.1709	.2704	.1061
	Percentage change	−5.3%	−4.8%	−6.0%
ii)	All men married both years	.1666	.2551	.1090
	Percentage change	−7.6%	−10.2%	−3.5%
iii)	All are white	.1495	.2550	.0809
	Percentage change	−17.1%	−10.2%	−28.3%
iv)	All are <35 years old	.2666	.4802	.1277
	Percentage change	47.8%	69.0%	13.1%
v)	All are aged 62–65	.1616	.1892	.1437
	Percentage change	−10.4%	−33.4%	27.3%
vi)	No one had kids	.1506	.2379	.0937
	Percentage change	−16.5%	−16.3%	−17.0%
vii)	On own (no kids and single)	.2067	.3532	.1114
	Percentage change	14.6%	24.3%	−1.3%
viii)	All at least a high school grad	.1095	.1890	.0578
	Percentage change	−39.3%	−33.5%	−48.8%
ix)	All single both years	.2405	.4043	.1340
	Percentage change	33.3%	42.3%	18.7%

values of selected variables on the probability of being poor or near poor in both 1982 and 1991 for the total population, and for the disabled and nondisabled subgroups. The results in Table 4 show the effect over both 1982 and 1991 of changing a single variable while holding the other variables constant, using both the level (columns 1 and 3) coefficients and the interaction (columns 2 and 4) coefficients of Table 3. These simulated probabilities are to be compared to the base probability (see top row of estimates). In effect, the simulations indicate the relative effects on the probability of being poor or near poor in both 1982 and 1991 for the total population, and for the disabled and nondisabled subgroups, if we assume that all individuals have the specified value of the characteristic indicated.[28]

The effect of age is clearly seen in Table 4 (rows iv and v). If all the disabled men were young (<35 in 1982) when they became SSDI recipients, we would observe a *far* higher probability of being poor or near poor in both years. Conversely, if all the disabled men were older (62–65 in 1982) when they first received SSDI benefits, the probability (relative to the omitted prime-age category) of being poor or near poor would be reduced by one-third. The pattern among the nondisabled is quite different. For nondisabled men, being younger (<35 in 1982) is associated with only a slightly higher

---

[28] The results are read as follows: In row ii, if we assume that all men in the sample are married in both years (as opposed to not being married in both years), the rate of poverty or near poverty will fall by 7.6 percent for the entire population, 10.2 percent for the disabled, and 3.5 percent for the nondisabled.

probability of being poor or near poor, and being older (62–65 in 1982) is associated with a higher probability of being poor or near poor (in contrast to a lower probability for the disabled) relative to the prime-age group. The age variables suggest the sharply better economic status for men who enter the SSDI rolls at or near age-eligibility for Social Security retired-worker benefits relative to those who enter the rolls when young. Over time, the position of these men improves relative to both their nondisabled peers and the disabled who are younger when first receiving SSDI benefits.

Row viii indicates the independent effect of education. If men with less than a high school education are simulated to have graduated from high school (holding constant the education of all others), the probability of being poor or near poor is sharply reduced for both disabled and nondisabled men. We conclude that being young when first receiving SSDI benefits and having low education—two factors closely related to low labor market earnings—have especially serious negative effects on the well-being of disabled males; they are doubly disadvantaged.

Finally, consider the simulated effect of changes in family composition. If those who are single in 1982 are assumed to have a spouse by 1992 (row i), the probability of being poor or near poor falls somewhat for both the disabled and nondisabled groups. Similarly, the probability of being poor or near poor is (1) decreased if it is assumed that there are no children in the family (row vi) and if it is assumed that all men are married in both years (row ii), and (2) increased substantially for the disabled if it is assumed that there is no spouse or children present (row vii) or if the married men become single over the period (row ix). The risk of being poor or near poor falls substantially, especially for the nondisabled, if it is assumed that none of the men are racial minorities (row iii).

V. The antipoverty effectiveness of social security benefits

The evidence presented in Sections III and IV suggests that, although SSDI benefits provide an important cushion against the loss of earned income due to disability, the families of disabled men receiving SSDI benefits have substantially lower levels of economic well-being than do the families of men without disabilities and for a considerably longer period of their lives. In this section, we provide a quantitative assessment of the contribution of the Social Security program (primarily SSDI) to the well-being of the younger and older disabled men. We adopt three approaches to assessing the effect of the SSDI program on well-being, in each case measuring the effectiveness of SSDI benefits in maintaining well-being relative to a counterfactual in which Social Security income support is unavailable to people with disabilities.

In our first approach, we measure the effect of Social Security income in removing from poverty disabled men who, in the absence of these transfers, would be poor.[29] In our second measure, we first estimate the "poverty gap" for both the younger and older groups of SSDI recipients; we then calculate

---

[29] Our calculations here use the poverty threshold, as opposed to the poverty plus near-poverty thresholds in the analysis in Section IV. Our conclusions are robust with respect to the specific poverty indicator used. We have chosen the poverty threshold for this analysis to enable comparison with studies assessing the antipoverty effectiveness of other transfer programs.

Table 5. Antipoverty effectiveness of social security benefits disabled men, 1982 and 1991

		1981		1991	
		< 55	55+	< 55	55+
i)	Pre-Social Security poverty rate	65.9%	54.0%	60.1%	64.5%
ii)	Pre-Social Security with simulated SSI	61.9%	51.3%	56.4%	62.0%
iii)	Poor simulated removed from poverty by SSI	6.1%	5.0%	6.0%	3.9%
iv)	Actual post-Social Security poverty	29.6%	13.2%	24.3%	10.0%
v)	Poor actually removed from poverty by Social Security	55.1%	75.6%	59.6%	84.6%
vi)	Average poverty gap filled by Social Security	75.8%	85.4%	80.2%	93.5%

Notes: Poverty is defined as receiving total income below the needs threshold. "Aggregate poverty gap" is needs threshold minus pre-Social Security family income, summed over all poor families. "Poverty gap filled by Social Security" is the aggregate Social Security benefit received by pre-Social Security poor households divided by the aggregate poverty gap.

the extent to which Social Security benefits reduce that gap. Finally, we assess the "insurance" value of SSDI by comparing Social Security benefits actually received by disabled men with estimates of their predisability earnings.

The antipoverty impact of social security benefits

In estimating the success of the Social Security program in removing the families of disabled men from poverty, we compare the actual poverty rate of these groups with the poverty rate that would exist if no Social Security benefits were paid. This calculation requires several steps.

First, we calculate the family income of each disabled SSDI recipient if they did not receive SSDI and Supplemental Security Income (SSI) benefits. By comparing this pre-Social Security income level for each family with its family-specific poverty line, we calculate the proportion of this disabled population that would have been poor in the absence of Social Security benefits, a pre-Social Security poverty rate."[30] This is shown in row i of Table 5.

Then, because the families of some disabled people would be eligible for SSI disability payments were there no SSDI program, we estimate the SSI benefits that each family would receive, based on reported income other than Social Security and assets,[31] and add this amount to pre-Social Security income. Comparing this adjusted income value with the poverty line yields a "pre-Social Security with simulated SSI" poverty rate (row ii). Finally, for

---

[30] The pretransfer calculation is standard in the public economics literature for measuring the antipoverty effectiveness of income transfer programs. To the extent that the provision of transfer income reduces the work and earnings of the disabled person or members of his family, the calculation would overstate antipoverty effectiveness. Because the recipients of SSDI benefits have very low residual work capacities, we judge that this potential bias is small.
[31] The SSI benefits are simulated (rather than reported to the NBS) since we want to count the full SSI benefit for all persons who would be eligible for this program in the absence of SSDI.

each SSDI recipient, we compare the actual (post-Social Security) poverty rate (row iv) to these simulated poverty rates, which comparisons provide a measure of the extent to which Social Security benefits enable the population of disabled SSDI recipients who would be poor in the absence of Social Security benefits to escape poverty (row v).

Table 5 presents these calculations for both the younger and older groups of disabled men. In 1982, shortly after these men first received SSDI benefits, the pre-Social Security poverty rate stood at about 66 percent for the younger group and 54 percent for the older group. For both groups, SSI would provide very modest income support, reducing these very high poverty rates by only about 3 to 5 percentage points. However, with Social Security income included in the family income definition, actual poverty rates were less than one-half of this level—about 30 percent for younger disabled men and only 13 percent for older disabled men. We conclude that Social Security benefits removed 55 percent of the younger men and 76 percent of the older men from poverty. The greater antipoverty effectiveness of Social Security for older relative to younger men is attributable to two factors: (1) the higher average benefit levels paid to older men because of their higher predisability earnings and (2) the larger proportion of older disabled men who are married (and who therefore have spouses who are either working or also receiving Social Security benefits).

The antipoverty effectiveness of Social Security benefits is quite different 9 years after the disabled population first received SSDI benefits. By 1991, many in the older group (and their spouses, if married) are older than 62 years (when Social Security retired-worker benefits can first be claimed) and hence have fewer earners in the family unit.[32] As a result, the pre-Social Security poverty rate increases from 54 to 65 percent. Because the actual poverty rate for the older group *fell* from 13 percent in 1982 to 10 percent in 1991, the antipoverty impact of Social Security benefits increased over this period. In 1991, almost 85 percent of the older group who were pre-Social Security poor were boosted over their family-specific poverty line by Social Security benefits, an increase from the 76 percent in 1982. For the younger group, the percentage of pre-Social Security poor families removed from poverty by Social Security benefits increased from 55 percent in 1982 to 60 percent in 1991. Overall, then, Social Security programs had a large and sustained effect in reducing poverty for both the younger group and older group of disabled men who became SSDI recipients in 1982, but it was more successful at doing so for the older disabled.

The impact of social security benefits on the average poverty gap

An alternative measure of the antipoverty effectiveness of Social Security benefits is obtained by calculating the fraction of the "poverty gap"—the amount of perfectly targeted income that would have to be given to the fam-

---

[32] At age 65, SSDI beneficiaries are automatically converted to retired-worker status. This is an administrative conversion that does not in any way change the benefits for which they are eligible. The only effect is to make them subject to the retired-worker earnings limits rather than SSDI's substantial gainful work activity test.

ilies of the pre-Social Security (but with simulated SSI benefits) poor disabled men in order to bring the level of each family's income up to the poverty line[33]—that is eliminated by the receipt of Social Security benefits.

Row vi of Table 5 shows that, in 1982, Social Security benefits filled 85 percent of the poverty gap for older disabled men and 76 percent for younger disabled men. By 1991, these percentages had increased to 94 and 80 percent. Again, Social Security benefits are seen to play an important role in reducing poverty for the families of both younger and older disabled men, though the effectiveness of the system is substantially greater for those men who entered the disabled rolls close to retirement age. A substantial number of younger disabled men—nearly one-quarter of them—remained poor nearly a decade after first entering the SSDI rolls, and even with Social Security benefits, 20 percent of the 1991 pre-Social Security poverty gap remained unfilled.

The income replacement impact of social security benefits

Our third measure of the income-support impact of Social Security is based on a comparison of what a disabled person receives in the form of Social Security benefits relative to an estimate of what that person could have earned had he not experienced a disability (and, hence, had not been an SSDI recipient). We present two estimates of this SSDI "insurance value," both calculated from Social Security-covered earnings records linked to the NBS data set. The question asked is the degree to which SSDI insures the individual's or family's predisability level of income.

Our first estimated replacement rate assumes that the maximum reported covered earnings (in 1994 dollars) represent the amount the disabled male earned prior to becoming disabled, or his current potential earnings had he *not* been disabled. We add this estimated amount to the total income of the family less Social Security and SSI income, and interpret this sum as the value of family income had the person not become disabled and instead continued to work at a job paying this maximum amount. The ratio of the family's actual income (including receipt of SSDI and SSI benefits) to this potential income value yields an insurance-type replacement rate that reflects the effect of SSDI benefits in maintaining the family's simulated without-disability income.

Alternatively, we assume that average earnings over the years actually worked[34] reflect the person's predisability earnings. To the degree that the year of maximum earnings was an unusual year for individuals, the average earnings measure may be a better measure of the earnings against which dis-

---

[33] This gap is equal to zero if the pre-Social Security (but with simulated SSI) income of a family is equal to or larger than the poverty threshold.

[34] This procedure understates nondisability income to the degree that a person's disability is long-term, hence reducing potential earnings for several years. We note that private market insurance is and can only be provided against actual earnings, and not against "potential" earnings. Our procedure understates nondisability income to the extent that spouses compensate for the loss of husband's earnings by increasing their own work involvement. However, our prior analysis revealed little difference between the earnings of spouses of disabled and nondisabled persons (see Table 2)

Table 6. SSDI replacement rates of predisability earnings

| | Mean Predicted Family Income Using | | | Mean Replacement Rate Using | |
	Mean Actual Income	Maximum Predisability Earnings	Average Predisability Earnings Work Years	Actual/Max.	Actual/Ave.
1982					
Above poverty					
<55	$30,760	$51,220	$38,110	60%	81%
55+	$29,786	$54,198	$40,033	55%	74%
Near poverty					
<55	$13,190	$30,716	$19,729	43%	67%
55+	$12,104	$32,750	$20,362	37%	59%
In poverty					
<55	$7,631	$22,188	$13,245	34%	58%
55+	$8,026	$25,426	$14,683	32%	55%
1991					
Above poverty					
<55	$28,066	$47,692	$35,055	59%	80%
55+	$25,953	$49,558	$35,232	52%	74%
Near poverty					
<55	$11,183	$28,207	$17,689	40%	63%
55+	$11,538	$30,091	$18,309	38%	63%
In poverty					
<55	$7,082	$22,158	$12,900	32%	55%
55+	$8,297	$23,294	$13,140	36%	63%

Notes: Table includes survivors to 1991 only. Figures in 1994 dollars. Near poverty is between 1.0 and 1.5 times poverty threshold.

ability insurance could be purchased.[35] This value is then added to the non-Social Security/non-SSI income of the family and is used as the denominator in calculating a second replacement rate. (The family's actual income—including receipt of SSDI and SSI benefits—again serves as the numerator.) Because the estimate of potential family income is lower in this second estimate, it provides a higher estimate of the insurance value of SSDI.

These replacement rates are shown in Table 6 for three categories of families headed by disabled men—those whose actual incomes indicated that they were poor, near poor, and nonpoor—and distinguish between older and younger disabled men in these categories.[36]

---

[35] Because this average is calculated over the years that the person actually worked, it exceeds the average earnings value used to calculate SSDI benefits, which includes some years with zero earnings. We exclude the years of zero earnings because we are seeking an estimate of the insurance value of this benefit in terms of earnings replacement.

[36] An example will aid in the interpretation of Table 6. Consider younger disabled men classified as poor (line 5). Actual average family income for this group of men was $7,631 in 1982. Had these men received no benefits from Social Security, but instead earned an amount equal to the **maximum** of their covered annual earnings, average family income would have been $22,188. The ratio of these two values yields an insurance-type replacement rate of 34 percent. Alternatively, if

For both the high and low estimate of mean predicted family income, the simulated without-disability family income of the older men is generally higher than that of younger men, consistent with the standard age-earnings profile. This pattern holds across the three well-being categories. However, and despite the progressive benefit formula, the actual benefits (plus other income) of families of SSDI recipients who are poor is a lower percentage of their estimated nondisabled income than it is for more well-off families, reflecting the more sporadic working careers and lower earnings of men in poor families. Finally, the difference between the high and low estimates reflects the impact of averaging earnings for beneficiaries whose earnings may have deteriorated because of disability well before applying for SSDI.[37]

VI. Summary and conclusions

The disabled men in our sample—those who entered SSDI beneficiary status in 1982 and survived to 1991—have a substantially lower level of economic well-being than their nondisabled but SSDI-eligible peers. In 1982 about 50 percent of the families of the disabled men were either poor or near poor—56 percent of the younger group (those who first received SSDI before age 55) and 47 percent of the older group. The rate of poverty or near poverty for the nondisabled comparison group was about one-half this level.

Over the subsequent decade, as family structure changed (e.g., the death of spouses, with the loss of both their earnings and their income needs), SSDI benefits remained nearly constant, providing a reliable base of income support for the families of disabled men. By 1991, the poor-plus-near-poor rate for the SSDI recipients recorded for 1982 had fallen slightly to 47 percent for the younger disabled and 30 percent for the older disabled, while the rate for the nondisabled group edged up. As a result, the well-being gap between the two groups narrowed significantly as both groups aged. Indeed, by 1991 about 30 percent of the families of both the disabled and nondisabled older groups were either poor or near poor. For the younger groups, however, the poor-plus-near-poor rate for the disabled (47 percent) remained at nearly twice the level of the rate for the nondisabled population.

For both 1982 and 1991, the probability that the families of both groups of men (disabled and matched nondisabled) are poor or near poor is positively

---

their earnings potential had been taken as the **average** of their covered earnings, the average income of their families would have been $13,245, or 58 percent of their nondisability income. Both the maximum and average values are based on the **actual** prior earnings of disabled persons receiving SSDI benefits and hence reflect the likely period of deteriorating health and work capacity experienced by many SSDI recipients prior to receiving benefits (see Livermore, 1995). As an alternative to these measures, we could have compared the earnings potential of the disabled person, given his human capital characteristics, with the value of Social Security benefits received. However, this approach would overestimate the individual's true earnings potential by failing to reflect this potential predisability earnings deterioration. It should be noted that our two estimates of the difference between potential (without-disability) family income and actual family income are measures of the family's loss of well-being attributable to the disability of the male head.

[37] The SSDI recipients in poor families have more years with zero earnings prior to receipt of benefits, reducing the actual benefit award and the "insurance value" of SSDI against lost earnings, which are estimated only across the working years. The negative effect on predisability earnings of the ultimate onset of disability has been studied by Livermore (1995).

associated with their being young (less than 35 years old in 1982), having a low level of schooling, being unmarried, and having children under 18 living in the family. The effect of being young when first receiving SSDI benefits is especially strong and persists over the first 10 years of benefit receipt. This age pattern carries two implications. First, it suggests that, in spite of a progressive benefit formula, SSDI benefits have a greater effect in reducing the prevalence of poverty or near poverty for recipients who enter the rolls when they are older than it does for those who become disabled and, hence, recipients earlier in life. Second, it suggests that those who become disabled earlier in life are disadvantaged by sacrificing the experience-related earnings growth that accrues to the nondisabled. We conclude that those who first receive SSDI benefits early in life are doubly disadvantaged relative to their nondisabled peers—in addition to experiencing the disutility of the disabling condition, they sacrifice higher earnings for lower benefits, and they forgo the growth of future earnings associated with age and experience.

SSDI recipients who remain single over the period experience much higher rates of poverty or near poverty than continuously married men do, suggesting that the added spouses contribute more to family income than to income needs. Interestingly, however, moving from being single to being married appears to increase the probability of poverty among the disabled, and probably reveals the relatively low earnings capabilities of the potential spouses of disabled men. Having children in the family unit adds more to income needs, increasing the probability of being poor or near poor by about 5 percentage points for disabled men in both 1982 and 1991. This suggests that dependents' benefits fail to fully offset the greater economic needs of families with children.

Social Security benefits in the U.S. have played an important role in sustaining the economic status of families of disabled men. Nevertheless, the families of young men with disabilities remain a disadvantaged group, relative to their nondisabled counterparts and to older disabled men. Men who enter the SSDI rolls early in life cease work earlier; hence the gains that come with longer working careers are not reflected in their later Social Security (SSDI) benefits. Over time their relative economic position remains well below that of their nondisabled peers and of men who first receive SSDI at a later age. Although men who come on the SSDI rolls at a later age experience an increase in their poverty rates over time due to the partial replacement of earnings by Social Security retirement benefits, their longer working careers result in postretirement income levels that are higher than their younger peers. Indeed, over time, their economic status and that of their nondisabled peers converge, as those in the latter group substitute lower retirement benefits for earned income.

These findings contribute to our understanding of the economic well-being of families headed by a disabled male and are distinct from previous results by revealing decade-long trends in well-being for these families. The disadvantaged position of the families of disabled men (relative to their nondisabled counterparts), and especially the disadvantaged position of the families of disabled men who enter the SSDI rolls at young ages (relative to both older disabled men and their younger nondisabled counterparts), is cause for concern if, as many believe, the U.S. social insurance system has been assigned responsibility for reducing such inequities.

Several options are available if policymakers should desire to narrow these disparities via legislative measures. Here we simply mention a few, and note some important considerations associated with each.

Given that about 80 percent of the pre-Social Security poverty gap is already filled by Social Security benefits, adjustment of the SSDI benefit formula by raising the insured income level at which the replacement rate factor decreases could increase the insurance value of SSDI for recipients (especially unmarried recipients) who enter the roles at younger ages and could close much of the remaining gap. Similarly, a small across-the-board benefit increase would reduce poverty rates for these vulnerable groups.[38] Both of these approaches, however, lack target efficiency, with much of the aggregate increase in costs accruing to beneficiaries who are not poor.

A more targeted approach would involve increases in the level of SSI benefits for disabled persons, but this change would have to be integrated with the SSDI benefit formula. It would also raise the question of increasing SSI benefits for aged poor persons in order to reduce the poverty gap for this population.

Other options might include reintroducing a minimum benefit level, reducing the number of zero-earnings years that are included in the benefit formula, or crafting an adjustment factor to reflect forgone earnings growth experienced by those whose onset of disability occurs when they are young.

All of these measures have specific advantages and drawbacks, and they vary in the costs associated with equivalent reductions in the poverty rates of the targeted groups. Analysis of the economic and administrative costs and benefits of each is a necessary next step should an increase in the antipoverty effectiveness of U.S. social insurance policy be desired.

Appendix. The NBS and PSID data sets and creation of the PSID matched sample

The New Beneficiary Survey (NBS) was developed by the Social Security Administration and conducted by Temple University's Institute for Survey Research and Mathematica Policy Research. The NBS is a nationally representative household survey of retired workers, disabled workers, and wife or widow beneficiaries representing the nearly 2 million persons who had begun receiving Social Security benefits during a 12-month period in 1980–81. This sample was first interviewed in 1982. Surviving respondents and surviving spouses were resurveyed in 1991.

The disabled-worker sample is the basis for the present study. The initial survey in 1982 gathered information on demographic characteristics; employment, marital and childbearing histories; household composition; health; income and assets; and information about the spouses of married respondents. The 1991 reinterview updated these data as well as providing expanded information including a more extensive section on health. SSA administrative records have been linked to these data. Additional information and the data may be obtained and transferred from the web site: *http://www.ssa.gov/*

---

[38] Conversely, the effective reduction of benefits through downward adjustment of the price indexation formula would impose a high cost on these beneficiary groups with high remaining poverty rates.

statistics/nbdsindx.html. For a summary of studies using the NBS, see Ycas (1992).

The Michigan Panel Survey of Income Dynamics (PSID) is a longitudinal data set that began with about 6,000 families in 1968 and continues to this day. In addition to gathering data on each member of the original panel households, the PSID follows each member of those households as they form their own households, and follows new household members. This design helps the panel maintain its representativeness, as new households and new household members take the place of original panel members who are lost from the panel through attrition. Because the sample frame of the PSID includes an oversample of the low-income and minority populations, sample weights are provided for each wave of the PSID to make the PSID sample representative of the U.S. population.

For the purposes of building a sample of nondisabled men that is used as a comparison group to the disabled men from the NBS, information was drawn from the PSID waves covering the years 1980–1983, and 1992–1993. The nondisabled sample was drawn from PSID panel years that mirrored the 12-month period during which the NBS sample was selected. This assures a nationally representative sample of totally nondisabled individuals who could have been selected at the same time as the NBS sample. We used information from the PSID panel years that had reference periods equivalent to those of the 1982 and 1991 NBS interview dates.

Detailed information about the PSID can be obtained from the annual PSID codebooks, entitled "A Panel Study of Income Dynamics: Procedures and Tape Codes," from the Survey Research Center of the Institute for Social Research at the University of Michigan. Additional information can be obtained from independent evaluations, such as Duncan and Hill (1989), Becketti, et al (1988), and Hill (1992).

The PSID matched sample was created to provide a nondisabled group comparable to the NBS sample of disabled individuals. After removing disabled individuals from the PSID sample, weights were applied to the remaining observations to match the NBS joint distribution of age, education, sex, race, and marital status. By matching, we are assured that differences in economic well-being across the two samples are not driven by differences in these demographic variables.

Disabled individuals were identified in the PSID by using self-reported health status and program participation information. Heads of household who reported their health status as "disabled" and indicated that their disability reduced the amount of work they could do "a lot" were defined as disabled. In addition, all individuals who reported their employment status as "permanently disabled," all individuals under 59 who received Social Security benefits, and all individuals who received Supplemental Security Income (SSI) or Workers' Compensation were defined as disabled and removed from the sample.

SSDI receipt requires that an individual be both "fully insured" and have 20 quarters of coverage (QC) in the last 40 calendar quarters, including the quarter of disablement. Prior to 1978 (and covering most of the covered earnings of the NBS sample) a QC was credited if a minimum amount was earned in a calendar quarter. Beginning in 1978, a QC was credited on the basis of units of dollars in annual earnings up to a maximum (in 1978 for each $250, with that amount increased annually by the rise in average covered wages). Four quarters (the annual maximum) may be earned now with sufficient covered earnings in one calendar quarter. A person is fully insured with the lesser of 40 QCs or QCs equal to the number of years elapsed between age 21 and the year before disablement. Receipt of SSDI also requires that, based on age, education, and work experience, the recipient be unable to engage in any kind of substantial gainful work and that the impairment must be expected to last at least 1 year or result in death. Using work histories in the PSID, we selected individuals who would have sufficient quarters to be eligible for Social Security should they become disabled and meet the disability standard for eligibility.

The NBS and PSID samples were matched nonparametrically. Each observation in the sample was classified into one of the 192 cells representing a particular combination of age, education, sex, race, and marital status. The possible values of the demographic characteristics were defined as follows:

Age (6 bins): 20–34, 35–51, 52–54, 55–58, 59–61, 62–65
Education (4 bins): ⟨HS, some HS, HS grad,⟩ HS
Sex (2 bins): women, men
Race (2 bins): white, nonwhite
Marital status (2 bins): married, single

The age categories were chosen to reflect key age groups relevant to eligibility for Social Security retired-worker benefits both in 1982 and as the cohort aged over the following 9 years. Matching was accomplished by creating a cell weight for each of the 192 cells defined as the cell frequency in the NBS divided by the corresponding cell frequency in the PSID. Weighting each observation in the PSID sample by the appropriate matching weight created a sample with the same joint distribution of demographics as the NBS.

Because economic well-being is one of the primary foci of our analysis, we gave careful attention to ensuring comparable income measures in the two data sets. There are two primary differences in the manner in which the questions are asked. First, the NBS is more specific about types of income (particularly asset and pension income). Second, the income measures in the NBS are the sum of the previous three months income which are then converted to annual amounts, while the PSID question inquires about income over the previous year.

With respect to income specificity, for example, the NBS poses the following questions with regard to the receipt of Social Security income: "In any of the last three months, did you receive any income from Social Security? How much did you receive last month from Social Security? How much did you receive the month before that, that is, 2 months ago, from Social Security? How much did you receive the month before that, that is 3 months ago, from Social Security?" Parallel questions are asked for each of the following income sources: asset income (income from rent on property, interest from money market, C.D., savings accounts, checking accounts, credit union accounts, bonds, mutual funds or stocks, roomers or boarders, estates, trusts, royalties, income from IRA or Keogh, and income from insurance or annuities), pension income (income from state or local employee pension benefits, military pension, federal employee pension, private employer or union pension, veterans pensions, black lung, and railroad retirement benefits), Social Security, SSI, state or local welfare benefits, workers compensation, unemployment insurance, alimony or child support, earnings, contributions from household members, contributions from nonhousehold members, and other income.

While the PSID asks respondents about annual income rather than monthly income, it also includes a very detailed set of income categories. The income variable is the combination of total taxable and transfer income where taxable and transfer income is generated by summing the sources of income. These sources of income include: labor income, asset income, rent, interest/ dividends, alimony, AFDC, SSI, other welfare, Social Security, VA Pension, other retirement, unemployment compensation, workers compensation, child support, help from relatives, and other transfer income. While there are differences in the depth of detail of the survey questions for the two data sets, the two income measures include virtually identical concepts of income.

References

Antonovics K, Haveman R, Holden K, Wolfe B (1999) Attrition in the national beneficiary survey and followup, and its correlates. University of Wisconsin-Madison, mimeo

Becketti S, Gould W, Lillard L, Welch F (1988) The panel study of income dynamics after fourteen years: An evaluation. Journal of Labor Economics 6(4):472–492

Berkowitz M (1997) Linking beneficiaries with return-to-work services. In: Reno V, Mashaw J, Gradison B (eds.) Disability: Challenges for social insurance, health care financing and labor market policy, National Academy of Social Insurance, Washington, DC

Bound J (1989) The health and earnings of rejected disability insurance applicants. American Economic Review 79(3):482–503

Bound J, Burkhauser R (1999) Economic analysis of transfer programs targeted on people with disabilities. In: Ashenfelter O, Card D (eds.) Handbook of labor economics, Vol. 3C, North Holland, Amsterdam

Burkhauser R, Haveman R, Wolfe B (1993) How people with disabilities fare when public policies change. Journal of Policy Analysis and Management 12(2):251–269

Danziger S, Gottschalk P (1995) America unequal. Harvard University Press, Cambridge, MA

Duncan G, Hill D (1989) Assessing the quality of household panel data: The case of the panel study of income dynamics. Journal of Business and Economic Statistics 7(4):441–452

Grad S (1989) Income and assets of social security beneficiaries by type of benefit. Social Security Bulletin 52(1):2–10

Haveman R, Jong P de, Wolfe B (1991) Disability transfers and the work decision of older men. Quarterly Journal of Economics 106:939–949

Haveman R, Holden K, Wolfe B, Smith P, Wilson K (2000) The changing economic status of disabled women, 1982–1991: Trends and their determinants. In: Salkever D, Sorkin A (eds.) Essays in the economics of disability, JAI Press, Stamford, CT

Haveman R, Warlick J, Wolfe B (1988) Labor market behavior of older men: Estimates from a trichotomous choice model. Journal of Public Economics 36:153–175

Haveman R, Wolfe B (1984) Disability transfers and early retirement: A causal relationship? Journal of Public Economics 24:47–66

Haveman R, Wolfe B (1990) The economic well-being of the disabled: 1962–84. Journal of Human Resources 25:32–54

Haveman R, Wolfe B (2000) The economics of disability and disability policy. In: Newhouse J, Culyear A (eds.) Handbook of health economics, North Holland, Amsterdam

Hill M (1992) The panel survey of income dynamics: A user's guide. Sage Publications, Newbury Park, CA

Hennessey JC (1997) Factors affecting the work efforts of disabled-worker beneficiaries. Social Security Bulletin 60(3):3–19

Leonard J (1986) Labor supply incentives and disincentives for disabled persons. In: Berkowitz M, Hill A (eds.) Disability and the labor market, Industrial and Labor Relations Press, Ithaca, NY

Levy F, Murnane R (1992) U.S. earnings levels and earnings inequality: A review of recent trends and proposed explanations. Journal of Economic Literature 30:1333–1381

Livermore GA (1995) The effect of pre-disability poor health on earnings and relative economic well-being of men with disability: An evaluation of the social security disability insurance benefit structure. Ph.D. dissertation, Department of Economics, University of Wisconsin–Madison

McCoy JL, Iams HM, Armstrong T (1994) The hazard of mortality among aging retired- and disabled-worker men: A comparative sociodemographic and health status analysis. Social Security Bulletin 57(3):76–87

Quinn J, Burkhauser RV, Myers DA (1990) Passing the torch: The influence of economic incentives on work and retirement. W. E. Upjohn Institute for Employment Research, Kalamazoo, MI

Weaver DA (1997) The economic well-being of social security beneficiaries, with an emphasis on divorced beneficiaries. Social Security Bulletin 60(4):3–17

Ycas MA (1992) The new beneficiary data system: The first phase. Social Security Bulletin 55(2):20–35

Ycas MA (1996) Patterns of return to work in a cohort of disabled-worker beneficiaries. In: Mashaw J et al. (eds.) Disability, work and cash benefits, W. E. Upjohn Institute for Employment Research, Kalamazoo, MI

The role of labour demand elasticities in tax incidence analysis with heterogeneous labour[*]

Keshab Bhattarai[1], John Whalley[1,2,3]

[1] Department of Economics, University of Warwick, Coventry, CV4 7AL, UK
(e-mail: K.Bhattarai@warwick.ac.uk)
[2] Department of Economics, University of Western Ontario, London Ontario, ONT N6A 5C2, Canada (e-mail: jwhalley@julian.uwo.ca)
[3] National Bureau of Economic Research, 1050 Mass. Ave., Cambridge, MA 02138-5318, USA

First version received: March 1998 / Final version received: April 1999

Abstract. Whether labour bears full burden of household level income and consumption taxes ultimately depends on the degree of substitutability among different types of labour in production. We find more variation in incidence patterns across households with less than perfectly substitutable heterogeneous labour than with perfectly substitutable homogeneous labour in production. This finding is based on results obtained from homogeneous and heterogeneous labour general equilibrium tax models calibrated to decile level income and consumption distribution data of UK households for the year 1994. We use labour supply elasticities implied by the substitution elasticity in households' utility functions and derive labour demand elasticities from the substitution elasticity in the production function.

Key words: Elasticities, labour demand, labour supply, welfare, tax incidence, redistribution

JEL classifications: J20, H22, C68

1. Introduction

This paper builds on the observation that existing empirically based incidence analyses drawing either on shifting assumptions[1], or on general equilibrium tax models treat labour as bearing the burden of its own income and payroll

---

* Bhattarai and Whalley acknowledge financial support from the ESRC under an award for a project on General Equilibrium Modelling of UK Policy Issues. We are thankful to Baldev Raj and two referees for comments on earlier versions of this paper.
[1] See Pechman and Okner (1974), and Gillespie (1965) as examples of this approach.

taxes[2]. The implicit assumption is that labour is a homogenous input which is perfectly mobile across industries and yields leisure which is consumed by households. A key set of parameters in incidence analyses conducted with these models have been presumed to be the labour supply elasticities which are the subject of some attention in both calibration and sensitivity analysis. Labour demand elasticities do not enter these analyses.

We argue that with homogeneous labour in production, the implicit labour demand function facing each household is highly elastic since, if small relative to the aggregate, each is a price taker in labour markets. The implication is that labour will bear most of the burden of its own labour taxes, independently of labour supply elasticities used. Conventional sensitivity analysis on labour supply elasticities will show little variation in tax incidence profiles. On the other hand, varying labour demand elasticities will allow for the shifting of tax burdens to other groups or households.

We investigate differences in model analyses of tax incidence using comparable nested models in which labour is either homogenous or heterogeneous in production, so that labour demand elasticities also enter. Each model is calibrated to a ten decile household data set containing data on consumption, taxes, and leisure for the UK for 1994. Labour supply elasticity calibration is based on estimates from Killingsworth (1983), with the labour demand elasticity used in calibration in the heterogeneous labour model drawing on estimates from Hamermesh (1993). Significant differences in incidence profiles are found across the two models. The heterogeneous model shows significant variations in incidence profiles as labour demand elasticities change, while the homogeneous good model shows little sensitivity to labour supply elasticities. The implication drawn is the need to more carefully specify labour demand elasticities in tax incidence analyses.

II. Tax incidence models with heterogeneous and homogeneous labour supply

It seems clear that if labour supplied by household groups is heterogeneous with imperfect substitutability in production across skill levels, then both labour demand and labour supply elasticities are needed in tax incidence analyses. If labour is treated as homogeneous across households, then if each household is small and a taker of wage rates, they implicitly face a perfectly elastic labour demand function. In this case, varying the labour supply elasticity will not change the conclusion that labour bears the burden of their own income taxes, even if tax rates differ across households.

If the labour demand elasticity is less than infinite, as labour supply functions shift due to household specific taxes, some of the burden of the tax is shifted elsewhere. The implication is that if heterogeneous labour models are used for tax incidence analysis and model parameters calibrated to both labour demand and labour supply elasticities, tax incidence results can

---

[2] See Shoven and Whalley (1972) for a simple 2 sector 2 household Harberger tax model; Piggott and Whalley (1985) for a 100 household model of the UK; Ballard, Fullerton, Shoven and Whalley (1985) for a 15 household model of the US; and Auerbach and Kotlikoff (1987) for a 55 overlapping generations dynamic structure applied to US data.

differ[3] (and potentially sharply so) from those generated by the homogenous labour model conventionally used.

We choose the household as the basic unit of tax incidence analysis not only because consumption and labour-leisure choice decisions are made at the household level, but also it is adapted in the data on income and consumption used in the empirical analysis of incidence profiles in the paper.

A heterogeneous labour household tax model

We consider an economy with households differentiated according to their skill levels, which, for our empirical application, we take to be collinear with income ranges. Each household is endowed with a fixed amount of time, which it can divide between leisure and work. A production function specifies how the various labour types combine to yield a single consumption good. Each of them buys the consumption good using income earned by selling its labour on the market along with transfers received from government, effectively buying back its leisure at its net of tax wage. Households maximize utility by choosing bundles of consumption goods and leisure subject to their budget constraint. Hours of work (labour supply), consumption and leisure are thus obtained by solving each household's optimization problem.

Taxes distort the consumption-leisure choice of households. Tax rates are household specific, and government budget balance holds with transfers the sole expenditure item. In empirical implementation, we use a single tax rate on labour income for each household to represent the composite of income and payroll taxes, and a composite indirect tax rate for each household which reflects sales (VAT) and excise taxes. These latter rates differ by household due to differing consumption patterns in the data.

More specifically, we assume CES preferences for each household as

$$U^h = [\alpha^h C^{h(\sigma^h - 1)/\sigma^h} + (1 - \alpha^h) L^{h(\sigma^h - 1)/\sigma^h}]^{\sigma^h/(\sigma^h - 1)} \qquad (1)$$

where U^h is utility, α^h is the share of income spent on the consumption good, $(1 - \alpha^h)$ is the share parameter on leisure, C^h and L^h are consumption and leisure respectively of household h, and σ^h is the elasticity of substitution between consumption and leisure of household h.

The income for household h equals the time endowment valued at the net of tax wage plus transfers received from government, i.e.

$$I^h = (1 - t_I^h) w^h \bar{L}^h + RH^h \qquad (2)$$

where I^h is the full income of household h, w^h is the gross of tax wage rate for household h, and t_I^h is the household specific income tax rate. $\bar{L}^h$ is the time endowment of household h to be divided between labour supply and leisure, and RH^h are transfers received by household h.

---

[3] One reason for the relative absence of heterogeneous labour models in empirically based general equilibrium work is the seeming difficulty of solution in the non-nested production function case. We solve it using the new PATH algorithm developed and employed with GAMS by Michael Ferris (see Appendix 2 for details).

Maximization of utility (1), subject to (2), yields demand functions for consumption and leisure for each household as,

$$C^h = \left[\frac{\alpha^h}{P(1 + t_C^h)}\right]^{\sigma^h} \left[\frac{I^h}{\alpha^h(P(1 + t_C^h))^{1-\sigma^h} + (1 - \alpha^h)(w^h(1 - t_I^h))^{1-\sigma^h}}\right] \quad (3)$$

$$L^h = \left[\frac{(1 - \alpha^h)}{w^h(1 - t_I^h)}\right]^{\sigma^h} \left[\frac{I^h}{\alpha^h(P(1 + t_C^h))^{1-\sigma^h} + (1 - \alpha^h)(w^h(1 - t_I^h))^{1-\sigma^h}}\right] \quad (4)$$

where w^h is the gross of tax wage rate for labor of type h (supplied by household h), P is the price of the consumption good, and t_C^h is the consumption (or indirect) tax rate faced by household h. The budget balance condition for households implies that on the expenditure side

$$I^h = P(1 + t_c^h)C^h + w^h(1 - t_I^h)L^h \quad (5)$$

Each household supplies labour to the market which reflects the difference between its labour endowment and its demand for leisure,

$$LS^h = \bar{L}^h - L^h \quad (6)$$

where LS^h is labour supplied by household h. The economy wide labour supply is the sum of labour supplied across the individual households. In equilibrium, equation (6) is also the labour market clearing condition for labour of type h.

In the model, we assume that the labour each household supplies is differentiated by skill level from the labour supplied by all other households, and we represent this through a CES production technology for the single output Y in which all labour types enter, i.e.

$$Y = \lambda \left(\sum_h \delta^h LS^{h(\sigma_p-1)/\sigma_p}\right)^{\sigma_p/(\sigma_p-1)} \quad (7)$$

where LS^h is the input (labour supply) of type h, δ^h is the share parameter in production on each category of labour, λ is a units term and σ_p is the elasticity of substitution among labour types in production.

Producers pay the gross of tax wage rate when hiring labour from each household, and households receive the net of income tax wage. For simplicity, we assume that only one consumption good is produced in this economy, and producers maximize profit, $\prod$, given by

$$\prod = PY - \sum_h w^h LS^h \quad (8)$$

where the P is price of the consumption good, and LS^h is the labour input of type h.

Profit maximization results in the labour demand function for each labour type h as,

$$LD^h = \frac{1}{\lambda}\left(\delta^h + \sum_{hh}\delta^{hh}\left(\frac{\prod\limits_{hh\neq h} w^{hh}}{w^h}\right)^{\sigma_p-1}\right)^{\sigma_p/(\sigma_p-1)}$$ (9)

where LD^h is labour demand of type h, and in equilibrium also equals labour supply LS^h.

The government in this economy raises revenues, R, by taxing income and consumption, i.e.

$$R = \sum_h t_l^h w^h LS^h + \sum_h t_c^h P C^h$$ (10)

We assume a single period in which all output is consumed (there is no saving). In equilibrium, P and the household wage rates, w^h, are endogenously determined such that there is market clearing in the consumption good

$$Y = \sum_h C^h$$ (11)

and there is market clearing for each labour type,

$$LS^h = LD^h.$$ (12)

As transfers to households are the only government expenditure item, government budget balance also requires that in equilibrium $R = \sum_h RH^h$. Thus, for each household h, in equilibrium labour supplied of each type equals its use in production, and a profile of skill specific equilibrium wage rates will be determined. For convenience, in this model, we can choose the numeraire of this system to be that the price of the consumption good is equal to 1.

A homogeneous labour tax model

In contrast to the heterogeneous labour model, when labour is homogeneous in production we need only specify a model with labour as the single input into production. We assume a constant marginal product of labour production function, which is linear in (total) labour[4].

$$Y = \lambda \sum_h LS^h$$ (13)

A single wage applies to all households' labour supply because of the homogeneity of labour inputs, and the relationship between the wage rate and

---

[4] This is a special case of the production function (7) in the model above, for the case where σ_p becomes infinite.

the price of the consumption good is given by

$$P = \frac{w}{\lambda}.$$ (14)

Households still differ in their preferences as in (1), still face household specific income and consumption tax rates, but unlike in the heteogeneous labour model face a common wage rate. Equilibrium in this case is given by market clearing for the single labour type in the model; with, in this case, one single wage rate endogenously determined.

This homogeneous labour model is thus a special case of the model presented above, and nests into the more general heterogeneous labour model.

III. Implementation of homogeneous and heterogeneous labour tax incidence models

We perform tax incidence analyses using two models above by calibrating[5] each to a base year data set, specifying labour demand and labour supply elasticity values, and performing counterfactual equilibrium analyses. The base case data set we use reflects the UK economy for the UK tax year 1994/95[6]. We use data on incomes, taxes and benefits by household decile compiled by the UK Treasury and reported in the UK government statistical publication Economic Trends (1996). This source reports data for non retired households grouped by income[7] decile, benefits received both in cash and in kind, and direct and indirect taxes paid by each household decile.

Base case data

For modelling purposes, we require a base case data set which is fully model admissible. This means that all variables which appear in each model should be identified in the data set, and all of the model equilibrium conditions need to be satisfied. Among these are conditions that the value of consumption across households should equal the value of production (a zero profit condition in production implies that income received from supplying labour equals the value of production). All households should also be represented by data which satisfies household budget balance, and government expenditures equal government receipts (government budget balance).

The basic data we use, while having most of the information we need, is deficient for our purposes in number of respects. Household leisure consump-

---

[5] Calibration, here, denotes the exact calibration of each model to a model admissible data set which is constructed from unadjusted data from a variety of statistical sources. This is the sense of calibration discussed by Mansur and Whalley (1984) and differs from the calibration procedures used by real business cycles researchers (see Kydland and Prescott (1982)). In this latter work, no readjustments are made to data, and model parameter values chosen by reference to literature sources with a view to seeing how close model solution can be made to actual data. See also Watson (1993).

[6] April 5th 1994 to April 4th 1995. This is the year used in recording tax and household income data by the UK tax authorities.

[7] The income concept used in the published data is "household equivalized disposable income".

tion is not identified. Government budget balance is violated in the data, since all taxes paid by households are identified but only those government expenditures leading directly to direct household benefits (cash transfers, education, and health care appear, but defence, for instance, is missing). In the basic data, government expenditures in aggregate are thus substantially less than tax revenues. Also, individual household budget constraints do not automatically hold.

A series of adjustments and modifications are therefore necessary to the basic data set before it can be used for model calibration. These are set out in more detail in Appendix 1, but can be summarised as follows. We scale the in kind portion of government benefits for each decile such that government expenditures equal taxes collected. Transfers received by each decile in the model are thus the sum of cash and in kind benefits provided by government. We use wage rate data by household and UK time use survey data to construct data on the value of leisure time by household for each decile, valuing time at the net of tax wage. We then make further adjustments to ensure full consistency of the data set to the model, including modifications such that household budget constraints hold in the data.

The resulting model admissible data set across ten UK households is displayed in Table 1. In this data, gross income is concentrated in the higher deciles, with transfers concentrated in the lower deciles. The household profile of leisure consumption reflects the interaction of hours (falling as we move to the higher income ranges) and wage rates at which leisure is valued (rising by income range). The two tax rate profiles are for average (not marginal) tax rates. For income taxes they rise by income range, but not by as much as might be thought from an examination of tax rate schedules. This is because of income tax allowances, caps on social (national) insurance contributions, untaxed housing capital income, and UK tax shelters (pensions, savings in tax sheltered vehicles), all of which have a major influence on the average tax rate profile. The indirect tax rates fall by income range due to the influence of excise taxes, particularly on petrol, but also on drink, both of which are a considerably larger fraction of expenditures for the poor than the rich.

Using information on elasticities, we calibrate both the homogeneous and heterogeneous labour models to this benchmark equilibrium data set. To do this, we first take the benchmark data set from Table 1 in value terms, and decompose it into separate price and quantity observations. Following Harberger (1962), and Shoven and Whalley (1992) we choose units both for labour by type, and for consumption, as those amounts which sell for £1 in the base case equilibrium. Using this convention all prices and wages are one in the base case, and all quantities are as given by the base case observations in Table 1. The calibrated versions of each model replicate this base case data as a model solution.

Elasticities

The elasticity parameters needed for the models are the ten household specific substitution elasticities in consumption (CES preferences) which are used in both models, and the substitution elasticity in production (in the CES production function) in the heterogeneous labour model. Direct estimates of these elasticities are not available in the literature. Elasticities in consumption over

Table 1. Model admissible household data set by deciles of income for non-retired households, UK 1994/95[8]

Households[9]	(a) Gross of tax labor income[a]	(b) Transfers[a]	(c) Income and other direct taxes paid[a,10]	(d) Indirect taxes paid[a,11]	(e) Consumption gross of indirect taxes[a,12]	(f) Leisure[a,13]	(g) Income tax rate[14]	(h) Indirect tax rate[15]
Decile 1 (Poor)	3079	14638	930	2139	16787	14491	0.05	0.13
Decile 2	5918	12880	1194	2183	17604	17085	0.06	0.12
Decile 3	11021	11040	1880	2759	20181	14076	0.09	0.14
Decile 4	16111	9867	2815	3213	23163	11934	0.11	0.14
Decile 5	21184	8559	3831	3572	25912	10895	0.13	0.14
Decile 6	26161	8205	4745	3957	29621	10455	0.14	0.13
Decile 7	30140	6858	5531	4266	31467	12293	0.15	0.14
Decile 8	34614	5645	6576	4362	33683	13895	0.16	0.13
Decile 9	41918	5166	8175	4537	38909	15449	0.17	0.12
Decile 10 (Rich)	71147	4440	15082	5551	60505	6871	0.20	0.09

Notes: All figures in this table noted with superscript **a** are millions of £, for the tax year 1994/95.

goods and leisure must be inferred from literature estimates of labour supply elasticities. Elasticities of substitution in production between labour types must be inferred from literature estimates of labour demand elasticities for various types of labour.

From the production function (7), we can use the first order conditions for profit maximization and the derived labour demand function (9). The elasticity of labour demand in production is given by $e_{LD}^h = \dfrac{\partial LD^h}{\partial w^h} \dfrac{w^h}{LD^h}$ and differentiating (9) w.r.t. w^h gives

$$
e_{LD}^h = \frac{-\sigma_p \sum\limits_{hh \neq h} \delta^{hh} \left(\prod\limits_{h \neq h} w^{hh} \right)^{\sigma_p - 1}}{w^{h^{\sigma_p - 1}} \left[\delta^h + \sum\limits_{hh} \delta^{hh} \left(\dfrac{\prod\limits_{h \neq h} w^{hh}}{w^h} \right)^{\sigma_p - 1} \right]}
\tag{15}
$$

In the base case all gross of tax wage rates are unity, and if, in addition, household labour shares are small, e_{LD}^h effectively collapses to $-\sigma^p$. We choose the elasticity of substitution between labour types in production which, from (15), we can calibrate numerically to values of labour demand elasticities found in the literature (Hamermesh (1993)), and use other sensitivity cases discussed below to reflect ranges around a central case value. As there are ten household demand elasticities in the model around the base case equilibrium, and only one free parameter, σ^p, in calibration we choose σ^p such that elasticities across households (which do not vary that much) are within a desired range.

Labour supply elasticities, in contrast, are found using the leisure demand function (4). Point estimates of labour supply elasticities for each household in the neighbourhood of the benchmark equilibrium can be generated by noting that

$$
\frac{\partial LS^h}{\partial w^h} \frac{w^h}{LS^h} = \frac{\partial LS^h}{\partial L^h} \frac{\partial L^h}{\partial w^h} \frac{w^h}{L^h} \frac{L^h}{LS^h} = (-1)\eta_{LE} \frac{L^h}{LS^h}
\tag{16}
$$

We use the leisure demand function (4) to derive the leisure demand elasticity, η_{LE} which is given by

$$
\eta_{LE}^h = -\left(\sigma^h + \frac{(\sigma^h - 1)(1 - \alpha^h)w^{h^{1-\sigma^h}}}{\alpha^h P^{1-\sigma^h} + (1 - \alpha^h)w^{h^{1-\sigma^h}}} \right)
\tag{17}
$$

---

[8] See Appendix 1 for more detail.

[9] These households are grouped by "original" household income as in Economic Trends (1995). Original income is pre tax/pre transfer income.

[10] This includes all social insurance contributions.

[11] This includes VAT and all excises (especially on petrol, tobacco, drink).

[12] This is gross of indirect taxes.

[13] This is from UK time use survey data; leisure time is valued at the net of tax wage.

[14] This includes income tax and social insurance contributions.

[15] This includes the VAT plus specific excise taxes.

Table 2. Model production and consumption side elasticities, and literature justification

A. Range of labour supply elasticities based on those reported in Killingsworth (1983)

Range of values	Labour supply elasticity assumed for each household	Range of elasticities of substitution in consumption implied for household deciles
High	1.0	0.52–10.5
Mid (central case)	0.3	0.38–3.50
Low	0.15	0.32–1.57

B. Range of labour demand elasticities based on those reported in Hamermesh (1993)

Range	Range of labour demand elasticities by decile	Elasticity of substitution used in production
High	−1.81 to −2.10	1.93
Mid Range (central case)	−1.05 to −1.24	1.32
Low	−0.58 to −0.67	0.71

The point estimate of the labour supply elasticity for each household, given σ^h, is:

$$e_{LS}^h = \left(\sigma^h + \frac{(\sigma_p - 1)(1 - \alpha^h)w^{h^{1-\sigma^h}}}{\alpha^h P^{1-\sigma^h} + (1 - \alpha^h)w^{h^{1-\sigma^h}}} \right) \frac{L^h}{LS^h} \tag{18}$$

In the neighbourhood of the base case, where the price of goods and all wage rates are unity, this collapses to

$$e_{LS}^h = (\sigma^h + (\sigma_p - 1)(1 - \alpha^h)w^{h^{1-\sigma^h}}) \frac{L^h}{LS^h} \tag{19}$$

and if $(1 - \alpha^h)$ is small[16] $e_{LS}^h \approx \sigma^h \dfrac{L^h}{LS^h}$.

We choose values for labour supply elasticities from literature estimates and using (16) these imply leisure demand elasticities. Using those as point estimates around the benchmark equilibrium, and using (18), elasticities of substitution in preferences are determined for each household decile. The equation (18) yields an implicit function for σ^h, which we solve numerically.

Table 2 sets out the elasticity ranges we use for in the two models and the implied substitution elasticities in consumption and production. These are approximately consistent with ranges of parameter estimates reported by Hamermesh (1993) for labour demand, and Killingsworth (1983) for labour supply.

---

[16] Typically, however, consumption share parameters on leisure are not small.

In the model, there are 10 separate labour demand elasticities for each labour type. These elasticities vary, and hence we calibrate the model to point estimates of these elasticities in the neighbourhood of the benchmark equilibrium. In addition, there is only one free model parameter (the elasticity of substitution among labour types in production) so that exact calibration for each household type labour demand elasticity is not feasible. We thus vary the single production side elasticity until the household labour demand elasticities, which are similar across households, are within the desired range.

IV. Results

We have used the heterogeneous and homogeneous labour models described above and calibrated to UK data for the 1995/96 tax year to investigate the behaviour of tax incidence results across models. We do this for different tax experiments, different labour supply elasticity (consumption/leisure substitution) configurations, freezing the labour demand elasticity specification; and for different labour demand elasticity specifications, freezing the labour supply elasticity specification.

The essence of tax policy analysis lies in comparing welfare changes between benchmark and counterfactual equilibria. How much a typical household has gained or lost because of changes in policy in money metric terms, or how much money is required to bring him/her back to their original welfare can be measured at either original or new prices. The Hicksian equivalent variation (EV) is a money metric measure of the welfare change between benchmark and counterfactual scenarios using benchmark (old) prices. It is the difference in money metric utility at old prices corresponding to benchmark and counterfactual model solutions; i.e.

$$EV = E(U^N, P^0) - E(U^0, P^0) \qquad (20)$$

where superscripts N and O represent new and old values for the variable on which they appear, U is the utility, and E is the expenditure function which depends on prices and utility level.

If utility functions are of the linear homogeneous type, then original and new equilibria can be thought of in terms of a radial expansion of the utility surface. In this case the change in money metric welfare between benchmark and counterfactual solutions of the model is proportional to the change in utility or the percentage change along the radial projection between the two consumption points.

$$EV = \frac{U^N - U^0}{U^0} I^0 \qquad (21)$$

where N and O represent new and old values of the variables as before, and I represents the income.

In Table 3 we report tax incidence calculations for a case where we replace the pre existing pattern of labour income tax rates by household by a yield preserving uniform rate income tax across households. We consider cases where we freeze labour supply elasticities first at 0.3, and then at 1.0, and vary the ranges we use for labour demand elasticities in the heterogeneous labour

Table 3. Comparing homogeneous and heterogeneous labour models

Specification
- Experiment: replacing existing labour income taxes by yield preserving uniform rate
- Elasticity specification: Labour supply elasticity 0.3 and 1.0 in two cases, labour demand elasticities range from −0.58 to −2.1.

Results:
Welfare gains/losses by decile in terms of Hicksian EV as a fraction of base income (with low labour supply elasticity (0.3))

Decile	Homogeneous Labour model	Heterogeneous Labour model Labour demand elasticities ranges as specified in Table 2		
		Low (−0.58 to −0.67)	Middle (−1.05 to −1.24)	High (−1.8 to −2.1)
1 poor	−0.0581	−0.0134	−0.0501	−0.0591
2	−0.0485	−0.0173	−0.0434	−0.0493
3	−0.0424	−0.0334	−0.0401	−0.0430
4	−0.0299	−0.0306	−0.0296	−0.0303
5	−0.0143	−0.0211	−0.0153	−0.0146
6	−0.0064	−0.0159	−0.0078	−0.0066
7	0.0044	−0.0059	0.0028	0.0042
8	0.0173	0.0060	0.0155	0.0171
9	0.0272	0.0154	0.0253	0.0270
10 rich	0.0670	0.0562	0.0660	0.0666

Results:
Welfare gains/losses by decile in terms of Hicksian EV as a fraction of base income (with high labour supply elasticity (1.0))

Decile	Homogeneous Labour model	Heterogeneous Labour model Labour demand elasticities ranges as specified in Table 2		
		Low (−0.58 to −0.67)	Middle (−1.05 to −1.24)	High (−1.8 to −2.1)
1 poor	−0.0577	−0.0376	−0.0503	−0.0585
2	−0.0481	−0.0709	−0.0442	−0.0486
3	−0.042	−0.2191	−0.0420	−0.0421
4	−0.0295	−0.2944	−0.0312	−0.0294
5	−0.014	−0.3300	−0.0150	−0.0140
6	−0.0061	−0.1114	−0.0060	−0.0061
7	0.0047	0.3908	0.0066	0.0045
8	0.0176	0.0739	0.0221	0.0172
9	0.0276	0.1476	0.0349	0.0270
10 rich	0.0676	−0.0025	0.0737	0.0670

model. We compare model results across the homogeneous labour model and the various specifications of the heterogeneous model for these labour supply elasticities.

Results in Table 3 show the redistribution across households in these cases. Richer households gain because their taxes fall, and poorer households lose since the replacement tax is at a uniform rate and their taxes rise. However, there is considerable variation in the redistribution profile across the two elasticity cases for the heterogeneous labour model. Considerably more redistribution occurs in the high elasticity case since wage rate changes in response to the tax replacement are small; low income households bear most of the burden of their higher taxes, and high income households gain by most of their tax saving.

As one moves across labour demand elasticity specifications the redistributive effects from the tax changes become larger, with wage changes less pronounced. Labour demand elasticities have a significant influence on the perceived tax incidence effects from the tax replacement. From various sensitivity analyses, we find that as labour demand elasticities increase, the income tax incidence profile in the heterogeneous labour model approaches that of the homogeneous labour model for any given value of the labour supply elasticity.

In Table 4 we explore how the model comparisons change as we vary labour supply elasticities. We consider the same tax replacement, i.e. replacing the existing profile of income tax rates by a uniform rate income tax across households, but only consider the mid range specification of labour demand elasticities, changing labour supply elasticities in both homogeneous and heterogeneous labour models.

Results in Table 4 show that the incidence profile changes relatively little between heterogeneous and homogeneous labour models as labour supply elasticities increase. The low income households lose about 5–6 percent of the base year income in both heterogeneous and homogeneous labour models irrespective of different values of labour supply elasticities. For middle range values of labour demand elasticities (irrespective to any specific value of labour supply elasticity), income tax incidence profiles of replacing base case labour income taxes by yield preserving labour income tax rates become comparable across two models.

As final sets of results in Table 5 we present incidence results for three different yield preserving tax changes; the first one only involves income taxes, the second one involves income and sales taxes, and the last one involves only sales taxes. We use a 0.3 labour supply elasticity and mid range labour demand elasticities.

In both the income tax case and the combined income and sales tax case we find low income households lose and high incomes households gain when base case taxes are replaced by yield preserving tax rates, but the pattern of gains is different in the upper tail of the distribution across heterogeneous and homogeneous models.

V. Conclusions

In this paper we analyze how labour demand elasticities, long neglected in empirically based tax incidence analysis, affect incidence conclusions. Using a data set for the UK for tax year 1994/95 covering 10 household deciles we

Table 4. Impacts of varying labour supply elasticities on incidence profile comparisons

Specification
- Experiment: replacing existing labour income taxes by yield preserving uniform rate
- Elasticity specification: Labour supply elasticity 0.3, mid range demand elasticities in the heterogeneous labour model.

Results:
Welfare gains/losses by households, Hicksian EV as a fraction of base income

Decile	Labour supply elasticity (0.15)		Labour supply elasticity (0.3)		Labour supply elasticity (1.0)	
	Homogeneous labour Model	Heterogeneous labour model	Homogeneous labour Model	Heterogeneous labour model	Homogeneous labour Model	Heterogeneous labour model
1 poor	−0.0582	−0.0500	−0.0581	−0.0501	−0.0577	−0.0585
2	−0.0486	−0.0431	−0.0485	−0.0434	−0.0481	−0.0486
3	−0.0426	−0.0395	−0.0424	−0.0401	−0.0420	−0.0421
4	−0.0300	−0.0290	−0.0299	−0.0296	−0.0295	−0.0294
5	−0.0144	−0.0149	−0.0143	−0.0153	−0.0140	−0.0140
6	−0.0065	−0.0075	−0.0064	−0.0078	−0.0061	−0.0061
7	0.0043	0.0028	0.0044	0.0028	0.0047	0.0045
8	0.0172	0.0150	0.0173	0.0155	0.0176	0.0172
9	0.0270	0.0244	0.0272	0.0253	0.0276	0.0270
10 rich	0.0668	0.0650	0.0670	0.0660	0.0676	0.0670

Table 5. Incidence comparison for different tax changes for the heterogeneous labour and homogeneous labour models

Specification
• Labour supply elasticity set at 0.3
• Labour demand elasticities set at mid range values in the heterogeneous labour model.

Results:
Welfare gains/losses by households, Hicksian EV as a fraction of base income

Decile	Only income tax		Income and sales tax		Only sales tax	
	Homogeneous labour Model	Heterogeneous labour model	Homogeneous labour Model	Heterogeneous labour model	Homogeneous labour Model	Heterogeneous labour model
1 poor	−0.0581	−0.0501	−0.0551	−0.0489	0.0029	0.0026
2	−0.0485	−0.0434	−0.0478	−0.0434	0.0006	0.0006
3	−0.0424	−0.0401	−0.0324	−0.0307	0.0101	0.0096
4	−0.0299	−0.0296	−0.0167	−0.0166	0.0132	0.0129
5	−0.0143	−0.0153	−0.0008	−0.0014	0.0134	0.0134
6	−0.0064	−0.0078	0.0039	0.0032	0.0100	0.0102
7	0.0044	0.0028	0.0164	0.0155	0.0116	0.0118
8	0.0173	0.0155	0.0235	0.0225	0.0058	0.0061
9	0.0272	0.0253	0.0217	0.0208	−0.0057	−0.0054
10 rich	0.0670	0.0660	0.0314	0.0307	−0.0337	−0.0338

use two models to evaluate the incidence effect of various tax changes, specially the replacement of the existing pattern of income tax rates by a uniform rate yield preserving alternative. We consider two models, one with labour heterogeneous in production, i.e. 10 different labour types (one for each decile) in production; and the other with labour homogeneous across households i.e. only one type of labour in production. The substitution elasticity among labour types in production determines labour demand elasticities. Our results suggest that labour demand elasticities do indeed matter for tax incidence conclusions.

Appendix 1. Data sources

This appendix presents details on various data sources and adjustments that underlie Table 1. The main data sources are Table 3A (Appendix 1) of Economic Trends, 1995/96, p. 36, New Earnings Survey 1995 and Time Use Survey reported in Dex et al. (1995).

The gross income in column (a) of Table 1 in the text comprises original income and direct taxes (see Table A1 below). Original income includes wages and salaries, imputed income from benefits in kind, self-employment income, occupational pensions, annuities and other income. Direct taxes include employees' national insurance (NI) contributions. The household average direct tax rate to be income and other taxes divided by gross of tax income plus transfers.

The UK Economic Trends data distinguishes five different concepts of income: original, income, gross income, disposable income, post tax income and final income. Original income plus cash benefits equal gross income, disposable income is gross income minus direct taxes. Post tax income is disposable income minus indirect taxes Final income equals post tax income plus in kind benefits.

The transfers presented in column (b) of Table 1 in the text include direct cash benefits, in kind transfers, and consumption of publicly provided goods services such as national defence. Direct cash benefits consist of retirement pension contributions, unemployment benefit, invalidity pension and allowance, sickness and industrial injury benefit, widow's benefits, and statutory maternity pay/allowance. Non-contributory benefits include income support, child benefit, housing benefit, invalid care allowances, attendance allowance, disability living allowance, industrial injury disablement benefit, student maintenance awards, government training schemes, family credit and other non-contributory benefits. Benefits in kind consist of education, national health service, housing subsidy, rail travel subsidy, bus travel subsidy, school meals and welfare milk.

The gross consumption of each household, included in column (e) of Table 1 in the text, is derived by adding cash, in kind and non-contributory benefits to original income and subtracting the direct and indirect taxes paid by the household. Consumption thus is gross of indirect taxes that include taxes on final goods and services, VAT, duty on tobacco, beer and cider, wines and spirits, hydrocarbon oils, vehicle excise duty, TV licences, stamp duty on house purchase, customs duties, betting taxes, fossil fuel levy, and Camelot national lottery fund. It also includes intermediate taxes such as

Table A1. Components of gross of tax labour income in table 1 (see text) (£ million 1995/1996 UK tax year)

	H1	H2	H3	H4	H5	H6	H7	H8	H9	H10	Total
Original income	2149	4724	9141	13296	17353	21416	24609	28038	33743	56065	210534
Direct taxes	930	1194	1880	2815	3831	4745	5531	6576	8175	15082	50759
Total	3079	5918	11021	16111	21184	26161	30140	34614	41918	71147	261293

Table A2. Gross consumption by households in table 1 (see text) (£ million 1995/1996 UK tax year)

Decile	H1	H2	H3	H4	H5	H6	H7	H8	H9	H10	Total
Gross income	3079	5918	11021	16111	21184	26161	30140	34614	41918	71147	261293
Transfers	14638	12880	11040	9867	8559	8205	6858	5645	5166	4440	86479
Direct taxes	930	1194	1880	2815	3831	4745	5531	6576	8175	15082	50759
Total	16787	17604	20181	23163	25912	29621	31467	33683	38909	60505	297013

Table A3. The value of leisure consumption by households in table 1 (see text)

	H1	H2	H3	H4	H5	H6	H7	H8	H9	H10	Total
Earnings/week/ households (£)	160	210	223	243	272	306	355	403	473	543	319
Working weeks	13	23	41	55	64	70	69	70	71	91	57
Leisure weeks	91	81	63	49	40	34	35	34	33	13	47
Value of leisure by household (£ million)	14491	17085	14076	11934	10895	10455	12293	13895	15449	6871	127444

commercial and industrial rates, employer's NI contributions, duty on hydrocarbon oils, vehicle excise and other duties.

The value of leisure reported in Table 1 in the text has been obtained by multiplying nonworking weeks by the weekly earnings rate. The number of non-working weeks is the difference between the working weeks and 104 weeks. The total working week represents the total labour endowment per household with two working members. Earnings per week for top and bottom deciles, and first and third quartiles are taken from the New Earnings Survey 1995. These are interpolated for other deciles. Working weeks are derived by dividing the original income by the weekly earnings.

Appendix 2. Solution method of the model

Both homogeneous and heterogeneous labour models discussed in this paper are set up as a mixed complementarity problems and solved in GAMS software using the PATH solver.

Dirkse and Ferris (1995) state the basic idea behind the PATH solver in terms of a "zero finding problem". For any function $F : \Re^n \to \Re^n$ with lower bound $-\infty \leq l$ and an upper bound $\leq u \leq +\infty$ the problem *is to* find $z \in \Re^n$ such that

either $z_i = l_i$ and $F_i(z) \geq 0$

or $z_i = l_i$ and $F_i(z) \leq 0$

or $l_i \leq z_i \leq u_I$ and $F_i(z) = 0$

PATH constructs a solution using a damped Newton method such as

$$0 = F_{B_{(x)}} = F_{x_{(B)}} + (x - x_B)$$

where x_B is the Euclidean projection of x onto the Box $B := [l, u]$. A vector x solves this nonlinear equation only if $z = x_B$ solves the MCP. A more detailed explanation of this algorithm is beyond the scope of this paper, many technical papers on the topic are available in Ferris's homepage: http://www.cs.wisc.edu/~ferris/.

GAMS syntax (Brook, Kendrick and Meeraus (1992)) permits us to generate a non linear mixed complemetarity model by declaring and assigning sets, data, parameters, variables, equations in the model. PATH is invoked by the "OPTION MCP = PATH" statement in the GAMS code and a command line "solve ⟨model name⟩ using MCP" instructs GAMS to solve the model using the PATH solver. We use batch files to compute incidence profiles across various scenarios for different values of elasticities and tax rates for households.

References

Auerbach AJ, Kotlikoff LJ (1987) Dynamic fiscal policy. Cambridge University Press
Ballard CL, Fullerton D, Shoven JB, Whalley J (1985) A general equilibrium model for tax policy evaluation. University of Chicago Press, Chicago

Dirkse SP, Ferris MC (1995) CCPLIB: A collection of nonlinear mixed complementarity problems. Optimization Methods and Software 5:319–345

Dex S, Clark A, Taylor M (1995) Household labour supply employment. Department Research Series No. 43, ESRC Center for Micro-social Change, University of Essex

Economic Trends (1996) Office of National Statistics. London

Gillespie W (1965) Effect of public expenditure in distribution of income. In Musgrave R (ed.) Essays in fiscal federalism, Brookings, Washington DC, pp. 122–186

Hamermesh DS (1993) Labour demand. Princeton University Press, New Jersey

Harberger AC (1962) The incidence of the corporation income tax. Journal of Political Economy 70:215–40

Killingsworth M (1983) Labour supply. Cambridge University Press

Kydland FE, Prescott EC (1982) Time to build and aggregate fluctuations. Econometrica 50:1345–70

Mansur A, Whalley J (1986) Numerical specification of applied general equilibrium models: Estimation, calibration and data. In: Scarf HE, Shoven JB (eds.) Applied general equilibrium analysis, Cambridge University Press

Pechman JA, Okner BA (1974) Who bears the burden of taxes? Brookings Institute, Washington D.C.

Piggott J, Whalley J (1985) UK tax policy and applied general equilibrium analysis. Cambridge University Press

Shoven JB, Whalley J (1992) Applying general equilibrium. Cambridge University Press

Shoven JB, Whalley J (1972) A general equilibrium calculation of the effects of differential taxation of income from capital in the U.S.. Journal of Public Economics 1:281–322

Watson MW (1993) Measures of fit for calibrated models. Journal of Political Economy 101:1011–1041

III Tax leakages and efficiency

Modelling the hidden economy and the tax-gap in New Zealand

David E. A. Giles*

Department of Economics, University of Victoria, P.O. Box 1700, STN CSC, Victoria, B.C., Canada, V8W 2Y2 (e-mail: dgiles@uvic.ca)

First version received: August 1997/Final version received: March 1999

Abstract. This paper develops and estimates a structural, latent variable, model for the hidden economy in New Zealand, and a separate currency-demand model. The estimated latent variable model is used to generate an historical time-series index of hidden economic activity, which is calibrated via the information from the currency-demand model. Special attention is paid to data non-stationarity, and to diagnostic testing. Over the period 1968 to 1994, the size of the hidden economy is found to vary between 6.8% and 11.3% of measured GDP. This, in turn, implies that the total tax-gap is of the order of 6.4% to 10.2% of total tax liability in that country. Of course, not all of this foregone revenue would be recoverable, as not all of the activity in the underground economy is responsive to changes in taxation or other policies.

Key words: Underground economy, latent variables, tax avoidance, tax evasion, tax-gap

JEL classifications: C32, C51, E32, E41

* I am grateful to Patrick Caragata, for initiating and supporting this research, and for his many contributions which have greatly improved this paper. Earlier versions were discussed at Workshops on the Health of the New Zealand Tax System, Wellington, 1995. I would like to thank Daniel Aldersley, Lief Bluck, Johannah Branson, Phil Briggs, Linda DeBenedictis, Erwin Diewert, Johannah Dods, Paul Dunmore, Michael Dunn, Ed Feige, Judith Giles, Chris Gillion, Anna Heiller, Knox Lovell, Ewen McCann, Michael O'Connor, Gerald Scully, John Small, Adolf Stroombergen, and Ken White for their many comments, suggestions, and assistance with data. The insightful comments of two referees led to a significant improvement of this paper, including the addition of Appendix II. The content this paper is the responsibility of the author, and should not be attributed to Inland Revenue New Zealand, which financed this study. The author's related papers on the hidden economy and tax evasion are available in Adobe pdf format on the internet at *http://web.uvic.ca/econ/economet_he.html*.

I. Introduction

Foregone tax revenue resulting from the underground economy is a major, and apparently growing, problem. We describe a modelling methodology which yields a time-series of the underground economy for New Zealand, from which a series of the "tax-gap" can be obtained. There have been no attempts to obtain such measures for New Zealand previously, but this is a topical issue in view of the current political debate on taxation policy and taxation compliance in that country.

The hidden economy and tax-gap have sizeable budgetary implications, and implications for taxation incidence and income distribution. For instance, if a principal cause of growth in the hidden economy is an actual, or perceived, increase over time in the tax burden, then an increase in (average or marginal) tax rates may reduce revenue and *worsen* the budget deficit. Similarly, if there is a significant hidden component to economic activity, then many economic indicators will be measured with error. Finally, there are political and social implications – a flourishing informal sector may reflect dissatisfaction, on the part of the electorate, with the degree of regulation of their activities.

There is an extensive literature on the measurement of the hidden economy, and section II discusses the major methods that have been used to address this issue. Our own econometric methodology is described in section III; data issues are discussed in section IV; and sections V and VI discuss the formulation and estimation of our models. Section VII provides estimated time-paths for the hidden economy and the tax-gap in New Zealand, and our conclusions are summarized in section VIII.

II. Measuring the hidden economy

The evidence on the actual size of the hidden economy is very mixed. Frey and Weck-Hanneman (1984) report that for seventeen OECD countries in 1978, the size of the underground economy (relative to GNP) varied from 4.1% for Japan, through 8.0% for the UK and 8.3% for the USA, to 13.2% in the case of Sweden, and with Canada at the sample mean of 8.8%. In more recent work, Schneider (1997) found that the average OECD figure had risen to about 15% of GDP by 1994, with Canada still close to this international average. The latter figure can be compared with the 5% to 7% of GDP that Mirus and Smith (1994) estimate for Canada in 1976, rising to almost 15% in 1990. Spiro (1994) estimates the Canadian underground economy at between 8% and 11% of GDP in 1993.

Other studies summarised by Aigner *et al.* (1988) report figures for the USA in 1978 which range from 4% (Park (1979)) to 33% (Feige (1982)) of GNP. On the other hand, evidence for the USA in 1970 yields a range, for this ratio, from 2.6% (Tanzi (1983)) to 11% (Schneider and Pommerehne (1985)). Bhattacharyya (1990) estimates the hidden economy for the UK to be 3.8% of GNP in 1960, with a peak of 11.1% in early 1976, and averaging around 8% during 1984; while a British Inland Revenue analysis reported by Chote (1995) suggests that the hidden economy comprises 6% to 8% of GDP. The available evidence is varied and imprecise, but the results of our study are consistent with the more robust of the above numbers. There are several surveys of the literature on measuring the hidden economy, including those of Blades (1982), Boeschoten and Fase (1984), Carter (1984), Frey and Pommerehne (1982, 1984), Gaertner and Wenig (1985), Kirchgaessner (1984), Weck (1983), and Tedds (1998).

As well as providing information about the range of the international estimates, these surveys discuss the different techniques (and their strengths and weaknesses) that have been used by various authors. One criticism of most of these approaches is that they focus on one cause of underground economic activity, and one indicator. In contrast, Frey and Weck-Hannemann (1984), Aigner et al. (1988), and Tedds (1998) use "latent variable" structural modelling to measure the size of the hidden economy. The (unobservable) latent variable here is the extent of underground activity, perhaps expressed as a percentage of measured real GDP. The MIMIC ("Multiple Indicators, Multiple Causes") model of Zellner (1970), Goldberger (1972), Jöreskog and Goldberger (1975), and others allows for *several* "indicator" variables and *several* "causal" variables in forming structural relationships to "explain" the latent variable. This latent variable/MIMIC model approach forms the basis for our own analysis here.

III. A modelling methodology

The MIMIC model is a variant of the LISREL ("Linear Interdependent Structural Relationships") models, of Jöreskog and Sörbom (1993a,b) and others. A MIMIC model uses observable data on a range of "causal" variables, and a range of data on observable "indicator" variables, to "predict" the values for one or more unobserable ("latent") varaibles. This type of model yields only a time-series *index* for the latent variables – in our case there is just one such variable, namely the size of the underground economy relative to the size of measured GDP. Accordingly, some sort of extraneous information is needed to calibrate the index so that we can then construct a cardinal time-path of the underground economy. Once the underground activity is measured, the effective tax rate (*i.e.*, the ratio of tax revenue to GDP) can be used to obtain an estimate of the size of the "tax-gap", and to address other policy issues.

We calibrate our hidden economy index via the estimation of a particular currency demand equation. Our currency-demand equation differs from the interesting model proposed by Bhattacharyya (1990), also in the context of underground activity. We allow for different velocities of circulation in the "hidden" and "recorded" sectors; explicitly "explain" hidden activity; and avoid a functional approximation in his approach. We allow for the non-stationarity of our time-series data, which he, and others, do not. Interestingly, our results imply a long-run average value for the "size" of the hidden economy that is almost identical to that obtained by using Bhattacharyya's approach in an earlier version of our work (Giles (1995, 1997a)), as is discussed briefly in Appendix II.

In our model, measured (nominal) currency demand is:

$$M_t = \beta_0' Y_{Rt1}^{\beta} Y_{Ht2}^{\beta} R_{t3}^{\beta} P_{t4}^{\beta}, \tag{1}$$

where Y_{Rt} and Y_{Ht} are "recorded" and "hidden" real output or income, R_t is a short-term interest rate variable, and P_t is the price level. The unobservable ratio of "hidden" to "recorded" activity is taken to be a function of variables such as the rate of growth in measured output; the inflation rate and the change in the latter; variables measuring the extent of the tax burden; and one to allow for the introduction of the Goods and Services Tax (GST) in October 1986. The latter is included because Inland Revenue Department (IRD) records suggest that the introduction of this tax in 1986 (together with the simultaneous abolition of sales taxes and dramatic changes to the personal and corporate tax scales) had a negative impact on unrecorded activity, especially among the self-employed. The inflation rate is included to allow for the upward "creep" of taxpayers through the tax brackets that it causes, and the associated incentive for tax-payers to engage in unreported activities. A more pervasive effect of inflation is that, as it tends to be uneven across sectors, it alters income distribution, and this may induce disrespect for tax law. The change in the rate of inflation is included in equation (2) below because such variability adds to uncertainty, and strengthens the incentive to enter the hidden economy as a means of risk or cost reduction. So, we have:

$$(Y_{Ht}/Y_{Rt}) = \alpha_1 + \alpha_2 \text{GST}_t + \alpha_3 \Delta \log Y_{Rt}$$

$$+ \alpha_4 \Delta \log P_t + \alpha_5 \Delta(\Delta \log P_t). \tag{2}$$

Solving (2) for Y_{Ht}, substituting in (1), taking (natural) logarithms, adding an error term and dummy variables to allow for deterministic seasonality, and for the introduction of "EFTPOS" ("Electronic Fund Transfer at Point of Sale"), bank debit card electronic retail transactions in lieu of cash in 1987.2:

$$m_t = \beta_0 + (\beta_1 + \beta_2)y_{Rt} + \beta_2 \log[\alpha_1 + \alpha_2 \text{GST}_t + \alpha_3 \Delta \, gd \, p_t + \alpha_4 \Delta p_t$$

$$+ \alpha_5 \Delta(\Delta p_t)] + \beta_3 r_t + \beta_4 p_t + \delta_1 S_{1t} + \delta_2 S_{2t} + \delta_3 S_{3t} + \delta_4 \text{DEFT} + \varepsilon_t, \tag{3}$$

where $\beta_0 = \log(\beta_0')$, lower case symbol denote natural logarithms of the variables, S_i is the i'th seasonal dummy, and DEFT is the EFTPOS dummy. (We also considered adding a variable for the *value* of EFTPOS transactions as a regressor, without success. A "dynamic" version of the model, incorporating a lagged value of the dependent variable as an additional regressor was also considered, as were the inclusion of various "tax burden" variables in equation (2). None of these refinements produced satisfactory results

In Table 1 below we also report on specifications of (1) which include $(P_t/P_{t-1}), (P_t/P_{t-4})$, or their lagged values, as regressors with a coefficient denoted β_5. Estimates of the α_i's can be used with (2) to measure (Y_{Ht}/Y_{Rt}) at each point in the sample. These values are of less interest than those obtained from the MIMIC model, as they are based rather narrowly on a single-equation model, but they provide a useful cross-check on orders of magnitude. The estimate of α_1 in Table 1 is also especially important in its own right as it measures the "long-run average" value for this ratio, and is used for the calibration of the MIMIC model.

Our MIMIC model of the hidden economy is formulated mathematically as follows: η is the scalar (unobservable) "latent" variable (the size of the hidden economy); $\mathbf{y}' = (y_1, y_2, \ldots, y_p)$ is a vector of "indicators for η; $\mathbf{x}' =$

$(x_1, x_2, \ldots, x_q)$ is a vector of "causes" of η; λ and γ are $(p \times 1)$ and $(q \times 1)$ vectors of parameters; and ε and ζ are $(p \times 1)$ and scalar random errors. It is assumed that ζ and all of the elements of ε are Normal and mutually uncorrelated, with Var.$(\zeta) = \psi$, and Cov.$(\varepsilon) = \Theta_\varepsilon$. The MIMIC model is:

$$\mathbf{y} = \lambda\eta + \varepsilon \tag{4}$$

$$\eta = \gamma'\mathbf{x} + \zeta. \tag{5}$$

Substituting (5) into (4), the MIMIC model can also be viewed as a multivariate regression model,

$$\mathbf{y} = \Pi\mathbf{x} + \mathbf{z}, \tag{6}$$

where $\Pi = \lambda\gamma'$, $\mathbf{z} = \lambda\zeta + \varepsilon$, and Cov.$(\mathbf{z}) = \lambda\lambda'\psi + \Theta_\varepsilon$.

The p-equation model in (6) has a regressor matrix of rank one, and the error covariance matrix is also constrained. Accordingly, we cannot obtain cardinal estimates of all of the parameters. Only certain "estimable functions" of the parameters can be identified, so we can estimate the *relative* magnitudes of the parameters, but not their levels. Thus, the estimation of (4) and (5) requires a normalization for (4), which is generally achieved by constraining one element of λ to a pre-assigned value. As both $\mathbf{y}$ and $\mathbf{x}$ are observable data vectors, the multi-equation model in (6) can then be estimated by conventional (restricted) Maximum Likelihood Estimation – in our case we have used the LISREL package (Jöreskog and Sörbom (1993a,b)) to obtain consistent and asymptotically efficient estimates of the elements of Π, and hence of λ and γ.

Given an estimate of the γ vector, and setting the error term ζ to its mean value of zero, equation (5) enables us to "predict" ordinal values for η (which in our case is the hidden economy) at each sample point. Then, if we have a specific value for η at some sample point, obtained form some other source, we can convert the within-sample predictions for η into a cardinal series. We use the "average" value for (Y_{Ht}/Y_{Rt}) from our estimated currency demand equation (*i.e.*, our estimate of α_1) to calibrate our time-series for the hidden economy by setting the latter to this value in 1981.

IV. Data issues

The variables are defined in Appendix I. Given the limitations of quarterly New Zealand time-series data, our MIMIC models have been estimated with annual data, for 1968 to 1994, but some experimentation with simple quarterly MIMIC models yielded strikingly similar results. Our currency demand model has been estimated with quarterly data for 1975.1 1994.4. Considerable attention has been paid to testing for stationarity and cointegration, and this appears to be the first application of a MIMIC model which addresses these issues.

The logarithms or levels of the series, as appropriate, have been tested for unit roots at the appropriate frequencies. Complete details of these unit root test results are given by Giles (1995, 1997a). Following Dickey and Pantula (1987), we test I(3) against I(2). If we reject I(3) we then test I(2) against I(1).

Table 1. Outcomes of unit root tests
Currency demand models: Quarterly logarithmic data

| Variable | ADF Tests | | | HEGY Tests |
	I(3) vs. I(2)	I(2) vs. I(1)	I(1) vs. I(0)	
CPI	Reject I(3)	I(2)		SI(1)
CURR	Reject I(3)	I(2)		SI(1)
GDP	Reject I(3)	Reject I(2)	I(1)	SI(1)
RBILL	Reject I(3)	Reject I(2)	I(1)	Zero

Then we test I(1) against I(0), as appropriate. We have used the "augmented" Dickey-Fuller (ADF) test (*e.g.*, Said and Dickey (1984)) to test for unit roots at the zero frequency. The quarterly data are *not* seasonally adjusted, and in this case we include a drift and seasonal dummy variables in the ADF regression and choose an augmentation level of at least three. This is based on the evidence provided by Ghysels *et al.* (1994). The lower limit of $p = 3$ was never binding. The dummy variables (S_{1t}, S_{2t}, and S_{3t}) allow for deterministic seasonality in the data, and in this case the ADF regression is always fitted with a "drift" term. Dods and Giles (1995) show that for samples of our size a preferred method involves choosing the value of p so that the autocorrelation and partial autocorrelation functions for the residuals of the ADF regression are "clean", and this is the procedure followed here. To determine if a time-trend should also be included in the ADF regression, we follow the Dolado *et al.* (1990) sequential testing strategy. The series PUBEMP exhibits a major structural break in its trend from 1988, and as this will distort the ADF "*t*-tests" in favour of *not rejecting* a unit root, Perron's (1989) modified test has been used in this case.

With the quarterly data we also allow for stochastic seasonality, and test for unit roots at the zero, π, and $(\pi/2)$ frequencies, following Hylleberg *et al.* (1990) (or HEGY hereafter) and Ghysels *et al.* (1994). We have determined the augmentation levels in the HEGY regressions in the same way as for the ADF tests. Following the recommendations of Ghysels *et al.* (1994), we include a trend, drift, and seasonal dummy variables in the HEGY regressions.

V. Estimating the currency demand model

Our currency demand model is given in equation (3), and it contains several non-stationary variables. The stationarity of the regressor in (3) whose coefficient is β_2 is unclear – this term is both non-linear and unobservable; but p_t and m_t are both I(2), and y_t and r_t are I(1), so we have an "unbalanced regression". We cannot simply "filter" the series according to their orders of integration, as this generates many negative observations, making the estimation of the model impossible. Estimating the model without filtering the data would result in a "spurious regression" (Granger and Newbold (1974)). One possibility is to exploit any cointegration among the variables, and estimate (3) directly as a long-run cointegrating relationship, resulting in valid asymptotic inferences. Testing for cointegration is complicated, here, given the mixture of I(1) and I(2) variables, the non-linear model, and the possibility of *seasonal* cointegration. Given these problems, a simple but somewhat indirect

Table 2. ADF tests for unit roots
MIMIC models : Annual levels data

Variable	ADF Tests		
	I(3) vs. I(2)	I(2) vs. I(1)	I(1) vs. I(0)
AATR	Reject I(3)	Reject I(2)	I(1)
AMTR	Reject I(3)	Reject I(2)	I(1)
log(CPI)	Reject I(3)	I(2)	
(CURR/M3)	Reject I(3)	Reject I(2)	I(1)
log(GDP)	Reject I(3)	Reject I(2)	I(1)
MPRT	Reject I(3)	Reject I(2)	I(1)
PUBEMP	Reject I(3)	Reject I(2)	I(0)
REGS	Reject I(3)	Reject I(2)	I(0)
RPDI	Reject I(3)	Reject I(2)	I(1)
TAXC	Reject I(3)	Reject I(2)	I(1)
TAXG	Reject I(3)	Reject I(2)	I(0)
TAXLEG	Reject I(3)	Reject I(2)	I(1)
TAXO	Reject I(3)	Reject I(2)	I(1)
UN	Reject I(3)	Reject I(2)	I(1)

cointegration testing strategy has been followed. The HEGY tests indicate that the only potential for cointegration is at the zero frequency, but this is rejected when standard Engle-Granger tests are applied. We then apply Haldrup's (1994) tests for cointegration involving I(2) data, using within-sample predictions for the series, $\log[\alpha_1 + \alpha_2 GST_t + \alpha_3 \Delta \, gd \, p_t + \alpha_4 \Delta p_t + \alpha_5 \Delta(\Delta p_t)]$. The null of *no cointegration* is again easily rejected, providing reasonable justification for treating our estimated "unbalanced" regressions as long-run equilibrium relationships. More complete details of this aspect of the modelling work are given by Giles (1997a).

The results of estimating the currency demand model, by Maximum Likelihood, using the SHAZAM (1993) package, over the period 1975.1 to 1994.4, appear in Table 3 for our preferred specification, together with some alternative specifications, including several in which the inflation rate enters the basic equation (1), with a coefficient denoted β_5. (In Models 3 and 5 the regressor associated with β_5 is the current quarterly rate of inflation; in Model 2 it is this rate lagged one period; and in Model 4 it is the lagged annual inflation rate.) These results illustrate the robustness of our estimate of the long-run average ratio of "hidden" to "measured" output, α_1. A range of conventional diagnostic tests for the preferred specification appear in Table 4.

The within-sample *averages* of the "predicted" (Y_{Ht}/Y_{Rt}) ratio, from equation (2), range from 8.4% to 8.7% across the models. In "Model 1" this estimated ratio varies from 5.5% to 10.8% over the sample, and these values may be compared with the data in Figure 1 below. The estimates of α_1, which represent long-run average values for (Y_{Ht}/Y_{Rt}) generally are very "sharp", and are consistent with the value arrived at from a different currency-demand model – a modification of that of Bhattacharyya (1990) – in Appendix II. The estimate of α_1 is 8.9% for Model 1, and that the corresponding sample average of (Y_{Ht}/Y_{Rt}) is 8.7%, so we use 8.8% in 1981.4, which is where the sample mean of the GDP series occurs, to calibrate our MIMIC models below by setting the "predicted" hidden economy series to this value in 1981.

Table 3. Estimated currency demand models

Coefficient ("t value")	Expected Sign	Model 1	Model 2	Model 3	Model 4	Model 5
β_0	$+/-$	0.213	-0.578	0.326	n.a.	1.044
		(0.13)	(-0.39)	(0.21)	(n.a.)	(0.69)
β_1	$+$	0.035	0.244	0.007	0.128	0.034
		(0.08)	(1.34)	(0.03)	(0.35)	(0.18)
β_2	$+$	0.276	0.141	0.302	0.222	0.128
		(0.61)	(3.72)	(10.43)	(0.41)	(8.47)
β_3	$-$	-0.104	-0.082	-0.100	-0.062	-0.101
		(-3.89)	(-3.70)	(-4.62)	(-2.40)	(-4.56)
β_4	$+$	0.729	0.694	0.724	0.680	0.746
		(18.11)	(19.26)	(19.26)	(19.73)	(19.23)
β_5	$+/-$	n.a.	-0.425	0.732	-0.350	1.272
		(n.a.)	(-0.64)	(1.14)	(-1.69)	(2.23)
α_1	$+$	0.089	0.088	0.089	0.087	0.104
		(3.23)	(11.11)	(21.93)	(1.56)	(14.99)
α_2	$-$	-0.027	-0.002	-0.010	-0.002	-0.050
		(-0.85)	(-0.08)	(-0.90)	(-0.16)	(-5.52)
α_3	$+/-$	-0.076	n.a.	n.a.	n.a.	n.a.
		(-0.82)	(n.a.)	(n.a.)	(n.a.)	(n.a.)
α_4	$+$	0.362	n.a.	n.a.	n.a.	n.a.
		(0.71)	(n.a.)	(n.a.)	(n.a.)	(n.a.)
α_5	$+$	0.044	n.a.	n.a.	n.a.	n.a.
		(0.26)	(n.a.)	(n.a.)	(n.a.)	(n.a.)
δ_1	$+/-$	-0.102	-0.135	-0.117	-0.126	-0.084
		(-3.99)	(-6.39)	(-5.46)	(-6.66)	(-4.12)
δ_2	$+/-$	-0.159	-0.135	-0.135	-0.135	-0.125
		(-4.62)	(-8.15)	(-8.06)	(-8.28)	(-5.38)
δ_3	$+/-$	-0.157	-0.140	-0.144	-0.142	-0.143
		(-7.05)	(-8.18)	(-8.48)	(-8.53)	(-6.86)
δ_4	$+/-$	n.a.	-0.098	-0.061	-0.089	n.a.
		(n.a.)	(-2.10)	(-1.32)	(-2.33)	(n.a.)

The sample correlation between actual and "fitted" m_t is 0.99 for all of the models in Table 3, and the estimated coefficients have the expected signs. As $\beta_0 = \log(\beta_0')$, its sign is ambiguous, even though we expect $\beta_0 > 0$. The anticipated sign of β_5 is also ambiguous: we might expect high inflation to lead to a *reduction* in the holding of nominal balances, including currency; or, as the estimated Models 2 to 4 are non-homogeneous in prices, a *positive* estimate of β_5 may reflect the effect of inflationary expectations. This is *not* an issue in the preferred Model 1. Although the significance of the individual parameter estimates is "mixed", many of the key parameters are precisely estimated. Testing the appropriate non-linear restrictions on the parameters with Wald tests, we *reject* income homogeneity, but *cannot reject* (short-run) price homogeneity at the 10% significance level, or lower in Model 1.

In Table 4, GOF is the goodness-of-fit test for normal errors, and JB is the corresponding Jarque-Bera (1980) test statistic. There is no evidence of non-normal errors. RESET2, RESET3 and RESET4 are asymptotic versions of Ramsey's (1969) test for a mis-specified functional form and/or omitted variables, constructed as Wald tests and using powers of the predicted values of m_t. The RESET2 and RESET4 statistics are significant at the 2.5% level, but

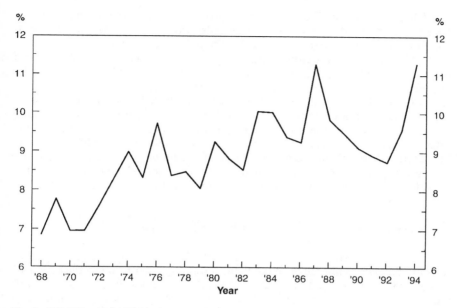

Fig. 1. MIMIC model 2 Hidden economy (% of measured GDP)

Table 4. Diagnostic tests for currency demand model 1

"Problem"	Test	Null Distribution	Statistic Value	p-Value
Non-Normality	GOF	$\chi^2(3)$	1.292	0.731
	JB	$\chi^2(2)$	0.536	0.765
Omitted Variables/	RESET2	$\chi^2(1)$	12.927	0.000
Wrong Functional	RESET3	$\chi^2(2)$	2.150	0.341
Form	RESET4	$\chi^2(3)$	10.745	0.013
	FRESET2	$\chi^2(4)$	0.314	0.990
	FRESET3	$\chi^2(6)$	4.283	0.638
	FRESET4	$\chi^2(8)$	5.051	0.752
Autocorrelation	LM1	$\chi^2(1)$	2.606	0.106
	LM2	$\chi^2(1)$	1.871	0.171
	LM3	$\chi^2(1)$	0.871	0.351
	LM4	$\chi^2(1)$	2.927	0.087
Heteroskedasticity	H1	$\chi^2(1)$	2.479	0.115
	H2	$\chi^2(1)$	2.463	0.117
	H3	$\chi^2(1)$	2.491	0.115

the latter is not significant at the 1% level. DeBenedictis and Giles (1998) show that the RESET test has extremely poor power, and is often a "biased" test. (That is, its power can fall below its significance level over part of the parameter space.) They propose an alternative test using a Fourier approximation, and show that it has excellent power. Their FRESET2, FRESET3 and FRESET4 tests in Table 4 are asymptotically valid in the present context. FRESET2 is based on two sine terms plus two cosine terms, *etc.* The outcomes of these tests clearly support this model's specification.

LM1 to LM4 are Lagrange Multiplier tests for serial independence against the respective alternatives of first, and general second, third and fourth order autoregressive (or moving average) errors. There is no evidence of serial correlation. H1, H2 and H3 are tests for heteroscedasticity based on regressing the recovered squared residuals from the non-linear regression on the fitted values, the square of the fitted value, and the logarithm of the square of the fitted values respectively. Although the various tests have only asymptotic justification here, given the non-linearity of the model, the results in Table 4 strongly support our preferred currency demand model, and its use as the basis for calibrating the predictions from our structural MIMIC model.

VI. Estimating the "mimic" model of the hidden economy

Prior to the estimation of the MIMIC model by the LISREL package, all of the data have been filtered to make them stationary, according to the orders of integration in Table 2. For instance, logCPI is second-differenced, logGDP and UN are first-differenced, but PUBEMP and REGS are not differenced at all prior to the estimation of the model. The coefficient of the labour force participation rate "indicator" is constrained to unity, without loss of generality, in order to ensure the identification of the models, in view of the shortage of rank noted earlier in section III. The Maximum Likelihood estimates of the coefficients (γ) of the "causal" variables ($\mathbf{x}$) in the structural equation for the hidden economy (η) in equation (5) provide the basis for predicting η (the size of the hidden economy) over the sample period. These estimates of the elements of γ are obtained only up to a scale factor, and they are used as relative weights to obtain a time-series index for η. The *actual* (not differenced) values of the causal variables are used with the estimated elements of γ. This index is then scaled to take a value of 8.8% in 1981, and this provides a series for the hidden economy, as a percentage of *recorded* real GDP.

Several MIMIC model specifications have been considered. Following earlier such studies for other countries, our "causal" variables allow for unemployment and income effects; the degree of economic regulation; the development of taxation legislation; the tax-bracket "creep" effect of inflation; and measures of the "tax burden". Up to three "indicator" variables are incorporated – the rate of growth in real GDP; the proportion of currency to M3; and the male labour force participation rate. As noted already, we have constrained the coefficient of the latter variable to unity to identify the models. Although Frey and Weck-Hanneman (1984) and Aigner *et al.* (1988) argue that this variable should be a *negative* indicator of the size of the hidden economy, in the New Zealand case it is clear from audit records and other evidence that most unrecorded economic activity is undertaken by agents who are also in the recorded workforce, suggesting a *positive* relationship. Indeed, we have found no models involving a negative coefficient for MPRT, and in which the signs of the various causal variable coefficients are all of the anticipated signs.

The implied series for the hidden economy are generally *insensitive* to the model specification. Representative results appear in Table 5. Model 1 is very

Table 5. MIMIC model results: parameter estimates

	Model 1	Model 2	Model 3	Model 4	Model 5
Indicators					
logGDP	1.234	2.759	2.546	2.358	1.427
[+]	(1.89)	(1.88)	(2.02)	(2.13)	(2.72)
MPRT	1.000	1.000	1.000	1.000	1.000
[?]	(n.a.)	(n.a.)	(n.a.)	(n.a.)	(n.a.)
CM3		0.700	0.711	0.668	0.863
[+]		(1.49)	(1.47)	(1.41)	(2.00)
Causes					
AATR	0.126	0.054	0.058	0.060	
[+]	(0.57)	(0.93)	(0.97)	(0.94)	
AMTR	0.146				
[+]	(0.65)				
CPI		0.289	0.310	0.330	0.340
[+]		(1.65)	(1.83)	(1.94)	(2.58)
GST	−0.149	−0.095	−0.198	−0.122	−0.731
[−]	(−0.91)	(−0.56)	(−1.33)	(−1.32)	(−2.59)
GST2		−0.075			
[−]		(0.56)			
PUBEMP					−0.582
[−]					(−2.51)
REGS		0.078	0.071	0.094	0.252
[+]		(0.98)	(0.93)	(1.12)	(1.97)
RPDI		0.090	0.091	0.104	0.268
[?]		(0.82)	(1.10)	(1.16)	(2.10)
TAXC	0.272	0.153	0.156	0.170	
[+]	(1.55)	(1.47)	(1.56)	(1.62)	
TAXG			0.097		
[?]			(0.84)		
TAXLEG		−0.060	−0.055	−0.069	−0.307
[−]		(−0.76)	(−0.75)	(−0.86)	(−2.50)
TAXO	0.216	0.242	0.282	0.295	0.400
[+]	(1.24)	(1.63)	(1.77)	(1.86)	(2.65)
UN		0.064			
[?]		(0.45)			

Notes: Anticipated signs appear in brackets.
Asymptotic "*t*-values" appear in parentheses below the estimated coefficients.

sparsely specified, and Model 5 generates an implausible historical time-series for the hidden economy. It is included, however, to illustrate that the statistical significance of the individual variables may not be the most important issue. The overall "fit" of the model is also important, as is the economic "believability" of the model's implications. For reasons given below, Model 2 is our preferred specification.

The results in Table 5 permit some interesting interpretations. Unlike the situation in a conventional regression model, because of the normalizations that have been introduced in the estimation of a MIMIC model the values of the estimated coefficients can be compared in relative terms. For instance, as we have normalized the coefficient of the male labour force participation rate (MPRT) variable to unity when identifying the model, the estimated coefficients on the "logGDP" indicator variable suggest not only a significant positive relationship between the size of the hidden economy and growth in measured GDP, but they also suggest that the effect of the hidden economy on the rate of growth in GDP is 1.2 to 2.8 times as great as its effect on the male labour force participation rate. The predicted positive effect of the hidden economy on the ratio of currency to M3 (*i.e.*, CM3) is more stable (and quite significant) across the different versions of the model, being of the order of 0.75 times that of the effect of the hidden economy on the male labour force participation rate. These values have obvious implications regarding the relative merits of these "indicator" variables as reflections of movements in the unobservable underground economy in New Zealand.

Although the "causal" variables have the anticipated signs, many of them lack individual significance. Exceptions include the inflation rate and the (separate) ratios of corporate and "other" taxes to GDP in most of the models. An inspection of the coefficients of the causal variables is also revealing. For example, if we consider Model 2 (which we focus on below as a "preferred" specification), then the following emerges if we "distribute" the sum of the absolute coefficients across the various general types of causal factors: taxation effects (in terms of both the overall "burden" and the make-up of the tax-take) account for 52% of the causal effects; inflation accounts for 24%; regulatory effects for 11%; real personal income for 8%; and the unemployment rate for 5%. So, for example, the (positive) effects of an increase in inflation on the size of the underground economy are estimated to be roughly twice as important as the (positive) effects of an increase in the amount of regulation in the economy. This is not surprising when one takes into account the secondary effect of inflation whereby it induces "bracket-creep" with respect to the statutory tax schedule, and effectively increases the average marginal tax rate, *ceteris paribus*.

Other inferences are also interesting. For instance, the introduction of the GST (and the simultaneous dramatic reductions in direct taxes) in 1986 were roughly twice as important in *reducing* the size of the hidden economy as are reductions in the average tax rate for average tax payers. Similarly, the increase in the GST rate from 10% to 12.5% in mid-1989 took effect in conjunction with a halving of the land tax rate, and a very recent reduction of the corporate tax rate from 45% to 28% and a simplification of the personal tax schedule to a two-step system. These changes to the tax burden and tax-mix led to a reduction in the hidden economy, but the effect of these changes was only about 80% as important as the earlier such changes in 1986. Finally, we see increases in the unemployment rate lead to an *increase* in the size of the underground economy, and the associated impact is almost identical to the *reduction* in the underground economy that results from a tightening of taxation regulations.

The Chi Square statistics in Table 6 test the specifications of the MIMIC models against the alternative that the covariance matrix of the observed variables is unconstrained (see Jöreskog and Sörbom (1993a, pp. 121–122)). Small values reflect a good "fit" of the models. The other statistics relate to criteria for measuring the overall performance of a MIMIC model. (See Jöreskog and Sörbom (1993a, Chap. 4).) *Small* values of Akaike's (1974) Information Criterion (AIC); of Bozdogan's (1987) CAIC measure; of the single-sample Cross-Validation Index (ECVI); and of the Root Mean Square Residual (RMR) measure favour the model. *Large* values of the Adjusted Goodness of Fit Index (AGFI), and the Parsimony Goodness of Fit Index

Table 6. MIMIC model results: Goodness-of fit

	Model 1	Model 2	Model 3	Model 4	Model 5
		Summary Statistics			
Chi Square	1.57	31.77	26.02	24.41	34.75
(n.c.p.; d.o.f.)	(0; 4)	(11.8; 20)	(8.0; 18)	(6.4; 16)	(20.8; 14)
[p-value]	[0.81]	[0.47]	[0.46]	[0.36]	[0.47]
AIC	49.57	173.77	146.02	122.41	116.75
CAIC	103.77	334.10	281.51	235.32	209.33
ECVI	1.98	6.95	5.84	4.90	4.67
AGFI	0.88	0.43	0.48	0.52	0.31
PGFI	0.14	0.19	0.20	0.21	0.21
RMR	0.04	0.10	0.10	0.10	0.12

Notes: n.c.p. = non-centrality parameter; d.o.f. = degrees of freedom.

Table 7. MIMIC model 2: Diagnostic tests of "conventional residuals"

	GOF	JB	LM1	LM2	LM3	LM4
CM3	3.047	0.469	0.679	0.112	0.353	0.221
	(0.38)	(0.79)	(0.41)	(0.74)	(0.55)	(0.64)
logGDP	3.047	0.476	0.729	0.096	0.349	0.243
	(0.38)	(0.79)	(0.39)	(0.76)	(0.55)	(0.62)
MPRT	3.047	0.508	0.741	0.090	0.374	0.239
	(0.38)	(0.78)	(0.39)	(0.76)	(0.54)	(0.62)

Note: Asymptotic p-values appear in parentheses.

(PGFI), reflect a good model fit. These measures should *not* be compared across models with different sets of indicator variables (and hence different likelihood functions).

The results in Table 6 are satisfactory. The various measures favour Models 2 and 4 over Model 3, so we focus on the more comprehensive Model 2, this being least prone to mis-specification bias. We have used the estimated "Π matrix" to construct conventional regression residuals series, these being the difference between the fitted and actual values for these "dependent" variables at each sample point for the GDP, MPRT and CM3 equations, scaled to have a zero sample mean in each case. We have then tested them for normality and serial correlation, in Table 7. The notation is as in Table 4, and the results further support Model 2. The use of these diagnostic tests must be treated cautiously in the context of a MIMIC model. While the tests will have asymptotic justification, our sample is quite small, and diagnostic testing in such models is largely unexplored in the literature, and certainly worthy of further attention in the future.

VII. The hidden economy and the tax-gap

Figure 1 provides an annual time-series of the New Zealand hidden economy, as a percentage of real measured GDP. This series was generated by multi-

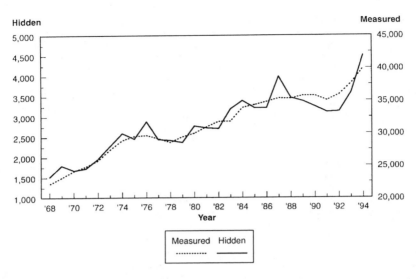

Fig. 2. Measured and hidden GDP (real 1982/1983 $ millions)

plying the causal variables' data, by their associated estimated coefficients (the elements of γ in equation (5)) as shown for MIMIC Model 2 in Table 5. The hidden economy series was then scaled to match the long-run average figure of 8.8% in 1981 implied by our currency demand equation results discussed earlier. Corresponding hidden economy series based on the other MIMIC models are given by Giles (1995). Except when the series for the number of public sector employees (which has a major distortive break in its trend in 1988) is included as a "causal" variable, the time-paths are strikingly similar in their overall cyclical movement, and differ only slightly in terms of actual magnitudes. In all cases there is a pronounced downward shift in the relative size of the hidden economy immediately after the introduction of the GST, and the simultaneous reductions in the sales, personal and corporate tax rates in October 1986. Actual real hidden and measured GDP are presented as separate time-series over our sample in Figure 2.

The hidden economy follows the phases of the business cycle in New Zealand. Unrecorded economic activity increased from around 6.8% of measured real GDP in 1968 to a peak of 11.3% in 1987, then fell to 8.7% of GDP in 1992 before increasing to around 11.3% in 1994. There is a secondary effect in the cyclical decline at the time of the *increase* in the GST rate from 10% to 12.5% on 1 July 1989. Clearly, underground economic activity in New Zealand is positively tied to the business cycle and to the tax burden. Giles and Caragata (1998) and Caragata and Giles (1998) provide simulation results for the responsiveness of the size of the hidden economy to changes in the tax burden and tax mix. The rapid rise in the size of the hidden economy in the early 1970's is consistent with the expansion in real output which took place at that time in New Zealand prior to the international oil price shocks. The cyclical movements during the mid-1970's to mid 1980's follow the (less pronounced) pattern in measured output; and the trough in 1992 (and subsequent

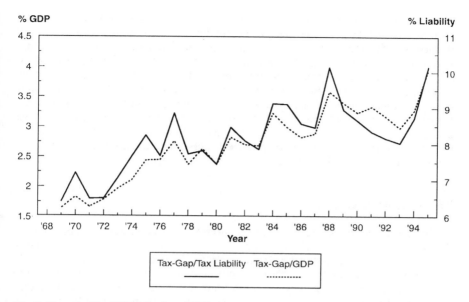

Fig. 3. Tax-gap (% of GDP & of tax liability)

expansion), is also associated with the general cyclical movements in the economy. The absolute size of the hidden economy exhibits greater volatility than does measured real output – the associated sample coefficients of variation are 25.9% and 15.0% respectively.

On the basis of these data, Giles (1997b) finds clear evidence of Granger causality from measured to hidden activity, and weak evidence of reverse causality. This poses a dilemma for policy-makers wishing to stimulate economic growth, but contain the "tax-gap". These data are also used by Giles (1997d, 1999) to test for asymmetries in the measured and hidden business cycles. No asymmetries are found, implying that fiscal and monetary policy changes that respond to the observed business cycle are likely to have consistent effects on the hidden cycle. Finally, Giles (1997c) finds strong evidence of Granger causality from tax-related prosecutions to the size of the hidden economy in New Zealand, suggesting that the compliance efforts of the IRD are pro-active, rather than reactive.

Unrecorded economic activity is untaxed, implying a shortfall between actual and potential tax revenue. The total "tax-gap" can be estimated by multiplying the hidden/measured GDP ratio by total tax revenue, and the associated results (as percentages of total tax liability or of *nominal* GDP) appear in Figure 3. (The tax-gap, as a percentage of total tax liability is a monotonic increasing function of the Hidden/measured GDP ratio, so the "shape" of the former graph in Figure 3 is identical to that of the latter in Figure 1.) The tax-gap ranged from 6.4% to 10.2% of total tax liability over the sample, representing NZ$0.07Billion to NZ$3.18Billion in foregone nominal revenue. This compares with IRS audit-based tax-gap estimates for the United States of the order of 19%, 18% and 17% (of total tax liability) in 1985,

1988 and 1992 for individual tax-payers (Internal Revenue Service (1996)). Of course, this measure of the tax-gap has to be qualified, as it assumes that all hidden activity is taxable, and that the incidence of the existing tax structure would be the same within the hidden sector as it is within the currently measured sector of the economy. Some aspects of these issues are addressed by Caragata and Giles (1998) and Giles and Caragata (1998): they provide simulation evidence indicating that in the New Zealand context, about half of the tax-gap is responsive to fiscal instruments (on average over the cycle), the rest being hard-core criminal evasion. They also show that a shift in favour of indirect taxation, and away from direct personal income tax, can have a significant impact on hidden activity and the tax-gap.

VII. Concluding comments

In this paper we have presented an econometric methodology for estimating the hidden economy, and have applied this methodology to New Zealand data. Our use of a structural MIMIC model, which treats the size of the hidden economy as a "latent" variable, is not novel in itself, but our coordination of this approach with a new currency demand model does distinguish our modelling methodology from others that have been used in this field. In addition, this study is the first such one to take proper account of the non-stationarity of the various economic time-series that are used in the estimation of the models.

We find that over the period 1968 to 1994, the New Zealand hidden economy averaged just under 9% of measured GDP, varying between 6.8% in 1968 and 11.3% in 1994. This ratio, and measured activity itself, were highly cyclical over this period, and these figures are consistent with the micro-economic evidence for New Zealand firms provided by Giles (1998a). The implied "tax-gap" ranged from 6.4% to 10.2% of total tax liability, or (equivalently) from 1.6% to 3.9% of GDP, in gross terms. Of course, only part of this tax-gap is recoverable in practice via fiscal means, and the results of Caragata and Giles (1998) and Giles and Caragata (1998) suggest that this amounts to about 50% of the total, on average over the cycle.

This same methodology can be applied to other countries, and recent such work for Canada by Tedds (1998) is being refined by her and the author. The availability of historical time-series data on the hidden economy provides new opportunities for empirical analyses of policy issues, with an explicit allowance for both measured and hidden sectors. For example, Giles (1998b) shows that the demand for money (M3) function in New Zealand is stable if its formulation allows for both hidden and recorded outputs. Johnson (1998) uses the data generated here to study money-income causality in New Zealand, and shows that allowing for the underground economy does not enhance the predictability of income from money. The results of these studies have important implications for monetary policy, but much more such work remains to be done if the policy implications of the underground economy in that and other countries are to be fully appreciated.

Appendix I: Data definitions

Variable	Definition	Source
AATR	Average Average Tax Rate (%)	IRD
AMTR	Average Marginal Tax Rate (%)	IRD
CM3	CURR/M3	RBNZ
CPI	Consumer's Price Index, All Groups (1993.4 = 1,000)	STATNZ
CURR	Currency (Notes and Coins) in Circulation ($ Millions)	RBNZ
DEFT	EFTPOS Transactions Dummy Variable	
GDP	Real Gross Domestic Product (1982/1983 $ Millions)	STATNZ
GST	GST Introduction Dummy Variable	
GST2	GST Increase Dummy Variable	
MPRT	Male Labour Force Participation Rate (%/100)	STATNZ
M3	Money Supply, M3 ($ Millions)	RBNZ
PUBEMP	Public Service Employees , Regulatory Depts. (Number)	BERL
RBILL	90-Day Treasury Bill Rate (Quarterly Average, % p.a.)	RBNZ
REGS	Index of Degree of Regulation of N.Z. Economy	BERL
RPDI	Real Personal Disposable Income/Labour Force	STATNZ
TAXC	[(TCOMP/CPI)/GDP]*10,000	IRD; STATNZ
TAXG	[(TGST/CPI)/GDP]*10,000	IRD; STATNZ
TAXLEG	Number of Sections in Income Tax Legislation	IRD; BERL
TAXO	[(TOTHER/CPI)/GDP]*10,000	IRD; STATNZ
TCOMP	Gross Tax Revenue – Companies ($ Millions)	IRD
TGST	Tax Revenue – Goods & Services Tax ($ Millions)	IRD
TOTHER	Gross Tax Revenue – Other Persons ($ Millions)	IRD
UN	Unemployment Rate (Total: Males + Females; %)	STATNZ

Note: BERL = Data Constructed by Business and Economic Research Limited; IRD = Series Compiled from Official Data by Inland Revenue Department; RBNZ = Official Data Supplied by Reserve Bank of New Zealand; STATNZ = Oficfial Data Published by Statistics New Zealand

Appendix II

An earlier version of this work formulated the currency demand model in the manner suggested by Bhattacharyya (1990) in his study of the hidden economy in the United Kingdom. As noted in section III above, our preferred currency demand model is more flexible than that of Bhattacharyya, and it does not involve any functional approximations. However, as the application of several versions of his model to our data provides estimates of the long-run average ratio of hidden to measured output are almost identical to our 8.8%, we present here a brief summary of these earlier results.

Demand for currency comprises two parts – that for recorded activity and that for hidden activity:

$$M_t = M_{Rt} + M_{Ht}$$

where, with lower case symbols (in our earlier notation) denoting natural logarithms,

$$m_{Rt} = \log \alpha_0 + \beta_1 y_{Rt} + \beta_2 r_t + \beta_3 p_t + \varepsilon_t$$

$$m_{Ht} = \beta_4 y_{Ht}.$$

Combining these equations, taking a first-order Taylor series approximation, and using the proxy:

$$Y_{Ht} = \alpha_1 Y_{Rt} + \alpha_2 Y_{Rt}^2 + \alpha_3 Y_{Rt}^3 + \alpha_4 Y_{Rt}^4 + \cdots\cdots\cdots + \alpha_n Y_{Rt}^n + \omega_t$$

we get the non-linear estimating equation (which includes the EFTPOS dummy variable):

$$m_t = \log \alpha_0 + \delta_1 \text{DEFT}_t + \beta_1 y_{Rt} + \beta_2 r_t + \beta_3 p_t$$

$$+ [(\alpha_1 Y_{Rt})_4^\beta / (\alpha_0 Y_{Rt1}^\beta R_{t2}^\beta P_3^\beta)] + \text{error},$$

where we have taken $n = 1$, so that α_1 is the long-run average ratio of Y_{Ht} to Y_{Rt}. Allowing for an AR(1) process in the error, with autocorrelation parameter ρ, we obtain the following results (with the diagnostic tests defined as in Table 4 above):

	α_0	α_1	β_1	β_2	β_3	β_4
Estimate	1.160	0.086	0.711	−0.100	0.731	−34.647
"t-value"	(2.443)	(20.143)	(8.287)	(−3.285)	(21.418)	(−19.406)

	δ_1	ρ
Estimate	−0.108	−0.009
"t-value"	(−2.981)	(−0.079)

$R^2 = 0.982$; LM1 = 0.016; LM2 = 0.668; JB = 10.262; GOF = 11.975
                 $[\chi^2(1)]$ $[\chi^2(1)]$ $[\chi^2(2)]$ $[\chi^2(3)]$

References

Aigner DJ, Schneider F, Ghosh D (1988) Me and my shadow: estimating the size of the hidden economy from time series data. In: Barnett WA et al. (eds) Dynamic econometric modeling: proceedings of the third international symposium in economic theory and econometrics, Cambridge University Press, Cambridge, pp. 297–334

Akaike H (1974) A new look at statistical model identification. IEEE Transactions on Automatic Control 19:716–723

Bhattacharyya DK (1990) An econometric method of estimating the 'hidden economy', United Kingdom (1960–1984): estimates and tests. Economic Journal 100:703–717

Blades D (1982) The hidden economy and the national accounts. OECD, Paris

Boeschoten WC, Fase MMG (1984) The volume of payments and the informal economy in the Netherlands, 1965–1982. Nijhoff, Dordrecht

Bozdogan H (1987) Model selection and Akaike's information criteria (AIC). Pychometrika 52:345–370

Caragata PJ, Giles DEA (1998) Simulating the relationship between the hidden economy and the tax mix in New Zealand. Econometrics Working Paper EWP9804, Department of Economics, University of Victoria

Carter M (1984) Issues in the hidden economy – a survey. Economic Record 60:209–221

Chote R (1995) 'Black economy' believed to exceed $100bn. Financial Times, 10–11 June

DeBenedictis LF, Giles DEA (1998) Testing the specification of regression models using Fourier series approximations: the FRESET test. In: Ullah A, Giles DEA (eds) Handbook of applied economic statistics, Marcel Dekker, New York, pp. 383–417

Dickey DA, Pantula SG (1987) Determining the order of differencing in autoregressive processes. Journal of Business and Economic Statistics 15:455–461

Dods JL, Giles DEA (1995) Alternative strategies for 'augmenting' the Dickey-Fuller test: size-robustness in the face of pre-testing. Journal of Statistical Computation and Simulation 53:243–258

Dolado JJ, Jenkinson T, Sosvilla-Rivero S (1990) Cointegration and unit roots'. Journal of Economic Surveys 4:249–273

Feige EL (1982) A new perspective on macroeconomic phenomena: the theory and measurement of the unobserved economy in the United States: causes, consequences and implications. In: Walker M (ed) International burden of government, The Fraser Institute Vancouver, pp. 112–136

Frey BS, Pommerehne WW (1982) Measuring the hidden economy: though there be madness, yet is there method in it?. In: Tanzi V (ed) The underground economy in the United States and abroad, Heath Lexington, pp. 3–27

Frey BS, Pommerehne WW (1984) The hidden economy: state and prospects for measurement. Review of Income and Wealth 30:1–23

Frey BS, Weck-Hannemann H (1984) The hidden economy as an 'unobserved' variable. European Economic Review 26:33–53

Gaertner W, Wenig A (eds) (1985) The economics of the shadow economy, Springer-Verlag, Heidelberg

Ghysels E, Lee HS, Noh J (1994) Testing for unit roots in seasonal time series. Journal of Econometrics 62:415–442

Giles DEA (1995) Measuring the size of the hidden economy and the tax-gap in New Zealand: an econometric analysis. Working Paper No. 5a, Working Papers on Monitoring the Health of the Tax System, Inland Revenue Department, Wellington

Giles DEA (1997a) The hidden economy and the tax-gap in New Zealand: a latent variable analysis. Discussion Paper 97–8, Department of Economics, University of Victoria

Giles DEA (1997b) Causality between the measured and underground economies in New Zealand. Applied Economics Letters 4:63–67

Giles DEA (1997c) The hidden economy and tax-evasion prosecutions in New Zealand. Applied Economics Letters 4:281–285

Giles DEA (1997d) Testing for asymmetry in the measured and underground business cycles in New Zealand. Economic Record 72:225–232

Giles DEA (1998a) Modelling the tax compliance profiles of New Zealand firms: evidence from audit records. Econometrics Working Paper EWP9803, Department of Economics, University of Victoria

Giles DEA (1998b) Measuring the hidden economy: implications for econometric modelling. Econometrics Working Paper EWP9809, Department of Economics, University of Victoria

Giles DEA (1999) The rise and fall of the New Zealand underground economy: are the responses symmetric?. Forthcoming in Applied Economic Letters

Giles DEA, Caragata PJ (1998) The learning path of the hidden economy: tax and growth effects in New Zealand. Econometrics Working Paper EWP9805, Department of Economics, University of Victoria

Goldberger AS (1972) Structural equation methods in the social sciences. North-Holland Amsterdam

Granger CWJ, Newbold P (1974) Spurious regressions in econometrics. Journal of Econometrics 35:143–159

Haldrup N (1994) The asymptotics of single-equation cointegration regressions with I(1) and I(2) variables. Journal of Econometrics 63:153–181

Hylleberg S, Engle RF, Granger CWJ, Yoo BS (1990) Seasonal integration and co-integration. Journal of Econometrics 44:215–28

Internal Revenue Service (1996) Individual income tax gap estimates for 1985, 1988 and 1992. Publication 1415 (Rev. 4-96), Doc. 96-13553, Research Division, Internal Revenue Service, Washington, D.C.

Jarque CM, Bera AK (1980) Efficient tests for normality, homoscedasticity and serial independence of regression residuals. Economics Letters 6:255–259

Johnson BJJ (1988) Money-income causality and the New Zealand underground economy. Unpublished M.A. Extended Essay, Department of Economics, University of Victoria

Jöreskog K, Goldberger AS (1975) Estimation of a model with multiple indicators and multiple causes of a single latent variable. Journal of the American Statistical Association 70:631–639

Jöreskog K, Sörbom D (1993a) LISREL 8: structural equation modeling with the SIMPLIS command language. Scientific Software International Chicago

Jöreskog K, Sörbom D (1993b) LISREL 8 user's reference guide. Scientific Software International Chicago

Kirchgaessner G (1984) Verfahren zur Erfassung des in der Schattenwirtschaft erabeiteten Sozialprodukts. Allegemeines Statistisches Archiv 68:378–405

Mirus R, Smith RS (1994) Canada's underground economy revisited: update and critique. Canadian Public Policy 20:235–252

Park T (1979) Reconciliation between personal income and taxable income, 1947–1977. Mimeo., Bureau of Economic Analysis, Washington, D.C.

Perron P (1989) The great crash, the oil price shock, and the unit root hypothesis. Econometrica 57:1361–1401

Ramsey JB (1969) Tests for specification errors in classical linear least-squares regression analysis. Journal of the Royal Statistical Society B 31:350–371

Said SE, Dickey DA (1984) Testing for unit roots in autoregressive-moving average models of unknown order. Biometrika 71:599–607

Schneider F (1997) Empirical results for the size of the shadow economy of Western European countries over time. Working Paper 9710, Institut Für Volkswirtschaftslehre, Linz University

Schneider F, Pommerehne WW (1985) The decline of productivity growth and the rise of the shadow economy in the U.S.. Mimeo., University of Århus

SHAZAM (1993) SHAZAM econometrics computer program: user's reference manual, version 7.0. McGraw-Hill, New York

Spiro PS (1994) Evidence of a post-GST increase in the underground economy. Canadian Tax Journal 41:247–258

Tanzi V (1983) The underground economy in the United States: annual estimates, 1930–1980. IMF Staff Papers 30:283–305

Tedds LM (1998) Measuring the size of the hidden economy in Canada: a latent variable/MIMIC model approach. Unpublished M.A. Extended Essay, Department of Economics, University of Victoria

Weck H (1983) Schattenwirtschaft: eine Möglichkeit zur Einschränkung der öffentlichen Verwaltung?. Peter Lang Verlag, Bern

Zellner A (1970) Estimation of regression relationships containing unobservable variables. International Economic Review 11:441–454

Tax efficiency in selected Indian states*

Raghbendra Jha[1], M. S. Mohanty[2], Somnath Chatterjee[2], Puneet Chitkara[1]

[1] Indira Gandhi Institute of Development Research, General Vaidya Marg, Goregaon (East), Bombay 400 065, India (e-mail: rjha@igidr.ac.in)
[2] Development Research Group, Reserve Bank of India, Central Office, Bombay 400 023, India

First version received: November 1997/final version received: November 1998

Abstract. This paper attempts to measure pure tax efficiency of fifteen major Indian states (Andhra Pradesh, Assam, Bihar, Haryana, Gujarat, Karnataka, Kerala, Madhya Pradesh, Maharashtra, Orissa, Punjab, Rajasthan, Tamilnadu, Uttar Pradesh and West Bengal) for the period 1980–81 to 1992–93 in a manner that allows this efficiency to vary both across time as well as across states. It is discovered that there is a moral hazard problem in the design of central grants in that higher grants by the central government to the state governments reduce efficiency of tax collection by these states. The less poor states are more efficient in tax collection. The rankings of states by tax efficiency for the various years do not converge. An index of aggregate tax efficiency is calculated and it appears that this index has been stagnating. It is argued that the weight placed on tax effort in the formula determining central grants to state governments should be increased to improve tax efficiency of state governments.

Key words: Moral hazard and grant design, tax efficiency

JEL classifications: H29, H77

---

* We would like to thank three anonymous referees of this journal for helpful comments and the editor, Baldev Raj, for encouragement. The research reported in this paper was funded by the Reserve Bank of India. R. Bird, C. Heady, C. Rangarajan, S. S. Tarapore, and A. Vasudevan gave helpful comments on an earlier version of the paper, which came out as DRG Study No. 11 of the Reserve Bank of India. We also thank participants in an ESRC development economics workshop in LSE and in the 1996 IIPF Congress in Kyoto for helpful comments and George Battese, for making available to us the program used to run the panel data estimation reported in this paper. All opinions expressed in this paper as well as any remaining errors are the responsibility of the authors alone.
The complete data set as well as details of all transformations effected in this paper can be obtained from the corresponding author Raghbendra Jha.

1. Introduction

Economic analysis with several layers of government has a long and distinguished tradition in public finance; (for a review see Jha (1998) and King (1984)). One of the most significant issues addressed in the literature is that of proper devolution of tax/expenditure authority between state and central governments in a federal country. Some economists argue that the level of government, which is legislatively superior, should have the mandate, in some sense, to treat the lower levels of government as equals. Moreover, they argue that there are economies of scale in collecting taxes. If states, for example, were to impose income taxes there would be considerable difficulties in the treatment of the incomes of taxpayers who migrate across state boundaries. Similarly, the bulk of commodity taxation is best carried out by the central government. State governments, left on their own, might opt for increasing their own tax revenues even at the risk of causing considerable allocative damage at the national level. Even under present arrangements in India, where the central government collects income taxes and excise duties and states play a relatively minor role and levy state sales taxes, in the main, considerable misallocation of resources occurs through the state tax structures. Vaillancourt (1992) and Vaillancourt and Rao (1994) estimate that subnational tax distortions are one of the highest in India among large federations.

Other economists argue that decentralization of tax and expenditure authority has innate advantages. Local governments would be more responsive to local needs and can be held accountable by residents in an easier and more transparent manner than higher level governments. This kind of reasoning, of course, does not preclude the arrangement whereby the degrees of decentralization in tax and expenditure authority are different. In particular, if lower level governments are assumed to be more responsive to the public expenditure needs of the people and higher level governments are deemed to have better ability to tax, then expenditure responsibilities may optimally be decentralized to a greater extent than tax authority. In this case, we would be setting up a rationale for fiscal transfers from higher to lower levels of government. The incentive effects of such transfers on tax efficiency of state governments have, hitherto, not been examined empirically. The present paper has this as one of its principal objectives.

One important maintained hypothesis of the extant literature is that state governments or, for that matter, the central government are raising taxes in an efficient manner. This is an assumption whose validity has to be tested and should not be assumed. Since local conditions are typically unknown to higher levels of government, it follows that state governments can easily conceal their tax efficiency and make claims on the federal government. This information theoretic approach to local public finance has a number of serious implications. The literature on this is very sparse and recent: see Boadway, Horiba, and Jha (1998) and Boadway (1997).

In the Indian context, historically, tax efficiency has played a relatively minor role in resource transfers from the central to state governments and much of this transfer is made on the basis of need and backwardness characteristics of the recipient states. (See Government of India (1994)). Nevertheless, there is increasing realization in recent years that efficiency in tax collection is important in the present context where there is considerable stress on state government finances. Further, it is generally agreed now, even in official circles, that much of the discussion on fiscal devolution has pre-supposed prudent fiscal behavior on the part of the center and states. The Tenth Finance Commission (an institution created to advise on center-state fiscal relations), for instance, in its report suggested that the weight placed on tax effort in the formula for distribution of transfers to states should be raised to 10 per cent. At least from the second oil price shock of 1979 the central government has been increasingly committed to lowering its fiscal deficit. This tendency became even more important after the structural adjustment pro-gram of 1991 was put in place. As a consequence, federal grants have become less important as sources of revenues for the state governments and their effi-ciency in tax collection has assumed greater importance. Buiter and Patel (1992, 1997) note that increasing tax efficiency at the state level will continue to be a matter of considerable urgency for quite some time to come. It might be the case that an appropriately structured federal grant formula might be able to induce greater efficiency in tax collection by the states. The issues concerning tax efficiency (both across states as well as time) in India certainly deserve a much deeper analysis than has hitherto been afforded to them.

State governments, which have essentially similar tax instruments at their disposal, can still differ with respect to the efficiency with which they collect these taxes. After factoring out the effects of tax base/capacity factors, an efficient state government would be able to collect more tax revenue than a less inefficient one. The analogy of tax efficiency with production efficiency is straightforward; however, this analogy has not yet been used to measure tax efficiency of sub-national governments. In the theory of production or cost, efficiency can always be defined relative to a production or cost frontier. [See Cornwell, Schmidt and Sickles (1990) and Jha and Singh (1994)]. Like pro-duction efficiency, tax efficiency can be measured relative to the best practice frontier.

We measure the tax efficiency of 15 major state governments in India for the thirteen year period 1980–81 to 1992–93 (the latest year for which con-sistent state level data are available) in a way that permits both cross-sectional as well as intertemporal variations in tax efficiency. We also identify the de-terminants of such efficiency. The performance of different states with respect to the same taxes can be compared across states as well as across time. Shome (1997) argues that the efficiency of tax collection by the central government in India is quite low. However, since the central government collects very diff-erent taxes from the state governments, it is not possible to compare the per-formance of state and central governments. Hence, in this paper we confine ourselves to analyzing efficiency in tax collection at the level of states.

The plan of this paper is as follows. In the next section we discuss some issues in tax efficiency in the Indian context. Section III discusses data and methodology and presents the results. Section IV offers some concluding remarks.

2. Tax efficiency in India: Some issues

When estimating tax efficiency at the state level, authors identify tax capacity factors (activity variables) such as State Domestic Product (SDP). Tradition-ally tax revenues of different states have been related in a cross-section equa-tion to these activity variables. In our opinion, this method does not give a good measure of tax efficiency by individual states because states with high values of activity variables will tend to have larger tax bases and larger tax revenues and will, therefore, end up showing higher tax efficiency because of this factor alone. Tax efficiency is more appropriately measured once we have filtered out the effects of the activity variables. Moreover, the tax efficiency analysis carried out using the extant approach does not allow for a comparison of tax efficiency across states and across time.

We, therefore, move to a completely novel approach, which considerably generalizes and improves upon the extant approach to tax efficiency and, at the same time, points to the shortcomings of the extant approach. The analysis in the present paper uses panel data and has two additional advantages over the extant approach. First we can now identify the determinants of tax efficiency. We discover, for instance, that the higher the proportion of central grants in the total expenditure of states, the lower is their efficiency in tax collection. Also it appears that, *ceteris paribus*, the less poor states are less inefficient in tax collection. Second, we can analyze whether tax efficiency of state governments has a tendency to converge over time and can compute an index of national tax efficiency. If gaps in state budgets are, ultimately, to be picked up by the central government, then states can afford to be lax in their tax efficiency if little weight is given to tax efficiency in the grant formula. Hence the analysis in this paper would have implications for the design of central government grants to state governments. To the best of our knowledge, this is the first attempt to measure tax efficiency by state governments in a panel framework for any country.

3. Tax efficiency: Analysis and results

We estimated tax efficiency in fifteen major Indian states: Andhra Pradesh, Assam, Bihar, Gujarat, Haryana, Karnataka, Kerala, Madhya Pradesh, Maharashtra, Orissa, Punjab, Rajasthan, Tamilnadu, Uttar Pradesh, and West Bengal. Tax capacity factors are represented by three variables: (i) state domestic product (henceforth SDP) (at 1980–81 prices) to represent the level of economic activity; (ii) proportion of agricultural income to total SDP (henceforth AGY) to proxy the degree of backwardness as also the low tax intensity of agricultural income (agriculture is hardly taxed in India); and (iii) per capita real rural household consumption expenditure (henceforth CO) to proxy the state of poverty conditions and its impact on tax potential. It was discovered that CO is not a significant determinant of tax revenue but it is a significant determinant of tax efficiency. We also used average tax rate for each state for each year. This is computed as follows. For any state for any year let t_i be the nominal tax rate on the ith tax source of that state. Let R_i be the revenue of the state from tax source i and let TR be the total tax revenue of the state. Then we define the weighted average tax rate (ATR) for that state for that particular year as:

$$ATR = \sum_{i=1}^{n} t_i(R_i/TR)$$

where n denotes the number of commodities taxed by the state government in question. States in India do not levy income taxes–only taxes on commodities and services. All of these are *ad valorem*. However, since *ATR* was insignificant, it was dropped. The appendix details data sources and some transformations that were performed.

The literature on technical efficiency in the theory of production (e.g. Cornwell, Schmidt and Sickles (1990) and Jha and Singh (1994)) usually estimates a panel stochastic production frontier and then regresses the residuals from the panel regression on the supposed determinants of efficiency. This procedure makes the assumption that the error terms in the two stages of the estimation are independent. This is restrictive and may make the estimates inefficient. The method of Battese and Coelli (1992, 1995), however, does not involve this restriction since the stochastic frontier, as well as the determinants of inefficiency, are estimated in a single stage. This is likely to improve efficiency considerably.

The frontier itself is defined by

$$TA_{it} = \exp(X_{it}\beta + V_{it} - U_{it}) \tag{1}$$

where

TA_{it} denotes real total own tax revenues of state i in year t, excluding the state's share in central taxes;

X_{it} represents a $(1 \times K)$ vector of values, which are functions of tax capacity factors, including time for the i-th state in the t-th year;

the V_{it} are assumed to be independently and identically distributed random error terms which have normal distribution with zero mean and standard deviation σ_v;

the U_{it} are non-negative unobservable random variables (with standard deviation σ_u) associated with the inefficiency of tax collection, such that, given the X_{it}, the observed level of tax collection falls short of potential.

Three different approaches to modeling the determinants of efficiency have been discussed in the literature. The first tries to model efficiency essentially as a function of time. The second models efficiency as a function of time and other variables whereas the third (the non-neutral stochastic frontier model due to Huang and Liu (1994)) permits interaction effects between the determinants of inefficiency (Z_{it}) and the X_{it}. In our case, the third model fits well both in terms of significantly higher value of the likelihood function as well as the significance of the variables determining the efficiency.

Concurrently with the stochastic frontier, then, we estimate

$$U_{it} = Z_{it}\delta + Z_{it}^* X_{it}\delta' + W_{it} \tag{2}$$

where Z_{it} is a $(1 \times M)$ vector of explanatory variables, including (possibly) time, associated with the technical efficiency effects, δ is an $(M \times 1)$ vector of unknown parameters to be estimated, δ' is a vector of parameters associated with the interaction terms ($Z_{it}^* X_{it}$) and W_{it} are unobservable random variables assumed to be independently distributed, obtained by truncation of the normal distribution with mean zero and variance, σ^2, such that the U_{it} is nonnegative. The second model would be a special case of specification (2) when δ' is assumed to be zero; the first model would be a special case of the second model.

Model selection proceeded as follows. We began by estimating a general version of the model with SDP, AGY, state level dummies, time and time squared, and CO as determinants of tax collected. Time, time squared, the share of central government grants in total state government expenditure (henceforth GTOE), CO and various interaction terms with determinants of tax collected were included in the set of variables affecting tax efficiency. We sought simpler models nested in this larger model on the basis of the likelihood ratio (LR) test. The LR test statistic is written as:

$$\lambda = 2(l(\rho^u) - l(\rho^r))$$

where $l(\rho^u)$ represents the value of the log of the likelihood function with unrestricted values of the vector of parameters and $l(\rho')$ represents the log of the likelihood function with maximum likelihood estimation of the parameter vector ρ with r restrictions. The statistic λ is distributed as a χ^2 with r degrees of freedom; (see Davidson and MacKinnon (1993)) under the null hypothesis that the restrictions hold. Several versions were tried. Some of these along with the values of the chi-squared values for the LR test, are reported in Table 1. None of the simpler functional forms could be accepted whereas forms more general than that reported in the paper could be rejected. The model selected had SDP, AGY, time and time squared as determinants of tax revenue and time and GTOE, GTOE*SDP, GTOE*AGY and CO as determinants of inefficiency.

Given the specification of the model, the hypothesis that the technical inefficiency effects are not random is expressed by $H_0 : \gamma = 0$, where $\gamma = \sigma_u^2/\sigma^2$ and $\sigma^2 = \sigma_u^2 + \sigma_v^2$. Further, the hypothesis that the technical inefficiency effects are not influenced by the level of explanatory variables in equation (2) is examined by testing the significance of δ and δ'. The estimation used Maximum Likelihood methods (see Coelli (1994)) with the Frontier 4.1 software.

In Table 2 we present the results of the maximum likelihood estimation. All coefficients are strongly statistically significant. It is interesting to note that the higher the central grant as a proportion of total state expenditure, the lower the tax efficiency. This effect works directly through the variable GTOE as well as indirectly through the interaction terms: GTOE*SDP and GTOE*AGY. The null hypothesis that $\gamma = 0$ is tested using both the t tables as well as the LR test and is decisively rejected.

In Table 3 we present the estimates of efficiency for each state for the beginning, mid-point and end of the sample period (results for all years can be obtained from the corresponding author). For each year Assam is the least efficient state followed, in that order, by Orissa and Bihar. These three also happen to be the poorest states (in terms of CO) in the sample period. Haryana and Punjab do well early in the sample period whereas the southern states of Tamilnadu and Andhra Pradesh and, to a lesser extent, Karnataka and Maharashtra, do well later on. For the other states, there is considerable variation in ranking over the years. A relatively economically underdeveloped state like Uttar Pradesh shows an improvement in performance whereas the performance of an advanced state like Punjab has deteriorated.

Table 1. LR tests for functional form
Base Model:
Determinants of Tax Collected: SDP, AGY, TIME AND TIME SQUARED
Determinants of Inefficiency: TIME, GTOE, GTOE*SDP, GTOE*AGY, CO
Value of Log of Likelihood Function for Base Model: -1236.029

Restriction Imposed on Coefficient of	Value of λ	Decision on H_0
CO $= 0$	6.2	Rejected
(in Z_{it}) TIME $= 0$ CO $= 0$	10.4	Rejected
All Cross Effects $= 0$	72.9	Rejected
(in X_{it}) TIME $=$ TIME2 $= 0$ (in Z_{it}) TIME $= 0$	8.1	Rejected
(in X_{it}) TIME2 $= 0$	28.0	Rejected
(in X_{it}) TIME $=$ TIME2 $= 0$	28.4	Rejected
(in X_{it}) TI2 $= 0$ (in Z_{it}) TI $= 0$	14.8	Rejected
(in Z_{it}) TI $= 0$	20.2	Rejected
(in X_{it}) TI $= 0$	14.4	Rejected
(in X_{it}) TI $=$ TI2 $= 0$	28.8	Rejected
(in X_{it}) TI $= 0$ (in Z_{it}) TI $= 0$	5.9	Rejected

N.B. (i) X_{it} refers to the variables determining tax revenue and Z_{it} to the variables determining inefficiency.
(ii) All H_0 except last rejected at 5% or less. Last rejected at 10%.

Indices of convergence

At this juncture, it is natural to ask whether the ranks of states by tax efficiency differ significantly across the years. To address this we calculate Kendall's coefficient of concordance (see Boyle and McCarthy (1997)) to track the mobility of individual states within the distribution of efficiencies over time. The motivation for calculating it in the context of our work is to determine if the states that were inefficient earlier are still inefficient or whether there has been any convergence. This could help in directing central funds, if there has been no convergence. Kendall's coefficient of concordance, W, is used to determine the association among the rankings obtained by various states in different years. (For a lucid discussion of this methodology as used in this paper as well as by Boyle and McCarthy (1997) see Seigel (1956)).

If all the states had the same ranks in all the years, then the variance of the sum of the ranks over the years of all the states would be the maximum. The coefficient of concordance can be thought of as an index of divergence of the actual agreement from the maximum possible (perfect) agreement. The degree of actual agreement in ranks obtained by the states in various years is reflected

Table 2. Estimates of production frontier and determinants of inefficiency
The final Maximum Likelihood Estimates are:
Determinants of
(i) Stochastic Frontier

Variable	Coefficient		Standard Error	t-ratio
Constant	446.9564		1.7030	262.4592
SDP	0.0911		0.0019	48.0477
AGY	−964.4124		22.2078	−43.4267
Time	50.5688		4.9012	10.3176
Time squared	−2.0140		0.1115	−18.0548
(ii) Inefficiency				
Constant	315.1587		24.7720	12.7224
Time	10.5026		3.4256	3.0659
GtoE	143.3539		11.1864	12.8150
GtoE*SDP	0.1421		0.0182	7.7888
GtoE*AGY	28.6853		1.9566	14.6605
CO	−2.3630		0.4291	−5.5075
Statistics				
Sigma-squared	3005.87	0.96	3126.98	
Gamma	0.9	0.0000859	10477.29	

by the degree of variance among the J (total number of states) sums of the ranks. Thus W is calculated as:

$$W = s/\{(1/12)(k^2)J(J^2 - 1)\}$$

where, s = sum of squares of the observed deviations from the mean of R_j (the sum of the ranks obtained by a particular state in different years), that is,

$$s = \left[\sum_j R_j - \sum_j R_j/N\right]^2$$

and

k = no. of years (the set of rankings.)

J = no. of states ranked.

Now, $(1/12)k^2(J^3 - J)$ = maximum possible sum of squared deviations, i.e. the sum of s which would occur with perfect agreement among k rankings.

The value of the rank concordance index ranges from zero to one. The coefficient of concordance is calculated for the first two sets of rankings (i.e. first two years), then for the first three set of rankings and so on for all the sets of rankings (i.e. for all the years). This enables us to study the mobility of ranks at each point in time. The probability associated with the occurrence under H_0 (rankings are unrelated to each other) of any value as large as an observed W can be determined by finding χ^2 by the formula

Table 3. Tax efficiency of Indian states: 1980–81 to 1992–93

State	1980–81 Efficiency	State	1986–87 Efficiency
Haryana	0.923556470	Andhra Pradesh	0.999946630
Punjab	0.804594720	Tamilnadu	0.911152480
Karnataka	0.797366800	Karnataka	0.873050590
Andhra Pradesh	0.779028060	Maharashtra	0.860045120
Gujarat	0.718350120	Madhya Pradesh	0.742590790
Tamilnadu	0.697422570	Punjab	0.733907360
Maharashtra	0.691915590	Gujarat	0.685532830
Kerala	0.650319580	Haryana	0.642210520
Rajasthan	0.579267970	Uttar Pradesh	0.627890000
Madhya Pradesh	0.546029590	Kerala	0.618550690
West Bengal	0.506593740	Rajasthan	0.602816670
Uttar Pradesh	0.499794010	West Bengal	0.582644670
Bihar	0.449040940	Bihar	0.440401840
Orissa	0.441748480	Orissa	0.397404370
Assam	0.291527920	Assam	0.263286490

State	1992–93 Efficiency
Tamilnadu	0.961665780
Andhra Pradesh	0.825862700
Gujarat	0.791400600
Karnataka	0.773042660
Maharashtra	0.763184780
Madhya Pradesh	0.691256740
Punjab	0.659759020
Uttar Pradesh	0.654959480
Rajasthan	0.641359910
Haryana	0.636910330
Kerala	0.627256300
West Bengal	0.584751720
Bihar	0.449062200
Orissa	0.361050170
Assam	0.220450290

N.B. States are arranged in descending order of efficiency.

$$\chi^2 = s/[(1/12)kJ(J+1)] = k(J-1)W$$

with degrees of freedom $J - 1$. In Table 4 we note the value of W over the years. In each case the null hypothesis is decisively rejected.

We also computed elasticity of tax with respect to the inputs. Battese and Broca (1995) show that the elasticity of tax with respect to the k-th input variable is

$$\beta_k + \sum_j \beta_{kj} X_{jit} + C_{it}(\partial \mu_{it}/\partial X_k)$$

where

$$\mu_{it} = \delta_0 + \sum_j \delta_j Z_{jit} + \sum_j \sum_k \delta_{jk} Z_{jit} X_{kit}$$

Table 4. Kendall's index of concordance

YEAR	W	Chi-Square
1980–81	0.8598	156.49
1981–82	0.8787	147.63
1982–83	0.9097	140.10
1983–84	0.9259	129.63
1984–85	0.9373	118.10
1985–86	0.9373	104.98
1986–87	0.9437	92.49
1987–88	0.9444	79.33
1988–89	0.9437	66.06
1989–90	0.9513	53.28
1990–91	0.9563	40.17
1991–92	0.9696	27.15

N.B.: Null Hypothesis of disagreements between the ranks rejected at 5% for all years.

and

$$C_{it} = -1 + (1/\sigma)[\phi\{(\mu_{it}/\sigma) - \sigma\}/\Phi\{(\mu_{it}/\sigma) - \sigma\} - \phi(\mu_{it}/\sigma)/\Phi(\mu_{it}/\sigma)]$$

where $\phi(\cdot)$ and $\Phi(\cdot)$ represent, respectively, the density and distribution functions of the standard normal variable, respectively. We calculated elasticities of tax collected with respect to SDP and AGY and report them for individual states for the beginning, mid-point and end points of the sample in Table 5. The former elasticity is always positive whereas the latter is always negative.

With so many states showing lackluster performance with respect to tax efficiency, it should not be surprising to find that the overall tax performance of Indian states has been disappointing. We compute an index of aggregate tax efficiency for any year t as follows. Let eff_i be the efficiency of state i. Aggregate tax efficiency for year t (μ_t) is defined as:

$$\mu_t = \sum_{i=1}^{15} \left[eff_i \left\{ TA_i \bigg/ \left(\sum_{i=1}^{15} TA_i \right) \right\} \right] \tag{3}$$

The results of this computation are shown in Table 6. These show that aggregate tax efficiency of Indian states has tended to stagnate.

4. Conclusions

The analysis in this paper has been quite revealing. Apart from tax capacity factors, which have a direct bearing on the amount of revenue that a state can collect at a given tax rate, the tax performance of the state depends on its revenue efficiency manifested in administrative and legislative efforts to expand the tax base, rationalize the tax structure and reduce avenues of tax avoidance and evasion. Moreover, the flow of resources to the state governments through the growth in tax capacity factors, or what is referred to as the built-in elasticity of the tax system, may often be inadequate. It is in this

Table 5. Elastcity of tax collected t SDP and AGY

	Elasticity to SDP	Elasticity to AGY
1980–81		
Andhra Pradesh	0.431977035	−0.714238126
Assam	0.4100987	−7.363534784
Bihar	0.434105484	−1.661299948
Gujarat	0.458492615	−0.671274341
Haryana	0.10345987	−2.217034341
Karnataka	0.210326616	−0.866122801
Kerala	0.064776348	−0.970144018
Madhya Pradesh	0.546750631	−1.097865228
Maharashtra	1.006420764	−0.211687709
Orissa	0.14887654	−3.712365647
Punjab	0.177309546	−1.33950718
Rajasthan	0.426895434	−2.059534923
Tamilnadu	0.65814168	−0.370765183
Uttar Pradesh	1.232092205	−0.746328133
West Bengal	1.009551581	−0.535576009
1986–87		
Andhra Pradesh	0.397719493	−0.356941386
Assam	0.588765498	−2.364433136
Bihar	0.729195093	−0.969373115
Gujarat	0.655959801	−0.360673954
Haryana	0.236591164	−1.285936159
Karnataka	0.323093906	−0.472204763
Kerala	0.101545324	−0.706563906
Madhya Pradesh	0.459026019	−0.758497301
Maharashtra	0.850643364	−0.110308651
Orissa	0.564682882	−2.278973536
Punjab	0.112103892	−1.000816089
Rajasthan	0.031596921	−1.141215988
Tamilnadu	0.55265194	−0.206617408
Uttar Pradesh	1.103892191	−0.449536228
West Bengal	0.794128576	−0.372300193
1992–93		
Andhra Pradesh	0.590378779	−0.280492281
Assam	0.509964875	−1.657557718
Bihar	0.951378205	−0.532549289
Gujarat	0.646140114	−0.204181646
Haryana	0.22128016	−0.749812709
Karnataka	0.584373541	−0.302729141
Kerala	0.348324241	−0.546235438
Madhya Pradesh	0.621355651	−0.433906866
Maharashtra	0.991902872	−0.079119919
Orissa	0.354429848	−0.999825957
Punjab	0.405991632	−0.676777206
Rajasthan	0.463194796	−0.613778598
Tamilnadu	0.557469189	−0.138216824
Uttar Pradesh	1.046694371	−0.255503851
West Bengal	0.981925908	−0.276053116

Table 6. Aggregate tax efficiency of Indian states

1980–81	0.657198
1981–82	0.667433
1982–83	0.689241
1983–84	0.651917
1984–85	0.681494
1985–86	0.711541
1986–87	0.746461
1987–88	0.728021
1988–89	0.700565
1989–90	0.738376
1990–91	0.749863
1991–92	0.707164
1992–93	0.714548

context that tax efficiency of states assumes critical importance for garnering resources for development. This apart, a sound tax system presupposes a certain degree of efficiency in tax collection.

State governments in India, by virtue of their very diverse economic conditions, collect different proportions of their gross revenue through their own resources, with the remainder being met by transfers from the central government. If the weight on tax effort in the formula for devolution of central funds to the states was to be reduced to zero, the incentive for a state to achieve higher tax efficiency, from the point of view of receiving higher levels of central transfers, would be completely absent. The analysis in this paper provides a framework to evaluate the temporal trend in states' tax efficiency, both inter-state and overall, and to see whether there is evidence of a close relation between central transfers and state tax efficiency.

There appears to be a problem of moral hazard in the design of central government grants to state governments. The greater the proportion of states' expenditure financed by central grants the lower is their tax efficiency. Furthermore, the less poor states, *ceteris paribus*, display greater efficiency in tax collection. In recent times, considerable concern has been voiced about the level of fiscal deficit of the central government. One way that the central government has chosen to reduce this deficit is by reducing grants to states. Against this backdrop, improvement in tax efficiency of Indian states assumes a degree of urgency. One way out of this problem could be to put greater weight on states' tax effort in the formula determining state government shares in central government revenues. This would address the moral hazard problem directly. The analysis in this paper, therefore, presents one method of reducing fiscal stress in the Indian economy.

Appendix. Sources and transformations of the data

Raw data was obtained from various publications of Central Statistical Organization (CSO) and National Sample Survey (NSS) (32nd. to 44th. rounds). Some transformation of the above data was needed to express them in a form that would provide estimable equations. Data on taxes collected by the states as well as their expenditures, and grants given to them by the central government were obtained from the various issues of **Finances of State Governments/RBI Bulletin** published by the Reserve Bank of India. A common set of taxes including sales tax, entertainment tax and the like for all fifteen states was considered. Data on Net State Domestic Product at constant prices is obtained from CSO documents, as is the proportion of total SDP originating from agriculture. The state-wise estimates of level of poverty for the period 1980–81 to 1992–93 were proxied by state specific real annual per capita rural household consumption expenditures. Nominal per capita rural household expenditure for 30 days are available for selected time points in publications of **Center for Monitoring the Indian Economy** (CMIE) and NSS. The annual nominal values so obtained were deflated to 1980–81 prices using the state-wise Consumer Price Indices for Agricultural Laborers (Base: 1980 $= 100$). The resulting real consumption expenditures were converted into index numbers to measure an individual state's position relative to the all-India average. Data on SDP are not available for 1992–93 in the case of Rajasthan and Tamilnadu. These were obtained by regressing SDP on time (for the period 1980–81 to 1991–92) and using the regression equations to project values for 1992–93. AGY for 1992–93 was obtained as an average of the previous three years in the case of both states. State-wise total own tax revenues, i.e., excluding their shares in central taxes were deflated to 1980–81 price levels using state-wise consumer price indices. These real tax revenues are referred to as TA_{it} for state i for year t.

References

Battese GE, Coelli TJ (1992) Frontier production functions, technical efficiency and panel data with applications to paddy farmers in India. Journal of Productivity Analysis 3:153–169

Battese GE, Coelli TJ (1995) A model for technical inefficiency effects in a stochastic frontier production function for panel data. Empirical Economics 20:325–332

Battese GE, Malik S, Broca SE (1995) Functional forms of stochastic frontier production functions and models for technical efficiency effects: A comparative study for wheat farmers in Pakistan. Mimeo, Department of Economics, University of New England

Boadway RW (1997) Public economics and the theory of public policy. Canadian Journal of Economics 30:753–772

Boadway RW, Horiba I, Jha R (1998) The provision of public services by government funded decentralized agencies. Public Choice (forthcoming)

Boyle GA, McCarthy TE (1997) A simple measure of β convergence. Oxford Bulletin of Economics and Statistics 59:257–264

Buiter WE, Patel U (1992) Debt, deficits and inflation: An application to the public finances of India. Journal of Public Economics 47:171–205

Buiter WE, Patel U (1997) Solvency and fiscal correction in India: An analytical discussion. In: Mundle S (ed.) Public finance: Policy issues for India, Oxford University Press, New Delhi, pp. 30–75

Coelli TJ (1994) A guide to FRONTIER Version 4.1: A computer program for stochastic frontier production and cost function estimation. mimeo, Department of Economics, University of New England

CMIE various publications, Bombay

CSO various publications, New Delhi

Cornwell C, Schmidt P, Sickles RE (1990) Production frontiers with cross-sectional and time-series variation in efficiency levels. Journal of Econometrics 46:185–200

Davidson R, MacKinnon JG (1993) Estimation and inference in econometrics. Oxford University Press, New York

Government of India (1994) Report of the tenth finance commission

Huang CJ, Liu JT (1994) Estimation of a non-neutral stochastic frontier production function. Journal of Productivity Analysis 5:171–180

Jha R, Singh SP (1994) Intertemporal and cross-section variations in technical efficiency in the Indian railways. International Journal of Transport Economics 21:57–73

Jha R (1998) Modern public economics. Routledge, London and New York

King DE (1984) Fiscal tiers: The economics of multi-layer government. Allen and Unwin, London

National Sample Survey, Government of India, various publications

Reserve Bank of India, various publications

Seigel SG (1956) Nonparametric statistics for the behavioral sciences. McGraw-Hill Book Company, New York

Shome P (1997) Economic liberalization, fiscal performance, and tax reform: Indian experience and cross-country comparisons. In: Mundle S (ed.) Public finance: Policy issues for India. Oxford University Press, New Delhi, pp. 76–103

Vaillancourt F (1992) Sub-national tax harmonization in Australia and comparison with Canada and the United States. Australian Tax Forum 9:51–64

Vaillaincourt F, Rao MG (1994) Interstate tax disharmony in India: A comparative perspective. Publius, The Journal of Federalism 24:99–114

IV Do governments act in the interest of their constituents?

Tax reforms and the growth of government*

Steven M. Sheffrin

University of California, Davis College Of Letters and Science, One Shields Avenue, Davis,
CA 95616-8572, USA (e-mail: smsheffrin@ucdavis.edu)

First version received: November 1997 / Final version received: February 1999

Abstract. This paper analyzes alternative approaches to measuring the effects
of structural tax changes on government growth. It first reviews traditional
time series approaches that attempt to disentangle the causal relationships
between taxes and spending. It explains why these methods are incapable of
uncovering the true causal links because of problems of observational equivalence and why institutional data can assist in making this determination. It
then presents the methods and results from two alternative approaches and
studies that analyze the effects of changes in tax structures on government
growth. Both methods rely on econometric and institutional analysis.

Key words: Causality, tax reforms, government growth

JEL classifications: C50, H10, B40

I. Introduction

In textbook public finance, the marginal benefits of government spending are
equated to the marginal cost of taxation while the mix of taxation is chosen to
minimize the inherent distortions from taxation. In this ideal world, there are
no agency problems with bureaucracy or politicians and no need for tax limitations to protect taxpayers from excessive government growth. Moreover,
since tax and spending decisions are jointly determined, there is no sense in
which tax changes or tax reforms can cause government growth unless they
fundamentally change the benefits of spending or the costs of taxation.

In actual tax systems, measures to restrain the growth of taxation and the

---

* Support for this research was provided by the Center for State and Local Taxation, UC Davis.

growth of government spending are ubiquitous. For example, as discussed by Sexton and Sheffrin (1995) for the United States, by 1994 all but four states had passed laws restricting state and or local governments tax or spending capabilities and efforts were underway to enact limitations in those states. States also have restrictions against deficit financing that in part are motivated by the desire to force explicit and politically costly taxation on politicians. At the federal level, proponents of constitutional amendments to balance the budget often insist on tax limitation measures within such amendments to reduce the growth of government.

The rationale given for these limitations is that, in their absence, government growth would be excessive. For example, voters will typically be less informed than government officials over the costs and alternatives for proposed spending. Since career prospects for bureaucrats and politicians are often increasing in the level of spending, this asymmetric information and difference in incentives naturally leads to potential overspending. Tax limitations are devices to change the costs of raising revenue and attempt to mitigate the agency problems.

In this world where agency considerations are important, structural tax changes or tax reforms can have significant and unintended effects on economic growth. To the extent that tax changes affect the incentives and information structures in budgetary settings, there is potential for additional effects on the size and scope of government. Of course, structural changes that reduce the excess burdens of taxation can also lead to government growth as well.

Compelling evidence of the effects of structural tax changes on government growth is scarce. Even the effects of such dramatic initiatives such as Proposition 13 in California have been disputed. Although Proposition 13 successfully reduced the growth of property tax revenues, other revenues grew more rapidly after the passage of Proposition 13 allowing significant government growth. As Sexton and Sheffrin (1995) report, both state and local government spending as a share of personal income declined in the United States for the period 1978–81 following a period of active tax limitations, but since then have exceeded their 1970 levels.

This paper analyzes alternative approaches to measuring the effects of structural tax changes on government growth. It first reviews traditional time series approaches that attempt to disentangle the causal relationships between taxes and spending. It explains why pure time series methods are incapable of uncovering the true causal links because of observational equivalence and how institutional data can assist in making this determination. It then presents the methods and results from two alternative approaches and studies that analyzed the effects of changes in tax structures on government growth. These methods relied both on econometric and institutional analysis. The need to utilize institutional information to untangle causal relations is a key focus of this paper.

II. Why pure time series methods won't uncover causal structure

In the United States, both politicians and economists have become fascinated with the notion that the potential availability of tax revenues lead to higher government growth. As reported by Hoover and Sheffrin (1992), a former

Secretary of the Treasury remarked that indexation of the income tax would reduce government spending because it reduced the flow of revenue to the federal government. Gramlich (1989) provides a representative economists perspective on this debate highlighting the notion that political behavior could be important in a world of asymmetric information and agency costs.

The empirical interest in this phenomena was motivated by regressions that show that deficit spending leads to lower government spending in the United States in the postwar era. More sophisticated approaches move beyond single equation models and look for Granger causality between taxes and spending in a vector autoregression. A representative example of this approach was taken by von Furstenberg, Green, and Jeong (1986).

Unfortunately, neither single equation nor multi-equation models can shed light on the causality between taxes and spending. It is important to distinguish between our common notion of causality as one of control and Granger-causality which is a statistical condition of incremental predictability. The question at hand is whether, for example, controlling government spending will eventually control the level of taxes or whether controls on taxation will eventually control the level of government spending. In other words, are government spending and taxes endogenous or exogenous? Granger-causality (and by implication any single equation time series models) is uninformative on this issue.

To understand this critical point, consider Barro's (1979) model of public debt. In his model, government spending follows an exogenous stochastic process. Because there are costs in changing taxes, politicians "smooth" tax rates in order to minimize intertemporal distortions subject to a present value constraint. With quadratic costs in taxation, this model becomes isomorphic to the standard linear model of permanent income.

As long as factors other than the past history of government spending help to predict government spending (and these factors are known to policy makers), then taxes will Granger-cause government spending even though taxes are endogenous and government spending is exogenous. The reason this occurs is that taxes are smoothed in anticipation of future movements of government spending and thus have incremental predictive power for government spending, in essence proxying for the other variables that cause government spending. Lagged taxes will therefore predict future movements in government spending over and above the past history of spending and therefore, by definition, Granger-cause spending.

This result depends on forward-looking policy makers. If policy makers use only feedback rules based on past information, then a regression which shows that lagged taxes assist in predicting government spending could be taken as evidence in favor of the view that taxes cause spending. The point, however, is that a simple regression could be given either interpretation and thus cannot shed light on the true causal relations between taxes and spending.[1] In other words, we are faced with a problem of observational equivalence- the same set of empirical relations are consistent with two radically different relations between spending and taxation.

---

[1] Hendry (1988) discusses how to distinguish forward-looking models from feedback models in situations where there are structural breaks in variables in the model.

III. Uncovering causal structure I: Using structural breaks

Sheffrin and Hoover (1992) show how to use time series methods and institutional knowledge to disentangle the causal relationships between taxes and spending. Their key insight is to uncover "structural" changes or breaks in the stochastic processes governing taxes and spending and to examine the stability of the empirical relationships of taxes and spending following these breaks.

To understand this method, suppose that taxes caused government spending and there was a sudden exogenous event that also influenced government spending, such as a war. Since, by hypothesis, government spending does not cause taxes; we should not see any change in the process governing taxes despite the fact that the war changed the process governing spending. Thus, we would have evidence that government spending did *not* cause taxes. Under these causal assumptions, however, a structural tax change would cause a corresponding break in government spending.

Under the alternative hypothesis that government spending caused taxes, changes in the processes governing taxes and spending would, of course, have the opposite implications. Thus, it is possible to distinguish these two cases from one another by looking at the behavior of taxes and spending following breaks in the stochastic processes for these variables.[2] It is also possible to determine if there is mutual causation or no causation between taxes and spending.

To implement this method empirically, it is first necessary to find a stable period in which there were no structural breaks and for which there are stable empirical models for taxation and spending. The next step is to look at the consequences of breaks in taxes and spending outside this sample period. Since empirical models can break down for any number of reasons, it is important to use institutional analysis to identify potential structural breaks in advance of the empirical analysis. It is then possible to be confident that, for example, a break in the series for government spending is a true "break" in government spending and not just a failure of the statistical model for government spending. A full range of statistical tests are now available to test for structural breaks when the precise date of the break point is unknown. The correspondence or non-correspondence of breaks in taxes and spending can then be used, as outlined above, to ascertain the causal relations between taxes and spending.

Using these methods, Hoover and Sheffrin (1992) studied the causal relationships between taxes and spending in the post-war era for the U.S. They first discovered that many tax changes, for example, those in the 1970s were not true structural breaks but were instead consistent with a stable empirical model for taxes. They then uncovered two different causal regimes. For the period after 1970, taxes and spending were essentially independent. During this era, breaks in either taxes or spending failed to cause breaks in the other series. For example, the tax cuts of 1981 did not cause any break in spending nor did the military build up in fourth quarter of 1982 lead to any break in the tax series. This provides evidence for the independence of taxes and spending. However, in the period from 1950 to the mid-1960s, taxes and spending were interdependent and there was mild evidence that taxes caused spending.

---

[2] If there is no forward looking behavior, conditional as well as marginal models for taxes and spending would be informative.

One episode is particularly instructive. At the onset of the Korean War, tax bills were enacted with built-in expiration dates at the end of 1953. The expiration dates clearly envisaged the end of the conflict by that time. The war and fighting actually ended prior to this period. The taxes were allowed to expire, requiring a fall in spending below wartime levels. This was consistent with taxes causing spending. On the other hand, if spending caused taxes and a "peace dividend" (a conversion of military to non-military spending) was anticipated, the level of spending would have remained at wartime levels and the expiration dates for the taxes could have easily been repealed. The statistical evidence is also consistent with the view that taxes cause spending.

While this approach to testing for the causality of taxes and spending is informative, it does have its limitations. First, it is often difficult to find episodes where there are independent shifts in taxes and spending. For example, looking at yearly data during the twentieth century, the two world wars and the Great Depression cause both breaks in taxes and spending, making causal analysis impossible. Second, statistical analysis of structural breaks is inherently a delicate process and it is difficult to pinpoint dates of breaks precisely. Finally, this approach does not take advantage of the fact that some tax changes are primarily revenue driven (and thus closely tied to spending initiatives) while others are primarily desired changes in the structure of existing taxes.

III. Uncovering causal structure II: Using episodes of tax reform

An alternative approach is to study tax reform episodes directly. If a tax reform is undertaken for structural reasons and not primarily revenue driven, then the consequences of such reforms for the course of government spending can be analyzed without fear that the initial change was directly or indirectly motivated by concerns for government growth. To illustrate this method, we turn to a case study of a major change in the structure of state taxation in California during the Great Depression.[3]

Economic historians have been keenly interested in the acceleration of governments' growth during the Great Depression. Robert Higgs argues that both the size and powers of government grow during perceived crises and that the Great Depression provides a classic example of this phenomenon.[4] John Wallis highlights both the growth of federal government at the expense of local government and the growth of state government during the 1930s.[5] He emphasizes the incentives provided by federal grants to change the nature of and size of government programs, particularly in the area of agricultural price supports and public welfare.

Here we focus on an alternative explanation for the growth of state government in the 1930s: the modernization of the tax systems that occurred during the very early part of the Great Depression. Voters, legislators, and government officials transformed state and local fiscal systems throughout the United States during the Great Depression. Retail sales taxes were introduced at a rapid rate during this period. Of the 46 states that now have retail sales

---

[3] This analysis draws on Hartley, Sheffrin, and Vasche (1996).
[4] Higgs, *Crisis and leviathan.*
[5] Wallis, "Birth of old federalism."

taxes, 24 initiated them during the 1930s, the vast majority by 1933.[6] Many states also introduced personal income taxes during this period. No other decade in this century has witnessed as dramatic a set of changes in state tax structures and fiscal systems generally.

Since the fiscal changes in the states occurred early in the 1930s, they potentially could constitute a third independent factor leading to the growth of government. The majority of these changes occurred before the bulk of the federal grant programs were implemented. To the extent that the modernization of the state tax systems permitted higher, sustained revenue growth by increasing the elasticity of the tax systems, they can also account for the "ratchet" effect emphasized by Higgs whereby the growth of government powers continues after the crisis appears to end.

The changes in the California fiscal system during the 1930s were as dramatic as anywhere in the country. In 1933, voters approved an initiative measure that quickly led to a major restructuring of the entire state and local system, the immediate introduction of a retail sales tax, and the introduction of a personal income tax two years later. The fiscal system enacted in California during the 1930s has persisted in its basic structure through today.[7] These changes have allowed real per-capita state expenditure to grow by a factor of approximately 10 from 1929/30 to 1989/90.

The key tax event in California was the passage of the Riley-Stewart initiative, which the voters approved in a special election on 27 June 1933. It had four main components: public utility property was to be returned to local property tax rolls and the gross receipts tax which had been levied on public utility property was to be abolished in 1935; the state would provide additional support for elementary and secondary schools; limits were to be placed on expenditure increases both at the state and local levels; and the Legislature was to be authorized to raise additional revenue to meet the cost for school aid. The source of this revenue was not described in the initiative but it was generally acknowledged that a sales tax would be necessary. After the Riley-Stewart amendment passed by nearly a two-to-one margin, the Legislature faced an enlarged state deficit from the additional school aid. It quickly adopted a retail sales tax based on New York's model and also passed a personal income tax. The personal income tax was vetoed by the governor but enacted two years later.

Despite these tax changes, California still suffered from fiscal deficits. The state began issuing registered warrants (essentially debt) in November of 1933 at an initial interest rate of 5 percent, a rate comparable that paid on Aaa corporate bonds. (Short-term US securities paid less than 1 percent at that time.) Initially there was no public market for the warrants but most banks did accept them. The outstanding stock of registered warrants reached a peak of over $98 million in July of 1940; shortly thereafter a rapidly improving economy created fiscal surpluses that allowed the warrants to be retired.

The driving force for tax reform in the early 1930s was the desire to reduce the burden of property taxation. As personal income fell during the initial years of the depression, property tax delinquencies rose in California as they did throughout the country. California experienced less severe problems than

---

[6] Ebel and Zimmerman "Sales tax trends," p. 8.

[7] The most significant modification occurred with the passage of Proposition 13 in 1978 which limited property taxation and increased the role of state expenditures.

did many other jurisdictions. In Los Angeles County, for example, the percentage of uncollected levies rose from 4.3 percent in 1931–32 to 10.1 percent in 1932–33. This was a far cry from the experience in the midwest with a 37.6 percent rate in Milwaukee in 1931–32 and a 40.6 percent rate and widespread tax resistance in Chicago in 1931–32.[8] Nonetheless, there were persistent demands for property tax relief emerging in California.

As the Depression widened, California fell into a fiscal crisis and budgetary plans proposed by the governor were rejected. The State Controller, Ray L. Riley, and a member of the Board of Equalization, Fred E. Stewart, assumed leadership in this crisis. They offered an initial plan which was substantially changed by the Legislature but nonetheless bore their names. The resulting constitutional amendment, which we have previously described, was offered to the voters in a special election on June 27, 1933.

Unlike an earlier proposition that failed, this measure was ideally framed and, indeed, seemed to promise something for all parties. It emphasized property tax relief through the reduction in school expenditures by counties and an increase in the property tax base. Local expenditure limits were designed to force counties to lower rates and not increase spending with the higher tax base. The utility industry would be free of the gross receipts tax and assessed by the state at a rate comparable to that for local property. And despite the fact that new taxes were clearly on the horizon, the nature of the taxes was sufficiently ambiguous so that debates about the relative desirability of income versus sales taxes could be postponed.

Although the ultimate effect of the passage of the Riley-Stewart amendment was to develop an elastic tax system that would permit the growth of government, at the time the support for the initiative was based on very different considerations. On the one hand, some parties supported Riley-Stewart in order to restrain government growth. Taxpayer organizations emphasized the state and local expenditure limitations and saw this as a method to restrain government. Proponents of the measure, such as the State Chamber of Commerce, stressed expenditure limitations along with taxpayer property tax relief. On the other hand, some parties viewed this as a change in the mix or composition of taxes, away from the property tax to a sales tax. It was commonly recognized that the passage of Riley-Stewart would bring forth additional state taxes. The strongest opposition in San Francisco was from the Retail Dry Goods Association which opposed a retail sales tax.

From the point of view of analyzing the effects of tax reforms on economic growth, it is important to insure that voters wanted to change the mix of taxation and not change the size of government. Because of the expenditure limitations contained in the initiative, it is possible that voters wanted to reduce the size of government. One way to address the question of whether the voters were primarily seeking changes in the tax mix or reductions in the size of government is to analyze the voting behavior across counties.[9] There are two parts to our analysis.

We first establish that the vote across counties was consistent with the

---

[8] For data on delinquencies, see *Tax Digest* (1935), p. 29. Bieto, *Taxpayers in Revolt*, provides an in-depth discussion of the organized tax resistance movement in the midwest.

[9] This approach is in the spirit of Attiyeh and Engle "Testing Some Propositions," pp. 131–146 in their work on the passage of Proposition 13. No contemporary observers believed that the tax changes would lead to larger government.

direct economic interests of the voters. The counties differed in the extent to which they would benefit from the state assumption of school expenditures and the return of public utility property to the tax rolls. Variables measuring these differences can capture the relative gain from changes in the mix of taxation. The regressions assume implicitly that consumers, who ultimately would bear the burden of a retail sales tax, take its effects into account as voters.[10] We also include other background variables in our baseline regression to capture differences in voter sentiment across the counties.

We then examine the effects of variables designed to explore whether the voters also wanted smaller government. To capture this, we use the fact that the counties differed on the absolute level of local property taxation and the rate of growth of property tax rates. If voters desired a lower level of government, we hypothesize that those counties with either the highest tax rates or, alternatively, the most rapid growing tax rates would be the ones most likely to vote for the measure. These regressions implicitly assume that tastes are the same across the counties; if tastes for public services differed, higher tax rates could be associated with a greater demand for public services.

We now turn to the specification of the baseline regression which establishes that voters were cognizant of their economic interests. The dependent variable in this regression is the percentage of votes in each of the 58 counties in favor of the Riley-Stewart measure. The first two independent variables we include are designed to capture the differences in ideological positions across counties. These can be viewed as proxies for "fixed effects" in the attitudes of voters across counties. The two variables we chose were the percentage of "yes" votes for Proposition 9 (the prior initiative that was similar in spirit but was defeated) and the percentage of registered Republicans. The support for the prior proposition captures the degree of general sentiment for radical reform of the property tax system. The Republican variable captures the significant but unobserved differences evident in voting behavior in prior elections between members of the two parties.

The next two variables in the baseline regression capture the tax-mix variables. The first is the ratio of average daily attendance in elementary schools to the total population. This measure captures the benefits from the state assumption of county school costs. The second variable is the estimated percentage decrease in property tax rates from the return of utility property to the rolls.[11]

The first column of Table 1 reports the baseline regression. It has an adjusted R-squared of 32 percent and significant coefficients for the prior Proposition 9 vote, the percentage of Republican registrants in the county, and the two tax mix variables. One way to measure the electoral significance of the variables is to calculate the effect of a one standard deviation change in each of the variables on the vote count. A one standard deviation increase in the Proposition 9 vote would increase the Riley-Stewart vote by 2.9 percentage points while a one standard deviation increase in the percentage of Republicans would have a 2.5 percentage point effect. Similar calculations for the

---

[10] We do not, however, have any variables that differentiate the burden across consumers in the different counties.

[11] Standard errors use the White correction for heteroskedascity. Regressions with a logistic transformation for the dependent variable yielded similar results.

Table 1. Riley-Stewart regressions

Variable	Dependent Variable: Percent Yes Vote				
	Baseline Model	Regressions With Added Variables			
Constant	.55 (.19)	.62 (.19)	.63 (.18)	.60 (.19)	.55 (.17)
Percent Vote for Proposition 9	.32 (.14)	.23 (.15)	.30 (.15)	.34 (.15)	.32 (.15)
Percent Republican	−.39 (.21)	−.49 (.21)	−.43 (.22)	−.41 (.22)	−.37 (.22)
Average Daily Attendance Proportion	1.99 (.68)	1.48 (.68)	1.98 (.63)	1.88 (.67)	1.96 (.67)
Reduction in Tax from Utility Property	.13 (.06)	.09 (.07)	.11 (.06)	.14 (.07)	.13 (.06)
Total Local Property Rate (All Districts)			−.000013 (.000013)		
County Tax Rate 1932–33		.00027 (.00053)		−.00029 (.00058)	
Percentage Change in County Rate 1929–30 to 32–33					−.10 (.07)
SF Dummy		−.27 (.12)			
Adjusted R^2	.32	.36	.32	.31	.31

Estimated by OLS over 58 counties. Heteroskedasticity Corrected Standard Errors in Parentheses.

two tax mix variables – average daily attendance and utility property – lead to a 4 and 2.6 percentage point effect respectively.

The remaining columns of Table 1 test for the hypothesis that the voters wanted lower government by including alternative measures of the size or growth rate of the local tax burden. None of these variables are statistically significant at conventional confidence levels. Tests were run for the total property tax burden (including counties, cities, schools and special districts) in 1934–35; the county tax rate in 1932–33 (adjusted for assessment ratios in counties); and the growth of the county tax rate between 1929–30 and 1932–33. The growth rate variable was the closest to being statistically significant (its p-value was 0.20) but its coefficient was small and negative. The mean change in this variable in the sample was .60 which translates into a decrease in the Riley-Stewart vote of .47 percentage points.

Since San Francisco was and is both a city and a county, its tax rate exceeded the other county measures. To insure that this one observation did not distort the regression, we effectively removed the observation by adding a dummy variable for San Francisco and then testing the 1932–33 county tax rate. The tax rate was still not significant. Alternative measures of fiscal distress (based on failures to meet debt obligations) were also not significant.

The regressions suggest that the vote was consistent with the direct economic interests of the counties and that there is no evidence in support of the view that voters were trying to reduce the size of government. These results suggest that the local expenditure limitations in Riley-Stewart were a means of insuring property tax relief, not a device to cut the existing provision of government services. However, local expenditure limitations provided important psychological support because of one technical feature of the initiative. The Riley-Stewart amendment called for assessment at "full cash value" because when utility property was returned to the property tax rolls it needed to be assessed at similar values across counties. Since assessments averaged forty-four percent of market value statewide, there was fear, manifest in newspaper editorials, that existing rates would be maintained and property tax bills would soar. Expenditure limitations would prevent this from occurring. As it turned out, the Board of Equalization chose a 50 percent assessment ratio as "full cash value."

Two cautionary notes about the results. First, our test for whether voters wanted to change the mix of taxation or reduce the size or growth of government is contingent upon our proxies for variables measuring government's size or growth. We do not have direct observations on voters' preferences for the size of government. Second, the regression results do not address the issue of whether the Riley-Stewart amendment was engineered by politicians seeking to create a more elastic tax structure to allow government spending to continue at rapid rates. While this is an intriguing possibility (in that spending grew rapidly in the 1930s), there is no direct evidence in favor of this hypothesis. Indeed, the politicians would have had to have fooled the taxpayer groups who were adamant about the expenditure limitations in the amendment. There were suggestions, however, that the Board of Equalization supported Riley-Stewart because it gave it a new tax to administer (the retail sales tax) and because the creation of the Franchise Tax Board in 1929 had sharply reduced the powers of the Board.[12]

Although it appears that voters in California did not recognize this at the time, their desire to reduce the property tax burden put into place an extremely elastic tax system, thereby permitting a rapid expansion of government in California since the 1930s. A change in the mix of taxes thus led to an increase in overall revenues. From 1929 to 1945, assessed valuations increased in the state by 21 percent while personal income increased by 148 percent. The base for the sales and income tax expanded much more rapidly than the base for the property tax. This provides an example of what Higgs terms the "ratchet" effects from fiscal crises. In this case, the ratchet arose from fundamental changes in the tax base.

Two final points. First, in retrospect it is clear that the tax reform of the early 1930s had the unintended consequence of allowing revenue to grow more rapidly than under the old tax structure. It is still possible that growth could have continued at the historical rate but with substantially more registered warrants being issued. However, at some point the markets might have rebelled at an additional supply of these warrants. Second, there is nothing inherent in this episode that suggests that tax reforms lead to higher government spending. In this particular case, the replacement taxes had a higher elasticity than the prior taxes, but this is not an inevitable outcome of tax reforms.

---

[12] Haig and Shoup, *Sales tax*, pp. 291–292.

IV. Conclusion

The relationship of tax reforms and government growth is quite important today. Despite their preference for consumption taxes over income taxes, many conservative economists in the United States oppose a value-added tax because they believe under this regime it would be easier to raise taxes and this would lead to higher government spending. This belief is predicated on a political judgment over the relationship of tax reforms and government growth.

This paper outlined two methods for studying the relationship between tax reforms or structural tax changes and government growth. Both required that institutional knowledge be combined with econometric studies. One could conjecture that any reforms of the tax system that reduce the inefficiencies of taxation could lead to additional government growth (perhaps both desired or undesired). But before jumping to that conclusion (and its pessimistic obverse), further studies of explicit tax reforms and government growth would be highly valuable.

Future studies could use a wide variety of tax reforms and use either econometric or "event-study" methodologies to examine the growth of government. It is important in designing these studies to have the proper set of controls for on-going government growth and to insure that the tax reforms are true reforms and not disguised attempts to increase revenues. There are also deeper structural issues that can, in principle, be addressed. For example, can we distinguish the growth in government that results from more efficient and less costly taxation from the growth of government that comes about solely from increasing the agency costs of monitoring politicians? How does the substitution of indirect for direct taxation affect the growth of government? Answering these questions will require us to move in the direction of imposing even more structure on our analysis of taxes and spending and move further away from pure time series models.

References

Advisory Commission on Intergovernmental Relations (1994) Significant features of fiscal federalism, Vol. I. Government Printing Office, Washington

Attiyeh R, Engle RF (1979) Testing some propositions about proposition 13. National Tax Journal 32:131–146

Barro RJ (1979) On the determination of public debt. Journal of Political Economy 87:940–71

Bieto DT (1989) Taxpayers in revolt. The University of North Carolina Press, Chapel Hill and London

Ebel RD, Zimmerman C (1992) Sales tax trends and issues. In: Fox WF (ed.) Sales taxation, Praeger, Westport, Connecticut and London, pp. 3–25

Gramlich EM (1989) Budget deficits and national savings: Are politicians exogenous? Journal of Economic Perspectives 3:23–35

Haig RM, Shoup C (1934) The sales tax in the American States. Columbia University Press, New York, Morningside Heights

Hartley J, Sheffrin SM, Vasche ID (1996) Reform during crisis: The transformation of California's tax system during the great depression. Journal of Economic History, forthcoming

Hendry DF (1988) The encompassing implications of feedback vs. feedforward mechanisms in econometrics. Oxford Economic Papers 40:132–49

Higgs R (1987) Crisis and leviathan., Oxford University Press, New York and Oxford

Hoover KD, Sheffrin SM (1992) Causation, spending, and taxes: Sand in the sandbox or tax collector for the welfare state? American Economic Review 82:225–248

Sexton TA, Sheffrin SM (1995) Five lessons from tax revolts. State Tax Notes 18:1763–1768
Tax Digest, various issues, 1931–1938, California Los Angeles
von Furstenberg GM, Green JR, Jeong J-H (1986) Tax and spend, or spend and tax? Review of
    Economics and Statistics 68:179–88
Wallis JJ (1984) The birth of the old federalism: Financing the new deal: 1932–1940. Journal of
    Economic History 44:139–159

Empirics of the median voter hypothesis in Japan*

Takero Doi

Faculty of Economics, Keio University, 2-15-45 Mita, Minato-ku, Tokyo 108-8345, Japan
(e-mail: tdoi@econ.keio.ac.jp)

First version received: December 1997/Final version received: February 1999

Abstract. This paper empirically analyses for the first time the median voter hypothesis in Japan as a means of investigating whether or not Japanese prefectural finance reflects the preference of the median voter. The hypothesis is tested by estimating the demand functions of local public goods in each prefecture. As official data on the income of the median voter is unavailable in Japan, respective prefectural data is constructed using official data on income distribution and taxation. Reasonable intuitive interpretation of results indicates that the median voter hypothesis is supported in prefectural finances, and that voter preference affects the outcome of gubernatorial elections, i.e., a governor's reelection probability, by estimating a probit model. When considering the centralized prefectural government system in Japan, these results indicate that central government management of prefectural expenditures via inter-regional grants ultimately reflects jurisdictional median voter preference.

Key words: Median voter hypothesis, local public goods, Japanese prefectural finance, gubernatorial elections, probit model

JEL classifications: H72, D72

I. Introduction

Numerous studies have empirically analyzed the median voter hypothesis and shown it to play an important role in determining expenditure-related local

---

* This paper was presented in the 53rd Congress of International Institute of Public Finance, August 1997 in Kyoto. I wish to thank Toshihiro Ihori and Isidoro Mazza for their helpful suggestions. I am also grateful for the comments of two anonymous referees. Any remaining errors are mine.

finance policy in the U.S. and European countries (e.g., see Borcherding and Deacon (1972), Bergstrom and Goodman (1973), Gramlich and Rubinfeld (1982), and Turnbull and Djoundourian (1994)). In Japan, however, the hypothesis has not been directly used for analysis of local (prefectural) finance system expenditures. This led to the present paper which provides a direct test of median voter hypothesis to analyze its corresponding role in Japan.

Presently, there exists an opinion in Japan that the central, prefectural, and local governments are suffering from unnecessary public expenditures and subsidies. If true, and the local populace is accordingly against such spending practices, then it seems only natural that governmental bodies will reduce them. In actuality, however, this is easier said than done in Japan; a situation which makes testing the median voter hypothesis particularly important, as in only this way can it be determined whether or not Japanese governments disburse expenditures and subsidies in a manner satisfying the needs of each jurisdiction.

Perhaps the main reason that the voter median hypothesis has never been comprehensively applied in this regard is that data used in testing it, i.e., median income for each jurisdiction, is not available. Accordingly, here the data is instead constructed using data acquired from various Japanese institutions.

In testing the hypothesis, it is assumed that the median voter is a person who earns median income. For this main assumption to hold, other key ones must hold as well, i.e., there must be a single-dimensional policy issue under majority voting, the level of the (quantifiable) policy issue must have a strong (positive) correlation to income, and heterogeneity must exist among voters.

The above assumptions are satisfied when considered from a prefectural standpoint, since (i) a prefecture's income taxation accounts for more than 70% of the total prefectural tax revenue, and (ii) each governor is directly elected under majority rule. Therefore, by obtaining official data on income distribution within each prefecture, prefectural expenditures are suitable for testing the hypothesis.[1]

Based on estimations of demand functions of local public goods, it is subsequently concluded that that the hypothesis holds under a prefectural framework. Such estimations also indicate that the preference of the median voter affects the outcome of gubernatorial election. Under the U.S. federal framework, the median voter hypothesis dictates how local governments determine expenditures based on median voter preference. This interpretation does not apply to a centralized local system such as in Japan, however. In-

---

[1] We cannot, however, investigate expenditures of municipalities, villages, and the central government for these reasons. First, we cannot obtain data on distribution of the central government's (ordinary) expenditures by prefecture in Japan. The Japanese central government directly provides public goods whose benefit is limited within a jurisdiction. Hence if we examine the demand function of public goods supplied by the central government, we must get data on spending by the central government in each prefecture. We cannot, however, obtain the data and measure their benefit. Secondly, we consider it is not suitable to argue the hypothesis in the level of central government. Because the Japanese national political system is an indirect democracy. Finally, data on income distribution we use in this paper are reported by prefecture in the surveys, but are not reported by municipalities and villages. So if we try to investigate a demand function of public goods provided by municipalities and villages, we cannot tell who is the median voter there. Therefore we can discuss prefectural expenditure but not expenditures on municipal, village, and the central government levels.

stead, we will show that the median voter hypothesis dictates how the central government determines their expenditures.

In Japan's centralized system, although each prefectural government can formally decide its own expenditures, the central government is able to manage prefectural finances without considering prefectural election results; in other words, without considering the median voter's preference for expenditures in their prefectures. If true, then the hypothesis does not hold. In contrast, however, when considering that (i) a governor of a prefecture must get support from the median voter in order to be reelected, and (ii) the prevalence in Japan of maintaining a sitting governor in office, then it is reasonable to assume that governors petition the central government as the agents of the median voters and that the central government accordingly reflects their wishes regarding prefectural expenditures.

This paper is organized as follows. After introducing Japan's local finance system in Section II, the models applied to it are constructed in Section III. This is then followed in Section IV by estimates of prefectural median and mean incomes, after which the results of testing the median voter hypothesis are presented in Section V. In Section VI, the superiority of the median income as the regressor on prefectural expenditures is closely examined; while in Section VII, the relation between median voter preference and the probability of reelection for an incumbent governor is directly tested. Section VIII concludes the paper.

II. Japanese local finance system

There are three levels of government in Japan: the central, prefectural, and municipal governments. As this paper is focused on prefectural expenditures, only the subjects of prefectural finance and politics are considered.

The Japanese prefectural finance system is centralized, especially with regard to the collection of prefectural revenues.[2] Revenues are divided into the following categories: 1) Local taxes, 2) Local Transfer Taxes, 3) Local Allocation Tax, 4) National Government Disbursements, 5) Local Public Bonds, and 6) Miscellaneous Revenue.

Revenues are almost entirely controlled by the central government, with the rates and sources of Local Taxes being basically determined by national laws such that prefectural governments have limited discretion over them. Moreover, issues of Local Public Bonds are controlled only through the central government, which also distributes to each prefecture Local Transfer Taxes, the Local Allocation Tax, and National Government Disbursements. Thus it is clear that prefectural revenues are managed by the central government.

On the other hand, through prefectural expenditures, prefectural governments can reflect the needs of their residents. Based on case studies, Reed (1986) suggests that Japanese prefectural governments have less authority than that of federal states, albeit more authority in comparison to other unitary states. If these prefectural governments want to manage their finances as considered necessary, then they must necessarily request the central government to distribute these revenues accordingly. In this regard, the inter-

---

[2] See Shibata (1993) for further details.

Table 1. The number of gubernatorial reelections in Japanese prefectures, April 1947~March 1995

	One	Two	Three	Four	Five	Six	Seven	Eight	Total
Total	55	62	50	35	14	7	1	2	226
Share	24.34%	27.43%	22.12%	15.49%	6.19%	3.10%	0.44%	0.88%	

Data Source: "Successive Governors in Japan"

regional distribution of national government disbursements is often affected by political pressure, as suggested by Doi and Ashiya (1997). That is, national Diet members and prefectural governors appeal to central bureaucrats to distribute more in their jurisdictions, which in turn benefits their chances of being reelected.

In Japanese prefectural election systems, the governor is elected not by indirect election among assemblymen but by direct election among the electorate. Hence, if incumbent governors are supported by the electorate majority, their reelection is assured. Table 1 indicates the number of times gubernatorial candidates have been reelected, where only about 25% of all successive governors after World War II in Japan have not been reelected; and in fact, many remain in office for several terms. Obviously then, the central government supports the needs of a particular governor, who in turn carries out the median voter preferences shown in prefectural elections, otherwise incumbent governors might be unseated more frequently in Japan than is the case. Therefore, the above facts imply that the median voter hypothesis may be held.

Analyzing the median voter hypothesis in Japanese prefecture is important to investigate whether or not prefectural expenditures reflect voter preference. Under a centralized local system as in Japan, if the hypothesis does not hold, this means that the central government can control prefectural finances without considering voter preference. In contrast though, if it does hold, this means that the governor-petitioned central government can control prefectural expenditures in accordance with said preference; phenomena which are descriptively supported by Reed (1986) who reported that Japanese central bureaucrats find it extremely difficult to deal with prefectural citizens such that governors tend to prominently emerge in conflicts between the central government and populace demands.

III. Model

In this section, models based on the previous studies on the median voter hypothesis are modified to confirm to the local (prefectural) finance system in Japan.

Borcherding and Deacon (1972) pioneered the test of the median voter hypothesis that use the demand function of local public goods on the assumption that the households maximize their utility.[3] The model in our paper is as follows.

---

[3] Borcherding and Deacon (1972) don't explicitly show the utility function.

We presume that household i living in jurisdiction j obtains the utility through per capita consumption of private good (X_j^i) and local public goods (Z_j). Their utility function is

$$U(X_j^i, Z_j), \quad \text{where} \quad \frac{\partial U}{\partial X_j^i} > 0, \quad \frac{\partial U}{\partial Z_j} > 0, \quad \frac{\partial^2 U}{\partial Z_j^2} < 0. \tag{1}$$

Assume that households maximize the utility without considering the effect of the migration across jurisdictions. We suppose that benefit of the local public goods is not spilled over the jurisdiction. The local public goods allow for congestion. The relation between consumption and provision (G_j) of local public goods is denoted

$$Z_j^i = \rho_j^i \frac{G_j}{N_j^\gamma} \quad 0 \le \gamma \le 1 \quad \text{where} \quad \rho_j^i \equiv (Y_j^i)^\alpha \Big/ \sum_{i=1}^{N_j} \{(Y_j^i)^\alpha / N_j\}. \tag{2}$$

where N_j is the population in jurisdiction j, and γ is its congestion parameter ($\gamma = 0$ when it is purely public, and $\gamma = 1$ when it is purely private). We usually assume $0 \le \gamma \le 1$. ρ_j^i is the benefit share of household i in jurisdiction j, parameter α "reflects in some sense the extent to which the distribution of the publicly provided good is biased towards the more affluent groups relative to the situation of equal shares" (Denzau and Mackay (1976) p. 72). $\alpha = 0$ when benefits are distributed to all households equally, $\alpha > 0$ when more is distributed to higher income households, $\alpha < 0$ when more is distributed to lower income households. We define $Y_j^* \equiv \sum_{i=1}^{N_j} \{(Y_j^i)^\alpha / N_j\}$. This formation proposed by Denzau and Mackay (1976) and used for empirical studies as Gramlich and Rubinfeld (1982), Preston and Ridge (1995), and so on, differs from Borcherding and Deacon (1972) in the relation between consumption and provision of local public goods. Borcherding and Deacon (1972) postulate $\alpha = 0$ (equivalent to $\rho_j^i = 1$ or $Z_j = G_j / N_j^\gamma$) a prior.

Suppose private good is the numeraire. The budget constraint of the household is

$$X_j^i + T_j^i + \tau_j^i = y_j^i \tag{3}$$

where y_j^i is pre-tax income, T_j^i and τ_j^i are respectively prefectural tax and national tax paid by household i in jurisdiction j.[4]

The central (national) government collects taxes from each household in each jurisdiction, and distributes general lump-sum grants (Local Allocation Tax) and matching grants (National Government Disbursements) to each prefectural government (omitting national public goods provided by the central government). Each prefectural government collects (prefectural) taxes, receives grants, and spends provision of local public goods. The budget

---

[4] As we will mention in Section III, τ includes any taxes excluding taxes levied by the prefectural government. That is, τ includes national and municipal taxes.

constraint of the prefectural government j is

$$(1 - m_j)E_j = \sum_{i=1}^{N_j} T_j^i + H_j, \tag{4}$$

where E_j is expenditure for the provision of local public goods, H_j is a general lump-sum grant (Local Allocation Tax) distributed to prefectural government j, and m_j is the ratio of the matching grants (National Government Disbursements) to total expenditures. Expenditures for local public goods, E_j, are expressed:

$$E_j = qG_j,$$

where q is the unit cost of local public goods.

The central government faces a budget constraint (there are J jurisdictions around the country):

$$\sum_{j=1}^{J}\sum_{i=1}^{N_j} \tau_j^i = \sum_{j=1}^{J}(m_j qG_j + H_j). \tag{5}$$

It decides H_j, m_j, and the prefectural tax system satisfying equation (5). The central government receives requested by prefectural governments or the households, and then it can control H_j (Local Allocation Tax) and prefectural tax systems.[5] In this paper, we focus on their demand for local public goods or revenues.[6]

We shall define the tax share of the household i in jurisdiction j,

$$t_j^i = T_j^i \Big/ \sum_{i=1}^{N_j} T_j^i.$$

Hence the budget constraint of the household i in jurisdiction j is rewritten by it

$$X_j^i = y_j^i - \tau_j^i + t_j^i H_j - t_j^i\{(1 - m_j)qG_j\}$$
$$= y_j^i - \tau_j^i + t_j^i H_j - \{t_j^i(1 - m_j)q Y_j^*(N_j)^\gamma/(Y_j^i)^\alpha\}Z_j^i. \tag{6}$$

---

[5] Under the present system, the distribution of Local Allocation Tax, and the rate and structure of prefectural taxes are prescribed by national laws. Therefore each prefectural government or household can hardly decide the revenue of Local Allocation Tax and Local Taxes directly. So prefectural governments or households require appropriate control of the revenue from the central government.

[6] Now, we do not explicitly consider the object function of the central government in this paper. Because we want to focus whether or not the central government disburses subsidies to answer the needs of each jurisdiction. In order to check it, we had better set the object function as a priori. We would say that its object is that it disburses subsidies required by the median voter in every jurisdiction.

Define $s_j^i \equiv t_j^i \{(1 - m_j)qY_j^*(N_j)^\gamma/(Y_j^i)^\alpha\}$ in the last term of the right hand side in equation (6), s_j^i is the (local) tax price in terms of consumption of local public goods. If $\alpha = 0$, then $s_j^i \equiv t_j^i \{(1 - m_j)qN_j^\gamma\}$. Now $Y_j^i \equiv y_j^i - \tau_j^i + t_j^i H_j$ denotes after-tax income of household i in jurisdiction j.

The household wishes the quantity of local public goods by maximizing its utility. Under appropriate conditions for utility function, we introduce the formulation that household i's demand function of local public goods is

$$Z_j^i = A(s_j^i)^\eta (Y_j^i)^\delta, \tag{7}$$

where A is constant, η is its elasticity of tax price (supposing constant), and δ is its elasticity of income (supposing constant).[7] Assume that each household is assessed national and prefectural taxes, but chooses the level of m_j as it desires. In the assumption, Z_j^i is a monotonic function of Y_j^i (and y_j^i as well). Hence from the supposition of the utility function (1), the median voter hypothesis holds in majority voting on the quantity of local public goods with (7). Namely, the level of prefectural government expenditures in each jurisdiction is optimal for the median voter in its jurisdiction. The hypothesis can be satisfied if the central government manages each prefectural expenditure to reflect the preference of voters in the jurisdiction (e.g. controlling the distribution of National Government Disbursements, after all m_j).[8]

On the supply side of local public goods, its production function is expressed, using the Cobb-Douglas assumption, by[9]

$$G_j = aL_j^\beta K_j^{1-\beta}, \quad 0 < \beta < 1 \tag{8}$$

where a is constant, L_j, and K_j are respectively labor and capital for its production. Each prefectural government decides the output to minimize cost for production of local public goods,

$$L_j = \frac{\beta C_j}{w_j}, \quad K_j = \frac{(1 - \beta)C_j}{r},$$

where w_j is wage in jurisdiction j (it varies from one jurisdiction and another), r is the rental rate of capital (it equalizes across jurisdictions).[10] From (8), the

---

[7] We adopt an assumption that household's utility function is additively separable with respect to public goods provided by each level of government. Under the assumption, the demand function of public goods provided by a prefecture is independent of public goods provided by the other level of government.

[8] Each m_j may be different. Though the rate of grant (the ratio of National Government Disbursements to expenditure) for some specific purpose is almost the same across jurisdictions, the quantity of each expenditure varies in each prefectural government. Hence each m_j, the rate of grant in the sense of aggregation, is not same.

[9] This function must be linearly homogenous in order to identify parameters in models when we estimate them.

[10] The cost minimizing problem is

$$\min C_j = w_j L_j + rK_j \quad \text{s.t.(8)}.$$

We posit that prefectural governments supply public good efficiently. Moreover, we suppose labor is imperfectly mobile across jurisdictions, and capital perfectly mobile.

unit cost function $c_j = C_j/G_j$ is

$$c_j(w_j) = \frac{1}{a}\left(\frac{w_j}{\beta}\right)^{\beta}\left(\frac{r}{1-\beta}\right)^{1-\beta} \equiv a'w_j^{\beta},$$

$$\text{where} \quad a' \equiv \frac{1}{a}\left(\frac{1}{\beta}\right)^{\beta}\left(\frac{r}{1-\beta}\right)^{1-\beta}. \tag{9}$$

Here $c_j = q$ (unit cost of local public goods).[11]

From (2), (7), and (9), as the result of majority voting on prefectural expenditures, total expenditures in jurisdiction j $E_j(= C_j = c_jG_j = c_jN_j^{\gamma}Z_j^m/\rho_j^m)$, are chosen for the following level preferred by median voter (superscript m denotes median voter).

$$E_j = A'w_j^{\beta(\eta+1)}[t_j^m(1-m_j)]^{\eta}N_j^{\gamma(\eta+1)}(Y_j^*)^{\eta+1}(Y_j^m)^{\delta-\alpha(\eta+1)}$$

$$\text{where} \quad A' \equiv A(a')^{\eta+1}.$$

Now we can $Y_j^* \cong \overline{Y}_j^{\alpha}$ ($\overline{Y}_j$ is mean income in jurisdiction j) from the definition of Y_j^*. In logarithmic form this becomes [12]

$$\ln E_j = \ln A' + \beta(\eta+1)\ln w_j + \gamma(\eta+1)\ln N_j$$

$$+ \eta\ln\{t_j^m(1-m_j)\} + \{\delta - \alpha(\eta+1)\}\ln Y_j^m + \alpha(\eta+1)\ln \overline{Y}_j. \tag{A}$$

If $\alpha = 0$, the above equation can be rewritten as

$$\ln E_j = \ln A' + \beta(\eta+1)\ln w_j + \gamma(\eta+1)\ln N_j$$

$$+ \eta\ln\{t_j^m(1-m_j)\} + \delta\ln Y_j^m \tag{B}$$

The model proposed by Bergstrom and Goodman (1973) deals with demand side only and tax price explicitly. In addition to Borcherding and Deacon (1972), i.e. their assumption $\alpha = 0$, we posit the marginal rate of transformation of local public goods for a private good is equal to 1 in each jurisdiction. Therefore, from (1), (2), (3), and (7),

$$\ln E_j = \ln A'' + \gamma(\eta+1)\ln N_j + \eta\ln\{t_j^m(1-m_j)\} + \delta\ln Y_j^m$$

$$\text{where} \quad A'' \equiv Aq^{\eta+1}. \tag{C}$$

After this section, in order to test the median voter hypothesis, we estimate

---

[11] We allow that not only the unit cost function, that is, wage w_j but q differs in each jurisdiction.
[12] In Borcherding and Deacon (1972), the left hand side in the above equation or (A) is not total expenditures but per capita expenditure.

Table 2. Models in this paper

Model	Demand Side		Supply Side
	congestion	benefit share	
(A)	Yes	Yes	Yes
(B)	Yes	No	Yes
(C)	Yes	No	No

model (A), (B), and (C).[13] The deference among them is shown in Table 2. Before that, we must estimate the median income as median voter, because we cannot get the data of median income from existing statistics. In the next section, we begin to estimate this.

IV. Estimating annual income and tax share of the median voter

In Japan, the data concerning median income (as the median voter) is not released explicitly. So we need to estimate it from income distribution. Statistics of (pre-tax) income distribution by prefecture are obtained from "Employment Status Survey," "Housing Survey of Japan," and "National Survey of Family Income and Expenditure." These are, however, taken every five years, and surveyed independently. Hence we analyze them separately using cross-sectional data in this paper.

We adopt a lognormal distribution, a popular specification, as income distribution in Japan.[14] Supposing annual pre-tax income of a household, y (omitting indexes), has a lognormal distribution, $\ln y$ has normally distributed with mean μ and variance $\sigma^2 (\ln y \sim N(\mu, \sigma^2))$. In standardizing $z \equiv (\ln y - \mu)/\sigma$, z is standard normally distributed $(z \sim N(0, 1))$. The cumulative distribution function of z is

$$\varphi = \Phi(z) \equiv \int_{-\infty}^{z} \frac{1}{\sqrt{2\pi}} \exp\left(-\frac{t^2}{2}\right) dt.$$

We define the inverse function $z = \Phi^{-1}(\varphi)$, and estimate

---

[13] We posit in these models that each household-voter is only interested in the quantity of local public goods (Total Expenditure). However we have no stylized evidence that this assumption is correct. In order to test the median voter hypothesis, we can use the expenditure for specific purposes (e.g. Ordinary Construction Works Expenditure, Social Welfare Expenditure). The spending which becomes an issue in an election is not always the same in every jurisdiction. In a cross-section analysis, unless we verify it, a test using the specific spending may be incorrect. When the issue in voting is Ordinary Construction Works Expenditure in one jurisdiction, or Social Welfare Expenditure in another jurisdiction, the test across jurisdictions using Ordinary Construction Works Expenditure is not meaningful. Therefore we can avoid this problem by testing the hypothesis of total expenditures.

[14] Previous works on the hypothesis (ex. Romer and Rosenthal (1979)) and on the income distribution in Japan have already used this distribution.

$$\Phi^{-1}(\varphi) = \frac{1}{\sigma}\ln y - \frac{\mu}{\sigma} \tag{10}$$

using these surveys. We can obtain the data on yearly income group and its density (distribution of households by yearly income group) by prefecture from each survey. Then we estimate the parameters, μ and σ, by prefecture.

$\hat{\mu}$, and $\hat{\sigma}$ respectively denote the OLS estimates of μ, and σ. The median and mean of y are as follows.

Median income : $y^m = \exp(\hat{\mu})$,   Mean income : $\bar{y} = \exp(\hat{\mu} + \hat{\sigma}^2/2)$.

The values of these and the ratio of separation between them $(= (\bar{y} - y^m)/\bar{y})$ by prefecture are reported in Table 3. We estimate those values in the 1984 National Survey of Family Income and Expenditure, the 1989 National Survey of Family Income and Expenditure, the 1992 Employment Status Survey, and the 1993 Housing Survey of Japan.

Table 3 implies that the ratio of separation differs from one prefecture to another, and the difference between maximum and minimum is 5% and over. In testing the median voter hypothesis, if the median income (as the median voter) is similarly proportional to the mean income in all prefectures, we can substitute the latter for the former. However we can not substitute, because Table 3 shows the former is not similarly proportional to the latter.

The income, y, in Table 3 is not levied any income taxes. In Japan, the central, prefectural, and municipal governments collect income taxes. So we calculate the national, prefectural and municipal tax burdens respectively on the condition that all income of the household is earned income, and it consists of the householder earnings,[15] an unearning spouse, and dependents under 16 years old.[16] Then we can make the data on τ (national and munici-pal taxes) and t (the (prefectural) tax share of the (median or mean) house-hold). Finally, we obtain the data on Y that is derived by $Y = y - \tau - tH$ (the definition). We suppose that the order of pre-tax income and that of after-tax income is the same among households gained income around median and mean. We set this supposition to guarantee that the median household in pre-tax income is the same household in after-tax income.

V. Estimating these models

In this section, we estimate models in Section III using prefectural data. Ex-cept for dependent and independent variables in models, we use the following

---

[15] We assume that all income of households gained income around median and mean is earned income, only when calculating tax burdens, because we cannot obtain official data on tax burdens by sources of income by household in each survey. In fact, most of income of household gained income around median and mean (income), not that of *all* household, is earned income in surveys. Also the composition of income sources of household gained income around median is almost similar to that of household gained income around mean in Japan. Hence, the result that the order of pre-fax income and that of after-tax income is the same among households gained income around median and mean is unchanged by calculating their tax burdens based on the assumption. We thank an anonymous referee for raising this point.

[16] We refer to Ministry of Finance, "Ministry of Finance Statistics Monthly" (various issues) for tax rates and various deductions.

data of socio-economic characteristics; the percentage of population aged 0 to 14 (PC14), the percentage of population aged 65 and over (PC65), the rate of increase in population (INCPOP), the rate of increase in Gross Prefectural Domestic Expenditure (at constant prices) (GROWTH), the share of gross prefectural domestic expenditure of the primary industry (IND1), the share of gross prefectural domestic expenditure of the secondary industry (IND2), the rate of change in land price at residential sites (LAND), the ratio of high school graduates who advanced to schools of higher education (ADVANCE), the area (AREA), the active job openings ratio (JOB), and the financial capability index (FCI) (in prefectural finance).

Considering the budget process of the prefectural governments and the Japanese prefectural tax system, we use the data of the regressand (prefectural expenditure) in *one* year, but that of the regressors (median income, and so on) in the *previous* year.[17]

Table 4 shows the results of estimation of models (A) ~ (C) using the data reported in Table 3. We don't report estimates with insignificant coefficients. There is no doubt that estimated coefficients differ widely from each other, as median income is estimated using different surveys. However the estimated coefficients reported in Table 4 are close. Therefore it is robust.

First, from estimates of model (A) in Table 4, there is not a significant coefficient every year. Especially, the coefficient of $\ln \bar{Y}$ and $\ln w$ characterizing model (A) is not significant. Therefore we reject model (A) as demand function of local public goods.

Second, see the result of estimating model (B). We obtain the result that each coefficient is significant in 1984 and 1989, but one of $\ln w$ is not significant in 1992 and 1993. Furthermore parameter β, denotes labor share in the production function of local public goods, is more than 1 in 1984, 1989, and 1993. In this sense, model (B) is not valid for the demand function of local public goods.

Finally, in model (C), we find for each year all coefficients are significant and well-behaved, and the model has good fitness. Thus there is no doubt that we can adopt the model as the demand function of local public goods.

Let us consider the implication of the results obtained in models (A) and (B). Minimizing the cost of production of local public goods is assumed in these models. On the contrary, model (C) is not imposed on this assumption. If provision of the local public goods is not efficient (minimizing the cost), these models may be rejected. Considering the known facts of prefectural governments in Japan, this interpretation is reasonable.

The result of model (C) leads to the conclusion that the median voter hypothesis is supported in Japanese prefectural expenditure, because parameters concerning the median voter are significant and valid economically in model (C). Furthermore this result is robust for it is obtained from estimations in 1984, 1989, 1992, and 1993, derived from various statistics.

Additionally, we try to test whether the estimation of this model by OLS is correct. We use the Hausman (1978) test. The null hypothesis is that the independent variables in the equation are exogenous variables, that is, the least square estimators are BLUEs. From the result shown in Table 5, the null

---

[17] In Japan, every fiscal years start from March. The budget in a year begins to formulate in the autumn of the last year.

Table 3. Median and mean income by prefecture

	1984 National Survey of Family Income and Expenditure (all household including one-person household)				1989 National Survey of Family Income and Expenditure (all household including one-person household)			
	Median Income y^m (¥10 thousand)	Mean Income $\bar{y}$ (¥10 thousand)	Separation (%)	R-square (Adj.)	Median Income y^m (¥10 thousand)	Mean Income $\bar{y}$ (¥10 thousand)	Separation (%)	R-square (Adj.)
Hokkaido	374.67	417.66	10.29	0.9890	387.92	435.08	10.84	0.9886
Aomori	372.56	419.12	11.11	0.9855	395.67	446.50	11.39	0.9776
Iwate	345.20	395.32	12.68	0.9913	392.71	442.98	11.35	0.9898
Miyagi	400.62	448.37	10.65	0.9802	442.51	500.95	11.67	0.9811
Akita	375.92	423.92	11.32	0.9801	422.84	478.19	11.58	0.9788
Yamagata	396.75	453.01	12.42	0.9768	488.94	552.63	11.53	0.9767
Fukushima	395.47	449.34	11.99	0.9781	443.91	503.13	11.77	0.9766
Ibaraki	415.35	472.48	12.09	0.9817	491.33	560.66	12.37	0.9621
Tochigi	456.35	507.22	10.03	0.9937	480.51	545.53	11.92	0.9618
Gumma	425.36	478.77	11.16	0.9875	450.66	511.58	11.91	0.9868
Saitama	449.99	507.44	11.32	0.9670	511.24	578.54	11.63	0.9836
Chiba	458.38	522.65	12.30	0.9732	490.93	568.52	13.65	0.9636
Tokyo	467.17	527.67	11.46	0.9904	443.52	536.62	17.35	0.9909
Kanagawa	478.79	542.89	11.81	0.9768	492.58	571.95	13.88	0.9759
Niigata	438.42	496.49	11.70	0.9775	462.59	524.33	11.78	0.9692
Toyama	469.00	532.57	11.94	0.9855	510.01	585.77	12.93	0.9453
Ishikawa	461.41	522.69	11.72	0.9723	485.43	551.89	12.04	0.9720
Fukui	476.54	546.67	12.83	0.9815	510.06	589.30	13.45	0.9711
Yamanashi	438.09	484.88	9.65	0.9911	469.49	522.73	10.18	0.9871
Nagano	432.35	482.58	10.41	0.9895	455.89	514.52	11.39	0.9738
Gifu	438.76	489.45	10.36	0.9877	475.12	545.26	12.86	0.9702
Shizuoka	433.34	489.27	11.43	0.9739	496.92	563.19	11.77	0.9832
Aichi	467.84	527.69	11.34	0.9779	475.49	553.61	14.11	0.9719
Mie	435.89	489.52	10.96	0.9815	479.90	558.09	14.01	0.9568
Shiga	467.39	535.87	12.78	0.9613	530.45	600.49	11.66	0.9865

Kyoto	422.07	488.06	13.52	0.9675	434.29	498.98	12.96	0.9587
Osaka	407.38	462.27	11.87	0.9806	439.33	508.98	13.68	0.9853
Hyogo	436.35	492.58	11.42	0.9871	447.34	519.92	13.96	0.9779
Nara	447.08	503.09	11.13	0.9800	501.25	566.15	11.46	0.9816
Wakayama	407.11	460.57	11.61	0.9846	382.00	446.24	14.40	0.9660
Tottori	402.86	462.23	12.84	0.9808	476.88	540.49	11.77	0.9770
Shimane	414.32	476.15	12.99	0.9825	445.72	505.73	11.86	0.9808
Okayama	406.77	463.15	12.17	0.9855	414.20	483.02	14.25	0.9752
Hiroshima	405.56	462.48	12.31	0.9769	418.82	477.51	12.29	0.9709
Yamaguchi	388.14	437.80	11.34	0.9868	410.98	466.31	11.87	0.9588
Tokushima	414.42	479.62	13.59	0.9864	421.38	485.40	13.19	0.9736
Kagawa	400.99	460.57	12.94	0.9873	444.25	500.81	11.29	0.9699
Ehime	364.10	410.81	11.37	0.9906	377.41	430.01	12.23	0.9857
Kochi	349.35	403.03	13.32	0.9942	369.37	433.41	14.78	0.9820
Fukuoka	384.08	438.01	12.31	0.9935	386.30	441.01	12.41	0.9817
Saga	380.71	434.73	12.43	0.9874	414.01	469.53	11.82	0.9781
Nagasaki	330.78	375.93	12.01	0.9834	379.01	423.12	10.43	0.9846
Kumamoto	365.15	408.19	10.54	0.9890	396.28	453.46	12.61	0.9842
Oita	348.19	390.27	10.78	0.9914	382.24	436.88	12.51	0.9819
Miyazaki	312.30	358.16	12.80	0.9962	350.44	400.46	12.49	0.9919
Kagoshima	290.23	324.67	10.61	0.9914	325.38	370.84	12.26	0.9920
Okinawa	278.85	328.25	15.05	0.9948	324.81	380.22	14.57	0.9939
Mean	406.99	461.37			438.90	501.71		
Std. Dev.	48.27	53.96			51.12	58.37		

Table 3 (continued)

	1992 Employment Status Survey (all household including one-person household)				1993 Housing Survey of Japan (ordinary household)			
	Median Income y^m (¥10 thousand)	Mean Income $\bar{y}$ (¥10 thousand)	Separation (%)	R-square (Adj.)	Median Income y^m (¥10 thousand)	Mean Income $\bar{y}$ (¥10 thousand)	Separation (%)	R-square (Adj.)
Hokkaido	343.26	436.79	21.41	0.9590	333.58	416.81	19.97	0.9699
Aomori	325.80	417.33	21.93	0.9562	304.17	378.94	19.73	0.9721
Iwate	352.16	446.74	21.17	0.9480	326.23	403.20	19.09	0.9685
Miyagi	394.40	514.98	23.42	0.9451	358.83	453.16	20.82	0.9620
Akita	356.90	452.42	21.11	0.9291	331.36	407.01	18.59	0.9669
Yamagata	418.98	535.71	21.79	0.9196	372.26	460.73	19.20	0.9564
Fukushima	393.10	505.51	22.24	0.9402	352.74	440.89	19.99	0.9635
Ibaraki	451.64	584.93	22.79	0.9275	403.93	510.36	20.85	0.9430
Tochigi	425.97	563.04	24.35	0.9168	398.09	504.44	21.08	0.9534
Gumma	411.76	541.83	24.01	0.9332	373.56	475.88	21.50	0.9543
Saitama	505.28	663.03	23.79	0.9197	452.04	574.63	21.33	0.9390
Chiba	493.08	648.98	24.02	0.9343	456.81	588.54	22.38	0.9440
Tokyo	461.78	641.77	28.05	0.9635	417.85	560.57	25.46	0.9686
Kanagawa	491.43	635.04	22.61	0.9631	469.13	608.76	22.94	0.9500
Niigata	421.53	547.21	22.97	0.9177	383.02	478.15	19.89	0.9510
Toyama	473.17	633.88	25.35	0.9077	411.66	519.50	20.76	0.9418
Ishikawa	399.72	549.90	27.31	0.9194	375.85	485.90	22.65	0.9498
Fukui	451.11	628.77	28.26	0.8962	402.60	521.39	22.78	0.9487
Yamanashi	408.26	541.96	24.67	0.9352	356.45	457.57	22.10	0.9514
Nagano	438.13	573.95	23.66	0.9270	377.49	475.28	20.58	0.9477
Gifu	446.58	590.09	24.32	0.9319	397.37	504.87	21.29	0.9492
Shizuoka	468.18	617.75	24.21	0.9403	421.38	533.43	21.00	0.9499
Aichi	465.78	619.09	24.76	0.9440	421.18	545.76	22.83	0.9461
Mie	423.09	571.87	26.02	0.9348	381.20	494.06	22.84	0.9442
Shiga	462.25	609.89	24.21	0.9118	429.55	546.83	21.45	0.9279

Kyoto	381.95	522.06	26.84	0.9368	360.70	480.25	24.89	0.9501
Osaka	404.83	536.80	24.58	0.9470	375.94	490.30	23.32	0.9600
Hyogo	429.58	561.94	23.55	0.9489	397.91	515.30	22.78	0.9539
Nara	432.56	607.78	28.83	0.9196	426.39	565.57	24.61	0.9422
Wakayama	353.97	471.55	24.94	0.9477	316.63	412.80	23.30	0.9637
Tottori	377.83	502.84	24.86	0.9200	343.04	441.28	22.26	0.9558
Shimane	343.12	454.58	24.52	0.9173	333.35	423.50	21.29	0.9575
Okayama	375.42	505.76	25.77	0.9341	351.84	451.77	22.12	0.9495
Hiroshima	390.34	508.16	23.19	0.9494	361.88	466.96	22.50	0.9518
Yamaguchi	347.52	455.49	23.70	0.9353	327.95	415.52	21.07	0.9546
Tokushima	335.77	457.67	26.64	0.9520	297.95	391.97	23.99	0.9637
Kagawa	381.14	511.99	25.56	0.9315	344.57	444.84	22.54	0.9560
Ehime	308.00	401.62	23.31	0.9607	292.94	373.35	21.54	0.9661
Kochi	293.03	389.97	24.86	0.9585	269.21	352.66	23.66	0.9695
Fukuoka	336.01	447.40	24.90	0.9490	323.75	418.76	22.69	0.9623
Saga	365.99	470.86	22.27	0.9407	339.01	424.61	20.16	0.9649
Nagasaki	307.23	402.35	23.64	0.9534	306.01	384.14	20.34	0.9703
Kumamoto	313.49	421.08	25.55	0.9440	305.91	393.16	22.19	0.9689
Oita	302.45	400.28	24.44	0.9488	296.51	378.74	21.71	0.9620
Miyazaki	301.08	393.97	23.58	0.9585	275.52	350.38	21.37	0.9714
Kagoshima	257.39	338.89	24.05	0.9638	242.65	313.13	22.51	0.9732
Okinawa	259.67	340.96	23.84	0.9720	229.94	298.49	22.97	0.9837
Mean	388.97	514.39			358.04	458.17		
Std. Dev.	63.44	86.65			54.89	71.97		

Table 4. Estimation of models using OLS

Dependent Variable: ln E						
Year	1984	1984	1984	1989	1989	1989
Model	(A)	(B)	(C)	(A)	(B)	(C)
Intercept	−13.787	−12.752	1.577	−7.026*	−6.836*	0.770
	(−1.965)	(−1.777)	(0.985)	(−2.379)	(−2.292)	(0.501)
ln w	1.567**	1.492*		2.017**	2.253**	
	(2.886)	(2.636)		(3.251)	(3.683)	
ln N	0.361**	0.363**	0.260*	0.272*	0.299*	0.248*
	(3.253)	(3.097)	(2.325)	(2.075)	(2.185)	(2.032)
$\ln\{t^m(1-m)\}$	−0.333**	−0.331**	−0.500**	−0.433**	−0.408**	−0.489**
	(−3.102)	(−2.960)	(−4.784)	(−3.465)	(−3.163)	(−4.374)
ln Y^m	1.156**	0.847**	1.200**	0.996	1.233**	1.110**
	(2.781)	(3.532)	(4.432)	(1.939)	(3.741)	(3.514)
ln $\bar{Y}$	−0.293			0.450		
	(−1.078)			(0.887)		
AREA	4.000**	4.065**	4.406**	3.754**	4.114**	4.781**
	(6.104)	(5.852)	(7.842)	(5.017)	(5.734)	(6.897)
IND1						
IND2	−0.012**	−0.012**	−0.013**	−0.010**	−0.010**	−0.0092**
	(−5.123)	(−5.123)	(−5.813)	(−4.069)	(5.224)	(−4.129)
PC14	−0.030*	−0.033*				
	(−2.083)	(−2.499)				
PC65			0.041**	0.049**	0.045**	0.037**
			(3.870)	(5.595)	(−4.064)	(4.324)
ADVANCE			−0.0067**	−0.0053*		
			(−2.925)	(−2.122)		
LAND						−0.0037*
						(−2.485)
INCPOP						
GROWTH	0.013*	0.013*				
	(2.087)	(2.180)				
NOB	47	47	47	47	47	47
$\bar{R}^2$	0.976	0.976	0.972	0.975	0.973	0.969

The above parentheses indicate the t-values using White's consistent covariance.
** and * denote significance at 1% and 5% level, respectively.

η	−0.333	−0.331	−0.500	−0.433	−0.408	−0.489
	(0.003)	(0.005)	(0.000)	(0.001)	(0.003)	(0.000)
δ	0.862	0.847	1.200	1.446	1.233	1.110
	(0.028)	(0.001)	(0.000)	(0.569)	(0.001)	(0.001)
γ	0.542	0.543	0.520	0.479	0.505	0.486
	(0.000)	(0.000)	(0.000)	(0.000)	(0.000)	(0.001)
α	1.734			1.758		
	(0.301)			(0.380)		
β	2.352	2.231		3.560	3.807	
	(0.002)	(0.003)		(0.003)	(0.004)	

These parentheses indicate the p-values of the hypothesis: the parameter is equal to zero.

Table 4 (continued)

Dependent Variable: $\ln E$

Year Model	1992 (A)	1992 (B)	1992 (C)	1993 (A)	1993 (B)	1993 (C)
Intercept	0.920	1.211	1.968	−4.452	−2.108	−0.173
	(0.394)	(0.546)	(1.870)	(−1.438)	(−0.853)	(−0.085)
$\ln w$	0.305	0.272		0.444	1.042	
	(0.397)	(0.352)		(0.465)	(1.156)	
$\ln N$	0.264**	0.262**	0.258**	0.306*	0.413**	0.382**
	(2.746)	(2.799)	(3.016)	(2.663)	(3.634)	(3.044)
$\ln\{t^m(1-m)\}$	−0.440**	−0.443**	−0.453**	−0.486**	−0.358**	−0.407**
	(−4.499)	(−4.627)	(−5.677)	(−3.930)	(−3.020)	(−3.395)
$\ln Y^m$	0.853**	0.918**	0.936**	1.074**	0.720*	1.096**
	(3.318)	(4.087)	(4.614)	(3.704)	(2.405)	(3.294)
$\ln \bar{Y}$	0.103			0.464*		
	(0.511)			(2.049)		
AREA	6.459**	6.431**	6.367**	4.530**	5.883**	4.657**
	(7.885)	(7.966)	(8.240)	(7.424)	(10.920)	(6.822)
IND1				0.043**		
				(3.796)		
IND2	−0.0058*	−0.0056*	−0.0057*			−0.0057*
	(−2.297)	(−2.306)	(−2.390)			(−2.072)
PC14						
PC65	0.034**	0.033**	0.033**	0.054**	0.070**	0.056**
	(6.851)	(6.670)	(6.871)	(5.443)	(5.128)	(5.082)
ADVANCE						
LAND	−0.014*	−0.014*	−0.013*		−0.037*	
	(−2.272)	(−2.513)	(−2.475)		(−2.042)	
INCPOP	−0.131**	−0.128**	−0.132**			
	(−3.991)	(−4.101)	(−4.748)			
GROWTH						
NOB	47	47	47	47	47	47
$\bar{R}^2$	0.976	0.977	0.977	0.971	0.967	0.967

The above parentheses indicate the t-values using White's consistent covariance.
** and * denote significance at 1% and 5% level, respectively.

η	−0.440	−0.443	−0.453	−0.486	−0.358	−0.407
	(0.000)	(0.000)	(0.000)	(0.000)	(0.004)	(0.001)
δ	0.956	0.918	0.936	1.538	0.720	1.096
	(0.055)	(0.000)	(0.000)	(0.057)	(0.021)	(0.002)
γ	0.472	0.470	0.472	0.595	0.644	0.644
	(0.000)	(0.000)	(0.000)	(0.000)	(0.000)	(0.000)
α	1.523			2.089		
	(0.607)			(0.117)		
β	0.545	0.488		0.863	1.624	
	(0.681)	(0.716)		(0.622)	(0.196)	

These parentheses indicate the p-values of the hypothesis: the parameter is equal to zero.

Table 5. Specification test (Hausman test)
Null Hypothesis: independent variables are exogenous.

Year	est statistic	p-value
1984	0.613	0.736
1989	1.290	0.525
1992	2.402	0.301
1993	0.014	0.907

hypothesis cannot be rejected every year. Therefore it is necessary for us to use the instrumental variable estimation, and so on when we estimate this model.

VI. Superiority of median income

Thus the median voter hypothesis holds true in Japanese prefectures. Until now, researchers on prefectural expenditure in Japan have not used median income but mean income (per capita income). We can not yet conclude that median income is more powerful than mean income as an explanation of prefectural spendings. As Mueller (1989) suggests, whether median income is better than mean income in order to explain prefectural expenditures depends on the differences between the two. The separation is shown in Table 3. This implies that estimation using mean income is not appropriate to the test the hypothesis. Table 3, however, is not adequate to judge its superiority. Let us check it directly using a specification test.[18]

We use J test introduced by Davidson and MacKinnon (1981). This specification test is as follows. We first set the hypotheses;

$$\mathrm{H}_0 : \ln E_j = \ln A_0'' + \gamma_0(\eta_0 + 1)\ln N_j + \eta_0 \ln\{t_j^m(1 - m_j)\} + \delta_0 \ln Y_j^m,$$

$$\mathrm{H}_1 : \ln E_j = \ln A_1'' + \gamma_1(\eta_1 + 1)\ln N_j + \eta_1 \ln\{\bar{t}_j(1 - m_j)\} + \delta_1 \ln \overline{Y}_j,$$

$$\text{where} \quad A'' \equiv Aq^{\eta+1}.$$

Suffix 0 or 1 denotes the parameter under the hypothesis 0 or 1. Next, we estimate these models (hypotheses). Then we define

$$E0_j \equiv \ln \hat{A}_0'' + \hat{\gamma}_0(\hat{\eta}_0 + 1)\ln N_j + \hat{\eta}_0 \ln\{t_j^m(1 - m_j)\} + \hat{\delta}_0 \ln Y_j^m,$$

$$E1_j \equiv \ln \hat{A}_1'' + \hat{\gamma}_1(\hat{\eta}_1 + 1)\ln N_j + \hat{\eta}_1 \ln\{\bar{t}_j(1 - m_j)\} + \hat{\delta}_1 \ln \overline{Y}_j.$$

Overscript $\hat{\ }$ denotes the estimator of the parameter. Finally, we estimate for

---

[18] Incidentally, Pommerehne and Frey (1976) estimate separately using median and mean income from the same data set (in Switzerland). They appreciate the superiority for the explanation by comparison of fitness and estimates between median and mean.

Table 6. Specification test

Year	J Test t-value		Jarque-Bera Test test statistic	
	Hypothesis:		Estimation:	
	$\lambda = 0$	$\omega = 0$	(11)	(12)
1984	−0.032	3.240	1.700	1.646
	(0.975)	(0.003)	(0.427)	(0.439)
1989	0.988	1.593	1.021	1.072
	(0.329)	(0.119)	(0.600)	(0.585)
1992	1.488	4.909	0.746	0.602
	(0.145)	(0.000)	(0.689)	(0.740)
1993	2.752	3.981	0.474	0.336
	(0.009)	(0.000)	(0.789)	(0.845)

The p-values are in parentheses.

this test

$$\ln E_j = \ln A_0'' + \gamma_0(\eta_0 + 1)\ln N_j + \eta_0 \ln\{t_j^m(1 - m_j)\}$$

$$+ \delta_0 \ln Y_j^m + \lambda E1_j + \varepsilon_{0j}, \tag{11}$$

$$\ln E_j = \ln A_1'' + \gamma_1(\eta_1 + 1)\ln N_j + \eta_1 \ln\{\bar{t}_j(1 - m_j)\}$$

$$+ \delta_1 \ln \bar{Y}_j + \omega E0_j + \varepsilon_{1j}, \tag{12}$$

where ε_0 and ε_1 denote the error terms, and λ and ω denote the parameters. If the hypothesis $\lambda = 0$ is not statistically rejected in the upper equation, H_1 is statistically rejected by H_0. Similarly if the hypothesis $\omega = 0$ is not statistically rejected in the lower equation, H_0 is statistically rejected by H_1.[19] In Table 6, we have the t-values of λ or ω, and p-values (probabilities). This shows that the hypothesis $\lambda = 0$ or $\omega = 0$ is statistically rejected. From the p-values shown in Table 6, the probability of rejecting the mean income's model is higher than the probability of rejecting the median voter's model in every year.

Therefore median income is better than mean income as the regressor of prefectural expenditures in Japan.

VII. Preference of the median voter and probability of reelection

We find that the median voter affects the level of prefectural expenditure in Japan. It means, described in Section I, that the median voter affects the administration of the governor in each prefecture, and the central government

---

[19] The J test is based on a maximum likelihood estimator being a consisten estimator. Hence we must check that residuals in the regressions (11) and (12) to use the J tests are distributed as the normal distribution. We use Jarque and Bera (1980) test in order to check it. We show the test statistics in (11) and (12) in Table 6. As the null hypothesis (the residual in the regression is distributed as the normal distribution) cannot be rejected in each regression in each year, we confirm that the assumption of the J test is satisfied. We thank an anonymous referee for this check.

manages prefectural finance by considering the results of gubernatorial elections. But we have never confirmed a relation between the median voter (or his preference) and the governor (or gubernatorial election).

If the governor's requests to the central government reflect the preference of the median voter, the probability of reelection for the incumbent governors raises as the difference between actual level of expenditure and the level required by the median voter becomes closer. We must test the relation econometrically.

A probit model is suitable for this test. We consider the following probit model:

$$\Pr(REELE_j = 1) = \Phi\left(const. + \lambda_1 RES_j + \sum_i \lambda_i \ \text{other variables}\right)$$

$$\text{where} \quad REELE_j = \begin{cases} 1 & \text{if the incumbent is reelected} \\ 0 & \text{if the incumbent is not reelected} \end{cases},$$

$$RES_j = |(\text{the actual value of } \log(E_j)) - (\text{the fitted value of } \log(E_j))|$$

in model (C).λ_i : the coefficient of explanatory variable i

We take RES_j as absolute value of the difference between the actual and fitted values of $\log(E_j)$ in model (C) of Section III. Because the fitted value of $\log(E_j)$ means theoretical level reflected the preference of the median voter, and the absolute value of the difference between them means the degree of difference between the expenditure level preferred by the median voter and the actual level.

We must obtain adequate data on gubernatorial elections and the governors not reelected in them after the year those surveys are examined. We show the data on gubernatorial elections and reelections in Table 7. In an election that the incumbent doesn't stand as a candidate, if the candidate who is supported by the same parties that supported the incumbent wins the election, such an election is classified as if the incumbent is reelected (R). It is difficult to obtain enough data on governors not reelected. However the data on the 1993 Housing Survey of Japan and the elections in 1994 and 1995 are suitable for our test, since we have data on the governor not reelected are sufficient in the 1994 and 1995 elections.[20] Thus we make $REELE_j$ based on the 1994 and 1995 elections and RES_j based on the estimations of Model (C) in 1993 reported in Table 4.

We estimate the probit model using those data. The result is reported in Table 8. We try to estimate including socio-economic characteristics and the number of candidates in the election (CAND) as other variables. Especially, we use the rate of increase in Gross Prefectural Domestic Expenditure (at constant prices) (GROWTH) and the active job openings ratio (JOB), associated with studies on the political business cycle, as well as other variables.[21]

---

[20] The 1993 Housing Survey of Japan was examined in October 1993. Almost all gubernatorial elections in 1993 had been held before October. We exclude elections in 1993 from observations in the test.

[21] JOB is a proxy of the unemployment rate because we cannot obtain it by prefecture in each year.

Table 7. Gubernatorial election

Prefecture	1989	1990	1991	1992	1993	1994	1995
Hokkaido			R				R
Aomori			R				N
Iwate			R				N
Miyagi	N				R, N		
Akita			R				R
Yamagata	R				N		
Fukushima				R			
Ibaraki			R		N		
Tochigi				R			
Gumma			R				R
Saitama				N			
Chiba	R				R		
Tokyo			R				N
Kanagawa			R				R
Niigata	R			R			
Toyama				R			
Ishikawa			R			R	
Fukui			R				R
Yamanashi			N				R
Nagano				R			
Gifu	R				R		
Shizuoka		R			R		
Aichi			R				R
Mie				R			N
Shiga		R				R	
Kyoto		R				R	
Osaka			R				N
Hyogo		R				R	
Nara			R				R

Table 7 (continued)

Prefecture	1989	1990	1991	1992	1993	1994	1995
Wakayama			R				R
Tottori			R				R
Shimane			R				R
Okayama				R			
Hiroshima	R				R		
Yamaguchi				R			
Tokushima	R				R		
Kagawa		R				R	
Ehime		R					R
Kochi			N				R
Fukuoka			R				R
Saga			R				R
Nagasaki		R				R	
Kumamoto			R				R
Oita			R				R
Miyazaki			R				R
Kagoshima	R				R		
Okinawa		R				R	
Number of election	8	8	23	9	10	7	23
Number of reelection	7	8	21	8	7	7	18

R: The Gubernatorial Election was held and the incumbent was reelected in the year.
N: The Gubernatorial Election was held and the incumbent was not reelected in the year.
Blank: The Gubernatorial Election was not held in the year.
Data Source: National Association of Prefectural Election Management Commission, "Senkyo (Election)," Various issues.

But when coefficients are not significant, we omit those variables. As shown in column (I) of Table 8, the coefficient of RES_j is significantly negative. It means that the smaller the difference between actual level of expenditure and the (estimated) level desired by the median voter is, the higher the probability of reelection for the incumbent governors is. Quantitatively, we estimate a marginal effect with respect to RES_j, and we report that it is -2.862 in Table

8.[22] It implies that 1% (marginal) increase of the difference between the expenditure level preferred by the median voter and the actual level leads about 2.8% decrease of the probability of reelection for the incumbent governors.[23] Thus we confirm the above-mentioned relation econometrically.

VIII. Conclusion

It was shown that the median voter hypothesis is supported within Japanese prefectures, based on the assumption that median income identifies the median voter. Hypothesis interpretation, however, is totally different compared to a decentralized country such as the United States where a decentralized local finance system allows an optimal level of local spending to be reached a particular median voter jurisdiction.

In contrast to this interpretation, within a centralized local system such as that of Japan, even though prefectural governments can freely decide prefectural taxes and expenditures for some purposes, the central government exhibits stronger expenditure control. Hence, under the present framework of politics and public finance, even if prefectural governments impose financial constraints, the central government nevertheless distributes inter-regional grants to each prefectural government in a manner reflecting prefectural election results, i.e., the jurisdictional preference of the median voter. If the central government ignores results of prefectural elections, i.e., median voter preference, then incumbent governors may not be reelected such that they are more frequently replaced every election. In actuality, however, many governors get reelected several times. As demonstrated here (Sec. VII), the probability of reelection for an incumbent governor increases as the difference between the actual level of expenditure and the estimated level desired by the median voter; a finding which supports our interpretation of the median voter hypothesis in Japanese prefectures.

Data sources

E_j (= Total Expenditures),
H_j (= Local Allocation Tax + Local Transfer Taxes), and
m_j (= National Government Disbursements/Total Expenditures):
    Ministry of Home Affairs, "Annual Statistical Report on Local Government Finance"
N_j (= Population):
    Ministry of Home Affairs, "Basic Resident Registers"
w_j (= Average monthly salary of prefectural employees: All occupations):
    Ministry of Home Affairs, "Survey on Wage of Local Government Employees"
t_j^m (= prefectural taxes paid by the median household/Prefectural Taxes):
    Ministry of Finance, "Ministry of Finance Statistics Monthly," and Min-

---

[22] By definition, the marginal effect with respect to RES_j is expressed as $\dfrac{\partial \Pr(REELE_j = 1)}{\partial RES_j}$.

[23] As $|(\log(1.01 \times E_j^*) - \log(E_j^*)| \approx 0.00995$, where E_j^* denotes the level requested by the median voter in jurisdiction j, $-2.862 \times 0.00995 \approx -0.02848$.

Table 8. Probit estimates, 1993

Dependent Variable: $\Pr(REELE_j = 1)$

	(I)	(II)	(III)	(IV)	(V)	(VI)	(VII)	(VIII)
Intercept	1.904*	4.677*	2.045*	1.618	5.816*	5.175	1.829	9.202
	(3.574)	(2.659)	(3.094)	(1.397)	(2.220)	(1.941)	(1.398)	(1.410)
RES	−14.439*	−12.195	−16.498*	−13.749*	−14.488	−12.798	−15.966*	−16.762
	(−2.383)	(−1.570)	(−2.259)	(−2.116)	(−1.582)	(−1.567)	(−2.055)	(−1.615)
CAND		−0.787			−1.035	−0.823		−1.490
		(−1.969)			(−1.702)	(−1.892)		(−1.385)
GROWTH			0.432		0.513		0.431	0.656
			(1.546)		(1.414)		(1.542)	(1.383)
JOB				0.361		−0.491	0.264	−2.007
				(0.272)		(−0.265)	(0.187)	(−0.659)
Log likelihood	−10.144	−7.289	−8.561	−10.106	−5.980	−7.253	−8.543	−5.734
Marginal Effect RES	−2.862*							
	(−2.197)							

Sample	All	REELE = 1	REELE = 0
NOB	30	25	5
Mean of RES	0.050	0.039	0.112
Mean of CAND	3.300	2.960	5.000
Mean of GROWTH	0.499	0.695	−0.483
Mean of JOB	0.721	0.747	0.592

The above parentheses indicate the *t*-values.
* denotes significance at 5% level.

istry of Home Affairs, "Annual Statistical Report on Local Government Finance"

The percentage of population aged 0 to 14, and the percentage of population aged 65 and over:

Statistics Bureau, Management and Coordination Agency, "Monthly Report on Current Population Estimates "

The rate of increase in gross prefectural domestic expenditure (at constant prices), the share of gross prefectural domestic expenditure of the primary industry, and the share of gross prefectural domestic expenditure of the secondary industry:

Economic Planning Agency, "Annual Report on Prefectural Accounts"

The rate of change in land prices at residential sites:

National Land Agency, "Prefectural Land Price Survey"

The active job openings ratio:

Ministry of Labor, "Annual Report on Labor Market"

The ratio of high school graduates who advanced to schools of higher education:

Ministry of Education, "School Basic Survey"

The area (in 1990):

Statistics Bureau, Management and Coordination Agency, "Population Census"

The financial capability index (in prefectural finance):

Ministry of Home Affairs, "Financial Index Table by Prefecture"

References

Bergstrom TC, Goodman RP (1973) Private demands for public goods. American Economic Review 63:280–296

Borcherding TE, Deacon RT (1972) The demand for the services of non-federal governments. American Economic Review 62:891–901

Davidson R, MacKinnon JG (1981) Several tests for model specification in the presence of alternative hypotheses. Econometrica 49:781–793

Denzau AT, Mackay RJ (1976) Benefit shares and majority voting. American Economic Review 66:69–76

Doi T, Ashiya M (1997) Distribution of interregional grant and government party: National Government Disbursement and LDP. Japan Center for Economic Research Economic Journal 34:180–195 (in Japanese)

Gramlich EM, Rubinfeld DL (1982) Micro estimates of public spending demand functions and tests of the Tiebout and median-voter hypotheses. Journal of Political Economy 90:536–560

Hausman JA (1978) Specification tests in econometrics. Econometrica 46:1251–1271

Jarque CM, Bera AK (1980) Efficient tests for normality, homoscedasticity and serial independence of regression residuals. Economics Letters 6:255–259

Mueller DC (1989) Public choice II. Cambridge University Press

Pommerehne WW, Frey BS (1976) Two approaches to estimating public expenditures. Public Finance Quarterly 4:395–407

Preston I, Ridge M (1995) Demand for local public spending : Evidence from the British Social Attitudes Survey. Economic Journal 105:644–660

Reed SR (1986) Japanese prefecture and policymaking. University of Pittsburgh Press

Romer T, Rosenthal H (1979) The elusive median voter. Journal of Public Economics 12:143–170

Shibata T (ed.) (1993) Japan's public sector: How the government is financed. University of Tokyo Press

Turnbull GK, Djoundourian SS (1994) The median voter hypothesis : Evidence from general purpose local governments. Public Choice 81:223–240

V Optimality of the public capital stock

Estimates of optimal public capital stocks in Japan using a public investment discount rate framework*

Jiro Nemoto[1], Kimiyoshi Kamada[2], Makoto Kawamura[3]

[1] School of Economics, Nagoya University, Furo-cho, Chikusa-ku, Nagoya 464-8601, Japan
(e-mail: A40402A@ibuki.cc.nagoya-u.ac.jp)
[2] Department of Economics, Chukyo University, 101-2 Yagoto-honmachi, Showa-ku, Nagoya 466-8666, Japan
[3] Department of Economics, Hosei University, 4342 Aihara-machi, Machida-shi, Tokyo 194-0211, Japan

First version received: March 1997/final version received: June 1998

Abstract. The purpose of this paper is to empirically assess the optimality of the level of public capital in Japan. We use a methodological approach based on Burgess's (1988) procedure for calculating the public discount rate. This approach involves estimating a production function, but does not necessarily require utility function estimation. The results indicate that, although the Japanese economy experienced a public capital deficiency over the period 1960–1982, public capital moved toward optimal levels throughout the period.

Key words: Public discount rate, optimal public capital, Japanese economy

JEL classifications: D24, H43, H54

1. Introduction

The purpose of this paper is to assess the optimality of the level of public capital in Japan by using a discount rate framework for public investment. For the past several decades, the supply of public capital in Japan has been considered insufficient, as suggested by the more rapid accumulation of private capital. Most arguments supporting such a view are based on a simple comparison with other developed countries, using an empirical approach lacking theoretical support. For example, the Economic Planning Agency (1990, pp. 243–244) typically argues that several kinds of infrastructures are deficient

---

* We wish to acknowledge helpful discussions with Nobuhiro Okuno and Akira Yakita. We are also grateful to Michiro Kaiyama and anonymous referees for their valuable comments on an earlier version of this paper, and Dennis Ray for kindly editing the English of our manuscript.

in Japan because their diffusion rates or per capita amounts are considerably smaller than those of the U.S., the U.K., Germany and France. In this paper, we present a procedure for evaluating the optimal public investment policy based on public discount rate theory. This procedure enables us to measure optimal levels of public capital and thereby any degree of deficiency.

A central concern of public discount rate theory has been the appropriate second-best discount rate in an economy distorted with taxes or market failures. Particularly, when a corporate income tax drives a wedge between the rate of return to private capital and the interest rate facing consumers, the appropriate public discount rate becomes a weighted average rate. Although a weighted average formula is empirically tractable, few empirical studies have concentrated on such a formula. In contrast, the contribution of public capital to private sector productivity has recently received increased attention. Many studies, including those of Aschauer (1989), Berndt and Hansson (1991), Shah (1992), Lynde and Richmond (1992) (1993), Evans and Karas (1994), Holtz-Eakin (1994), Nadiri and Mamuneas (1994), Dalamagas (1995), and Baltagi and Pinnoi (1995), estimate cost or production function including public capital. However, all of these studies fail to discuss optimal conditions for public capital. In this paper, we use Burgess's (1988) version of the weighted average formula in order to determine optimal levels of public capital.

The Burgess formula is appealing because it is so broadly applicable, especially as compared to previous studies such as those of Sandmo and Drèze (1971) and Ogura and Yohe (1977). In the Burgess' weighted average formula, the weights depend on two components. The first component, the degree of complementarity or substitutability between public and private capital, reflects the presupposition that the Burgess discount rate allows public capital to be complementary with or substitutable for private capital. The second component accounts for proportions of funding for public investment obtained from consumption and private investment. In contrast to the Burgess discount rate, the Ogura-Yohe discount rate consists of only the first component. This is because Ogura and Yohe exclude private investment as a source of funding for public investment by assuming an infinitely elastic supply of savings. Likewise, the Sandmo-Drèze discount rate consists of only the second component. As a result, Sandmo and Drèze confine their analysis to public capital, which is independent of private capital. In fact, it can be shown that the Burgess formula includes both the Sandmo-Drèze and Ogura-Yohe formulas as special cases.

Implementation of the Burgess formula requires the estimation of parameters representing the degree of intertemporal substitutability in consumption, and the technological relationship between private and public capital. To obtain the technological parameters, we estimate a variable profit function using annual time series data for Japan. However, for the intertemporal substitution parameter, we seek a pair of upper and lower boundary estimates and do not estimate a utility function. The boundary estimates of intertemporal substitution are then used to measure optimal levels of public capital within a given interval.

Two procedures are suitable for this measurement. First, upper and lower boundaries are set by two extreme cases, namely, infinitely elastic intertemporal substitution and perfectly inelastic intertemporal substitution. The former is equivalent to applying the Ogura-Yohe formula for public investment, and the latter to applying the marginal rate of returns on private capital as a public discount rate. In effect, two conventional formulas thus provide the boundaries for the more generally applicable Burgess formula. The second appropriate procedure for measuring intertemporal substitution is to set more precise boundaries by using estimates of the interest rate elasticity of consumption. Such estimates have been reported in previous studies. These serve as a proxy for intertemporal substitutability in consumption. Fortunately, existing estimates of the interest elasticity of consumption are quite consistent, in the present study, it is assumed to be -0.01.

Our results indicate that although the Japanese economy experienced a deficiency of public capital during the fiscal period 1960–1982, public capital moved toward optimal levels throughout that same period (Japan's fiscal year starts in April). The ratio of actual to optimal levels of public capital ranged from 0.66 to 0.82 in the early 1960s and from 0.96 to 0.98 in the early 1980s.

2. The Burgess formula for public discount rate

Let $F(L, K, G)$ be the production function where L, K and G represent labor, private capital and public capital, respectively. For notational simplicity, partial derivatives of the production function are denoted by subscripts attached to F. Burgess gives the discount rate for public investment F_G^* as

$$F_G^* - \mu_G = \frac{r\theta_1 + (F_K - \mu_K)\theta_2}{\theta_1 + \theta_2},$$ (1)

where

$$\theta_1 = \left(1 - \frac{F_{KG}}{F_{KK}}\right)\left(\frac{\partial C_1}{\partial r}\right)_U,$$

$$\theta_2 = \frac{1}{(1 - t)F_{KK}} + \frac{F_{KG}}{F_{KK}}\left(\frac{\partial C_1}{\partial r}\right)_U.$$

Here, r is the interest rate; C_1 is the current consumption rate; $(\partial C_1/\partial r)_U$ is the compensated interest derivative of current consumption; t is the rate of corporate income tax; μ_K and μ_G are depreciation rates of private and public capital, respectively. The net discount rate for public investment, $F_G^* - \mu_G$, is a weighted average of $F_K - \mu_K$ and r, where $F_K - \mu_K$ and r are, respectively, measures of marginal opportunity costs of forgone private investment and current consumption for financing public investment.

In the analytic model on which F_G^* is based, the economy consists of the private sector and government. The private sector maximizes its utility under certain budget constraints over time. If we let C_2 be the future consumption and $U(C_1, C_2)$ be the utility function, then first order conditions for the private sector's behavior are

$$U_1 - (1 + r)U_2 = 0,$$ (2)

$$F_L = w,$$ (3)

$$(1 - t)F_K = r + \mu_K,$$ (4)

where $U_i = \partial U / \partial C_i$ for $i = 1, 2$, and w is the wage rate.[1] The corporate income tax is defined as levied on $F(\cdot) - wL$.

Given eqs. (2)–(4), the objective of the government is to supply public capital such that the private sector achieves the highest feasible utility. The government borrows from the private sector to finance public investment in the current period, and redeems the borrowing with interest by future income tax from productive public capital. Since the tax rate is assumed to be exogenous, one cannot assume that the government's budget in the future period will be balanced; the government returns the net surplus to the private sector by a lump-sum transfer. We denote the amount of this transfer by the variable a. A comparative statics analysis on the system of eqs. (2)–(4) with an intertemporal budget constraint gives the following equation:

$$\left(\frac{\partial C_1}{\partial r}\right)_U = \frac{\partial C_1}{\partial r} - G \frac{\partial C_1}{\partial a}. \tag{5}$$

We will use eq. (5) in section 4 to place measurable boundaries on $(\partial C_1 / \partial r)_U$. Optimal public capital G^* is determined by solving

$$\frac{\partial F(K, L, G^*)}{\partial G} = F_G^*. \tag{6}$$

Eqs. (1), (5) and (6) show that production function parameters and the compensated interest derivative of consumption are required for measuring G^*. The following sections discuss how we obtain those parameters and implement eq. (6).[2]

3. Production function estimation

As discussed in section 1, Burgess's formula is appealing because it allows public capital to be substitutable for, or complementary with private capital. Therefore, to take advantage of the Burgess formula, a flexible functional form should be used for specifying the production technology. In addition, the duality approach is preferable to avoid estimation problems raised by the

---

[1] While Burgess assumes that labor demand is determined by the exogenous supply of labor, this paper assumes that the wage rate is determined so as to equate labor demand with the exogenous supply of labor. This switch on an assumption about the labor market does not alter the Burgess formula, except that $1/(1 - t)F_{KK}$ is no longer interpreted as $(\partial K / \partial r)$. A proof is obtained by a comparative statics analysis on eqs. (2)–(4) with an intertemporal budget constraint, in which endogenous variables are C_1, C_2, K and L. An example of such a comparative statics analysis is briefly outlined in Appendix B.

[2] Implementing the public discount rate framework requires that profits of the private sector include no rents to unpriced inputs except public capital. Our measurements of optimal public capital will be biased to the extent that such rents to natural resources or monopolies are important in the Japanese economy for 1960–1982. Fortunately, since few mining industries exist in Japan (accounting for 0.5 percent of GDP at most), the availability of unpriced natural resources is negligible. Monopolistic rents are also not considered large if the relatively strong performance of the Japanese economy in the 1960s and the 1970s can be attributed to the competitive environment. See Ito (1992, Chap. 7) for a discussion of this issue.

simultaneity between the production function and the input demand equations. Although the translog and generalized Leontief forms meet these requirements, these functional forms make it difficult to handle eq. (6). In this paper, we employ the normalized profit function of the quadratic form:

$$\Pi = \alpha_0 + \alpha_L p_L + \alpha_K p_K + \alpha_G G + \alpha_T T$$

$$+ \tfrac{1}{2}\beta_{LL} p_L^2 + \tfrac{1}{2}\beta_{KK} p_K^2 + \tfrac{1}{2}\beta_{GG} G^2 + \tfrac{1}{2}\beta_{TT} T^2$$

$$+ \beta_{LK} p_L p_K + \beta_{LG} p_L G + \beta_{LT} p_L T + \beta_{KG} p_K G + \beta_{KT} p_K T + \beta_{GT} GT \qquad (7)$$

where p_L and p_K are, respectively, the wage rate and unit capital user's cost normalized by the output price, and T is a time trend as a proxy for technology change.[3] Π is normalized profit given by

$$\Pi = \max_{L,K}\{F(K, L, G; T) - p_L L - p_K K\}. \qquad (8)$$

The quadratic profit function (7) is a member of the flexible form family in the sense that it provides a second order Taylor series approximation to any normalized profit function. Although the translog form has been the most widely used flexible functional form, it often violates required monotonicity and curvature conditions if no restrictions are imposed. Imposing global restrictions forces the translog form to meet those requisites, but also greatly restricts its flexibility. The quadratic form is much easier for accommodating theoretical requisites because all the second derivatives are constant.[4] In fact, Ornelas, Shumway and Ozuna (1994) give favorable evidence for the quadratic form against the translog form in specifying profit function.

The normalized profit function is well-behaved if it is nonincreasing in p_L and p_K, nondecreasing in G, convex in p_L and p_K, and concave in G. Concerning the monotonicity conditions, we check the estimated normalized profit function for $\partial\Pi/\partial p_L \leq 0, \partial\Pi/\partial p_K \leq 0$ and $\partial\Pi/\partial G \geq 0$ over the whole sample. Convexity in p_L and p_K is satisfied if the Hessian matrix with respect to p_L and p_K is positive semidefinite, that is, $\beta_{LL} \geq 0, \beta_{KK} \geq 0$, and $\beta_{LL}\beta_{KK} - \beta_{LK}^2 \geq 0$. Concavity in G requires $\beta_{GG} \leq 0$. These inequalities are also checked. Once inequalities confirmed, the normalized profit function globally satisfies the curvature conditions.[5]

Applying Hotelling's lemma to (7) yields demand equations for L and K as

$$L = -(\alpha_L + \beta_{LL} p_L + \beta_{LK} p_K + \beta_{LG} G + \beta_{LT} T), \qquad (9)$$

$$K = -(\alpha_K + \beta_{LK} p_L + \beta_{KK} p_K + \beta_{KG} G + \beta_{KT} T). \qquad (10)$$

---

[3] More specifically, $p_L = w/p$ and $p_K = (p_I/p)(r + \delta)/(1 - t)$, where p is the output price and p_I is the price of capital goods.

[4] An assumption of constant second derivatives is convenient and yet somewhat restrictive. A new flexible form family, such as the symmetric generalized McFadden, may be desirable because it can be globally proper without sacrificing any flexibility. However, the number of observations in our data set is not large enough to estimate such a functional form that is so rich in parameters.

[5] Linear homogeneity of nominal profit in output price, wage, and capital cost is incorporated into the normalized profit function by normalizing those variables with output price.

If the unit cost of capital is defined as $(r + \mu_K)/(1 - t)$, then eqs. (9) and (10) are exactly the dual counterparts of eqs. (3) and (4), respectively. The profit function is then estimable in a fully consistent manner with the Burgess formula. We append a homoscedastic and serially uncorrelated disturbance to each of eqs. (7), (9) and (10) and estimate them using the generalized method of moments (GMM). Although eqs. (7), (9) and (10) are seemingly uncorrelated, we employ the GMM to eliminate possible biases caused by the endogeneity of wage and interest rates.

Unlike the translog or generalized Leontief forms, the quadratic profit function is easily transformed to its "self-dual" production function [Lau (1978)]. Specifically, the dual production function also takes the quadratic form:

$$Y = \gamma_0 + \gamma_L L + \gamma_K K + \gamma_G G + \gamma_T T$$

$$+ \tfrac{1}{2}\delta_{LL}L^2 + \tfrac{1}{2}\delta_{KK}K^2 + \tfrac{1}{2}\delta_{GG}G^2 + \tfrac{1}{2}\delta_{TT}T^2$$

$$+ \delta_{LK}LK + \delta_{LG}LG + \delta_{LT}LT + \delta_{KG}KG + \delta_{KT}KT + \delta_{GT}GT, \tag{11}$$

and, as shown in Appendix A, its parameters $\gamma_0, \gamma_i, \delta_{ij}$ $(i, j = K, L, G, T)$ are retrievable from profit function parameters $\alpha_0, \alpha_i, \beta_{ij}$ $(i, j = K, L, G, T)$. The quadratic production function makes it easier to solve eq. (6) for public capital because $\partial F/\partial G$ is linear in G and the second derivatives, F_{GG} and F_{KG}, are constants. Given (11), solving (6) for G^* yields

$$G^* = \frac{1}{\delta_{GG} - \delta_{KG}\lambda} \{\lambda(\gamma_K + \delta_{LK}L + \delta_{KK}K + \delta_{KT}T)$$

$$- (\gamma_G + \delta_{LG}L + \delta_{KG}K + \delta_{GT}T) + (\mu_G - \mu_K)\} \tag{12}$$

where

$$\lambda = 1 - t\frac{\theta_1}{\theta_1 + \theta_2} = 1 - t\frac{\left(1 - \dfrac{\delta_{KG}}{\delta_{KK}}\right)\left(\dfrac{\partial C_1}{\partial r}\right)_U}{\left(\dfrac{\partial C_1}{\partial r}\right)_U + \dfrac{1}{(1 - t)\delta_{KK}}}.$$

In (12), G^* depends on unobservable $(\partial C_1/\partial r)_U$ through λ. As described in the next section, this paper applies two different procedures for obtaining $(\partial C_1/\partial r)_U$, and thereby for figuring λ. Where appropriate, we write estimates of G^* as $G^*(\lambda)$ to distinguish the procedures for λ in measuring G^*. In addition, we denote F_G^* associated with $G^*(\lambda)$ as $F_G^*(\lambda)$.

4. Measurement of the optimal public capital boundary

Although estimation of the utility function is a straightforward way to obtain $(\partial C_1/\partial r)_U$, the utility function itself is not necessary. It is easier to place boundaries on $(\partial C_1/\partial r)_U$, by which we obtain a pair of upper and lower boundary estimates of optimal public capital. From eq. (12), it is verified that G^* is a monotonic function of $(\partial C_1/\partial r)_U$ for each period. The monotonicity allows us to measure a pair of upper and lower boundaries of G^* from that of $(\partial C_1/\partial r)_U$.

First, since $(\partial C_1/\partial r)_U$ is negative, it is natural to examine the boundaries of G^* by taking the limits as $(\partial C_1/\partial r)_U \to -\infty$ and $(\partial C_1/\partial r)_U \to 0$. From the definition of λ, $\lambda \to 1$ as $(\partial C_1/\partial r)_U \to 0$ and $\lambda \to 1 - t(1 - \delta_{KG}/\delta_{KK})$ as $(\partial C_1/\partial r)_U \to -\infty$. We thus have

$$\min\{G^*(\lambda^a), G^*(\lambda^b)\} \le G^* \le \max\{G^*(\lambda^a), G^*(\lambda^b)\} \qquad (13)$$

where

$$\lambda^a = 1$$

$$\lambda^b = 1 - t\left(1 - \frac{\delta_{KG}}{\delta_{KK}}\right).$$

As noted by Burgess (1988), $G^*(\lambda^b)$, which is obtained by taking $(\partial C_1/\partial r)_U \to -\infty$, is equivalent to the optimal public capital implied by the Ogura-Yohe discount rate. On the other hand, $G^*(\lambda^a)$, which is obtained by taking $(\partial C_1/\partial r)_U \to 0$, implies that its discount rate follows the first best rule, $F_G^* - \mu_G = F_K - \mu_K$. Therefore, two conventional rules for public investment derived under less general conditions provide boundaries placed on the optimal public capital by the Burgess formula.[6]

However, one cannot know ex ante how precise and informative the boundary estimates, $G^*(\lambda^a)$ and $G^*(\lambda^b)$, are. In case they are unsatisfactory, more information should be utilized to improve the precision of the boundaries. Assuming that both the current and future consumptions are not inferior goods, we can obtain more precise alternative boundary estimates. It can be shown that the second term on the right hand side in eq. (5), the intertemporal income effect, is bounded as

$$0 \le G\frac{\partial C_1}{\partial a} \le \frac{G}{1+r}. \qquad (17)$$

A formal proof is given in Appendix B. It follows from eqs. (17) and (5) that

$$\frac{\partial C_1}{\partial r} - \frac{G}{1+r} \le \left(\frac{\partial C_1}{\partial r}\right)_U \le \frac{\partial C_1}{\partial r}. \qquad (18)$$

Most of the existing estimates of the interest elasticity of consumption for Japan are around -0.01. For example, the Nikkei Macro Econometric Model estimates it between -0.008 and -0.016 [Databank Bureau of Nihon Keizai Shimbun (1988)], and the Econometric Committee of the Economic Council (1984) gives estimates ranging from -0.005 to -0.01 in its Multi-Sectoral

---

[6] The Burgess formula is reduced to the first best rule if $\delta_{KK} = \delta_{KG}$ as well. If this is the case, $G^*(\lambda^a)$ coincides with $G^*(\lambda^b)$.

Econometric Model of Japan. Therefore, choosing the interest rate elasticity of consumption to be -0.01 and setting $(\partial C_1/\partial r) = -0.01 C_1/r$ to evaluate the upper and lower boundaries of $(\partial C_1/\partial r)_U$ using (18), we then obtain

$$\min\{G^*(\lambda^A), G^*(\lambda^B)\} \le G^* \le \max\{G^*(\lambda^A), G^*(\lambda^B)\}, \tag{19}$$

where

$$\lambda^A = 1 + t \frac{0.01\left(1 - \dfrac{\delta_{KG}}{\delta_{KK}}\right)\dfrac{C_1}{r}}{\dfrac{1}{(1-t)\delta_{KK}} - 0.01\dfrac{C_1}{r}},$$

and

$$\lambda^B = 1 + t \frac{\left(1 - \dfrac{\delta_{KG}}{\delta_{KK}}\right)\left(0.01\dfrac{C_1}{r} + \dfrac{G}{1+r}\right)}{\dfrac{1}{(1-t)\delta_{KK}} - \left(0.01\dfrac{C_1}{r} + \dfrac{G}{1+r}\right)}.$$

To be specific, G in λ^B should be G^*, which raises a complicated problem for solving (19). However, merely assuming the marginal productivity of G^* to be nonnegative, we recover the tractability of λ^B. The assumption of non-negative marginal productivity implies that G^* is smaller than or equal to $\hat{G}$, such that $\partial F(K, L, \hat{G})/\partial G = 0$. Then, $(\partial C_1/\partial r) - \hat{G}/(1+r)$ provides another lower boundary of $(\partial C_1/\partial r)_U$. Thus, it is possible to work with λ^B evaluated at $G = \hat{G}$ to obtain valid boundary estimates of G^*.

5. Empirical results

The set of equations to be estimated consists of the profit function (7) and demand equations for labor (9) and capital (10). We apply the GMM for estimating these equations using the Japanese aggregate time series from the fiscal years 1960–1982. To avoid spurious regression, the equations are first-differenced before estimation. Error correction terms are unnecessary because the augmented Engle-Granger test does not reject the null of no cointegration at the 5 percent significance level for both eqs. (9) and (10).

The data are compiled in consistence with the system of national accounts. Output Y is measured by real GDP, and labor L is man-hours worked, measured by the number of employees times the index of total hours worked. We obtain the data from *Annual Report on National Accounts* (the Economic Planning Agency) except private and public capital stocks. Private capital stock is taken from *Gross Capital Stock of Private Enterprises* (Economic Research Institute of the Economic Planning Agency) and public capital stock from *Social Capital Stock in Japan* (Planning Bureau of Economic Planning Agency). Public capital stock consists of ten sectors including roads, seaports, airports, railroads, telecommunications, posts, agriculture, forestry, fisheries and water supply for industrial use. We exclude public capital for improving the

Table 1. Profit function parameter estimates and transformed production function parameters [a]

Profit Function		Production Function	
α_L	−8198.8 (17113.0)	γ_L	107.82
α_K	−31370.4 (52314.5)	γ_K	2.6105
α_G	4.4739 (2.349)	γ_G	−2.1630
α_T	2355.0 (11258.1)	γ_T	−12671.
β_{LL}	76.039 (2.398)	δ_{LL}	−0.013151
β_{LK}	−0.013119 (−0.2715)	δ_{LK}	-0.14357×10^{-7}
β_{LG}	0.56158×10^{-2} (0.6170×10^{-2})	δ_{LG}	-0.73814×10^{-3}
β_{LT}	−139.36 (48.379)	δ_{LT}	1.8327
β_{KK}	12017.5 (36327.0)	δ_{KK}	-0.83212×10^{-4}
β_{KG}	−2.7743 (0.1263)	δ_{KG}	0.23086×10^{-3}
		δ_{KT}	0.20007×10^{-5}
β_{GG}	-0.14717×10^{-4} (0.3152×10^{-4})	δ_{GG}	-0.65561×10^{-3}
		δ_{GT}	0.010286
β_{TT}	−119.21 (1682.6)	δ_{TT}	−374.61
J	33.12	Critical J at 1% = 34.81 [b]	

a) The values in parentheses are asymptotic standard errors.
b) J is asymptotically distributed as $\chi^2(18)$ under the null.

living environment because in this paper the utility function does not include public capital. Additional details on our data are provided in Appendix C.

The estimated results for the profit function are given in Table 1. The first column shows the profit function parameters with asymptotic standard errors in parentheses. The list of instruments includes consumption expenditures of the government, working age population, official discount rate of the Bank of Japan, import price index, public capital stock at the end of the previous period, lagged wage rate, lagged capital user's cost, a time variable divided by the number of observations, and a dummy variable capturing the effect of the first oil crisis. The last row of Table 1 gives the J statistic for the over-identifying restrictions and its critical values. The overidentifying restrictions are rejected at the 5 percent significance level but not rejected at the 1 percent significance level, indicating no obvious signs of misspecification.

We restrict β_{KT} and β_{GT} to zero. If the profit function is estimated without these restrictions, the resulting profit function fails to satisfy the regularity conditions stated in section 3. In contrast, the parameter estimates shown in the first column in Table 1 satisfy these conditions. Specifically, the estimated profit function locally satisfies monotonicity conditions and globally satisfies

Table 2. Tests for parameters on technology

hypothesis	dual restriction to be tested	test statistic $\chi^2(1)$	critical value at 0.05
$\delta_{KG} = 0$	$\beta_{LK}\beta_{LG} - \beta_{LL}\beta_{KG} = 0$	6.17	3.84
$\delta_{KG} = \delta_{KK}$	$\beta_{LK}\beta_{LG} - \beta_{LL}\beta_{KG} + \beta_{LL} = 0$	2.73	3.84

curvature conditions. Furthermore, Newey and West's (1989) likelihood ratio type test for the GMM estimator cannot reject the null of $\beta_{KT} = \beta_{GT} = 0$ at the 5 percent significance level.

The second column of Table 1 shows the dual production function parameters obtained from taking the dual transformation presented in Appendix A. Since δ_{KG} is positive, public and private capital stocks are complementary in the sense that the marginal productivity of private capital increases with an increase in public capital.

It is of interest to test the null hypotheses of $\delta_{KG} = 0$ and $\delta_{KG} = \delta_{KK}$. The former implies that private and public capital are independent, so that the Burgess discount rate is reduced to the Sandmo-Drèze discount rate. The latter implies the first best rule that the proper public discount rate is the marginal rate of returns on private capital, that is, $F_G^* - \mu_G = F_K - \mu_K$. From the dual relationship shown in Appendix A, the restrictions on profit function parameters,

$$\beta_{LK}\beta_{LG} - \beta_{LL}\beta_{KG} = 0 \tag{20}$$

and

$$\beta_{LK}\beta_{LG} - \beta_{LL}\beta_{KG} + \beta_{LL} = 0 \tag{21}$$

are found to be identical to $\delta_{KG} = 0$ and $\delta_{KK} = \delta_{KG}$, respectively. We tested (20) and (21) using Newey and West's likelihood ratio type test. The results are reported in Table 2. The test statistic is distributed as chi-square with one degree of freedom under the null hypothesis in both cases. The parameter restriction (20) is rejected at the 5 percent significance level, indicating that the Sandmo-Dréze discount rate is not appropriate for public investment. On the other hand, the restriction (21) cannot be rejected, indicating that public investment can be discounted at the marginal rate of returns on private capital.

Table 3 provides components of the Burgess discount rate, F_K, r, μ_K and μ_G, together with the tax rate of corporate income and the relative price of capital goods to output. Marginal productivity of private capital is evaluated with eq. (10) at the estimated demand for private capital. This makes the marginal rate of returns on private capital identical to the normalized capital cost, that is, $F_K = (p_I/p)(r + \mu_K)/(1 - t)$ holds identically. Since p_I/p is close to unity in the 1970s and 1980s, the wedge between F_K and r is determined by the tax rate of corporate income. In the 1960s, p_I/p exceeded unity and also contributed to raising F_K and widening the difference between F_K and r. The expensive capital goods relative to output in the early 1960s reflects the fact that the Japanese economy at that time was still in a "catch-up" phase relative to the developed economies, importing most of its machine tools and producing mainly light industrial products.

The depreciation rate of private capital is around 0.10 over the 1960–1982 period. We calculated it for each year by dividing real private capital con-

Table 3. Components of the Burgess formula

Year	Marginal Pro- ductivity[a] of Private Capital F_K	Depreciation Rate of Pri- vate Capital μ_K	Interest Rate r	Tax Rate of Corporate Income t	Relative Price of Cap- ital Goods p_I/p
1960	0.483	0.0836	0.0817	0.458	1.583
1961	0.428	0.0901	0.0800	0.387	1.543
1962	0.456	0.0917	0.0821	0.428	1.503
1963	0.430	0.0986	0.0779	0.418	1.419
1964	0.444	0.1133	0.0790	0.414	1.353
1965	0.425	0.1124	0.0780	0.413	1.311
1966	0.401	0.1134	0.0748	0.400	1.278
1967	0.391	0.1164	0.0731	0.402	1.237
1968	0.390	0.1197	0.0746	0.402	1.200
1969	0.380	0.1229	0.0740	0.402	1.155
1970	0.375	0.1215	0.0766	0.413	1.111
1971	0.362	0.1195	0.0759	0.418	1.078
1972	0.343	0.1196	0.0704	0.418	1.049
1973	0.334	0.1116	0.0718	0.416	1.063
1974	0.362	0.0979	0.0911	0.437	1.076
1975	0.341	0.0933	0.0909	0.435	1.044
1976	0.330	0.0930	0.0825	0.460	1.014
1977	0.313	0.0934	0.0756	0.468	0.984
1978	0.286	0.0951	0.0630	0.469	0.960
1979	0.291	0.0935	0.0629	0.469	0.988
1980	0.332	0.0931	0.0832	0.471	0.994
1981	0.325	0.0954	0.0778	0.484	0.968
1982	0.315	0.0948	0.0722	0.496	0.951

Depreciation rate of Public Capital: $\mu_G = 0.0784$ for 1960–1982

a) One billion yen at 1980 prices

sumption by the private capital stock. However, the same procedure is inapplicable for obtaining the depreciation rate of public capital. This is because data on capital consumption is not available. Instead, the value of $\mu_G = 0.0784$ is calculated by assuming the durable period to be 28.2 years over the whole period. It is plausible that the depreciation rate of public capital is smaller than that of private capital. The public capital considered here is infrastructure which includes publicly owned assets in transportation, telecommunications, posts, industrial water supply, forestry, agriculture and fisheries. Those are plausibly more durable than privately owned structures and equipment.

Table 4 summarizes the measured results of optimal public capital based on eq. (13). The first two columns present the upper and lower boundaries of the net public discount rate, $F_G^*(\lambda^a) - \mu_G$ and $F_G^*(\lambda^b) - \mu_G$. As mentioned above, $F_G^*(\lambda^a) - \mu_G$ is the net marginal productivity of private capital, while $F_G^*(\lambda^b) - \mu_G$ is the public discount rate proposed by Ogura and Yohe. As expected by the complementarity between private and public capital, $F_G^*(\lambda^b)$ is smaller than $F_G^*(\lambda^a)$.

The third and fourth columns of Table 4 present the boundary estimates of the optimal public capital, $G^*(\lambda^a)$ and $G^*(\lambda^b)$. Our primary interest is in examining whether the actual levels of public capital are indeed optimal. To see this, the fifth and sixth columns in Table 4 present the ratios of actual public

Table 4. Measurements of the public discount rate and the optimal public capital by eq. (13)

Year	Net Discount Rate		Optimal Public Capital[a]		Actual to Optimal Ratio	
	$F_G^*(\lambda^a) - \mu_G$	$F_G^*(\lambda^b) - \mu_G$	$G^*(\lambda^a)$	$G^*(\lambda^b)$	$G/G^*(\lambda^a)$	$G/G^*(\lambda^b)$
1960	0.400	−0.800	15969	19993	0.823	0.658
1961	0.338	−0.637	17378	20387	0.825	0.703
1962	0.365	−0.702	18772	22316	0.845	0.711
1963	0.332	−0.626	20860	24248	0.856	0.737
1964	0.331	−0.619	22836	26165	0.872	0.761
1965	0.312	−0.572	25458	28738	0.883	0.783
1966	0.288	−0.515	28523	31613	0.894	0.807
1967	0.275	−0.487	31983	35056	0.906	0.826
1968	0.270	−0.467	35861	38859	0.917	0.845
1969	0.257	−0.434	39904	42910	0.926	0.861
1970	0.253	−0.413	44482	47579	0.935	0.874
1971	0.242	−0.386	50346	53440	0.943	0.888
1972	0.223	−0.353	57518	60538	0.950	0.903
1973	0.223	−0.346	64252	67174	0.957	0.915
1974	0.264	−0.387	70191	73297	0.964	0.923
1975	0.247	−0.343	76602	79605	0.967	0.930
1976	0.237	−0.345	82841	86070	0.970	0.934
1977	0.219	−0.322	90458	93680	0.973	0.940
1978	0.191	−0.292	99155	102279	0.976	0.946
1979	0.198	−0.311	107490	110496	0.979	0.953
1980	0.238	−0.347	115051	117970	0.983	0.959
1981	0.230	−0.344	122602	125567	0.985	0.962
1982	0.220	−0.338	130217	133200	0.986	0.964

Weights in λ^a : $\theta_1/(\theta_1 + \theta_2) = 0.0$ for 1960–1982 ($\lambda^a = 1$)
Weights in λ^b : $\theta_1/(\theta_1 + \theta_2) = 3.77$ for 1960–1982 ($\lambda^b = 1 - t(1 - \delta_{KG}/\delta_{KK})$)

a) One billion yen at 1980 prices

capital G to $G^*(\lambda^a)$ and $G^*(\lambda^b)$, and Figure 1 illustrates the development of
those ratios over time. The results reveal that actual levels of public capital
had continuously approached optimal levels since 1960 and were almost optimal in the early 1980s. The lower boundary of actual to optimal public
capital ratio rose from 0.66 in 1960 to 0.96 in 1982, while the upper boundary
rose from 0.82 to 0.99 in that same period. The degree of deficiency in public
capital had fallen to 1–4 percent in the early 1980s from the 18–35 percent
levels in the beginning of the 1960s.

Clearly, $G^*(\lambda^a)$ and $G^*(\lambda^b)$ tend to converge over time, meaning that optimal levels of public capital become less sensitive to intertemporal substitution in consumption. It can be shown that the sensitivity to intertemporal
substitution is proportionate to the marginal productivity of private capital.
Manipulating (13) with eqs. (1) and (4), we have[7]

$$\left| \frac{G^*(\lambda^a) - G^*(\lambda^b)}{\lambda^a - \lambda^b} \right| = F_K \left| \frac{\delta_{GG} - \delta_{KG}\lambda}{(\delta_{GG} - \delta_{KG}\lambda^a)(\delta_{GG} - \delta_{KG}\lambda^b)} \right|. \tag{22}$$

[7] Eq. (22) is obtained by subtracting $G^*(\lambda^b)$ from $G^*(\lambda^a)$ and using eqs. (1) and (4) to eliminate
$F_G - \mu_G$ and r.

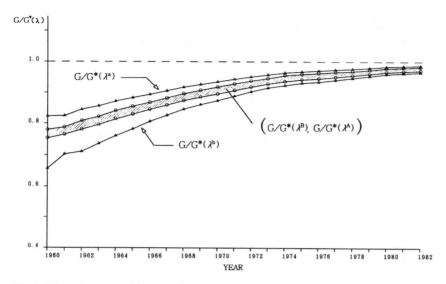

Fig. 1. The ratios of actual to optimal public capital

Since λ^a and λ^b are constant over time, the tendency for $G^*(\lambda^a)$ and $G^*(\lambda^b)$ to converge is due to the decreasing trend of F_K. An intuitive explanation for this is indicated by noting that the Burgess formula can be rewritten as $F_G^* - \mu_G = [\theta_2/(\theta_1 + \theta_2)][(F_K - \mu_K) - r] + (F_K - \mu_K)$, and that $(\partial C_1/\partial r)_U$ relates to F_G^* only through the weights $\theta_2/(\theta_1 + \theta_2)$. It is, then, considered that the sensitivity of G^* to $(\partial C_1/\partial r)_U$ is determined by the magnitude of $(F_K - \mu_K) - r$, the difference between opportunity costs of foregone private investment and current consumption for financing public investment. In the weighted average formula, one of the weighting factors, intertemporal substitution in consumption becomes less influential as the wedge between $(F_K - \mu_K)$ and r shrinks. Recalling the first order condition for private capital (4), we have $(F_K - \mu_K) - r = tF_K$, which explains why the sensitivity of G^* to $(\partial C_1/\partial r)_U$ is proportionate to F_K[8].

Although the boundary estimates $G^*(\lambda^a)$ and $G^*(\lambda^b)$ are satisfactory after the mid-1970s, they are somewhat less informative as regards the 1960s. Exploiting information on the ordinary interest elasticity of consumption, we obtain more precise boundary estimates, $G^*(\lambda^A)$ and $G^*(\lambda^B)$, using eq. (19). Table 5 presents $G^*(\lambda^A)$ and $G^*(\lambda^B)$ together with their corresponding net discount rates, $F_G^*(\lambda^A) - \mu_G$ and $F_G^*(\lambda^B) - \mu_G$, and weights $\theta_1/(\theta_1 + \theta_2)$. The weights are no longer constant because $(\partial C_1/\partial r)_U$ varies over time. The net discount rates are negative in the lower boundaries and are very close to zero, even in the upper boundaries. Since negative discount rates seem to be unreasonable, $G^*(\lambda^B)$ may give loose upper boundaries. However, the gross rates in the upper boundaries, $F_G^*(\lambda^A)$, turn out to be positive during the

---

[8] Furthermore, the decreasing trend in the relative price of capital goods to output also contributes to a converging tendency of the boundary estimates of G^*. As noted in footnote 4, we assume $F_K = (p_I/p)(r + \mu_K)/(1 - t)$ in empirical practice, so that the difference between $F_K - \mu_K$ and r is $F_K[(p_I/p) + t - 1]$.

Table 5. Measurements of the public discount rate and the optimal public capital by eq. (19)

Year	Weights $\theta_1/(\theta_1 + \theta_2)$		Net Discount Rate		Optimal Public[a] Capital		Actual to Optimal Ratio	
	in λ^A	in λ^B	$F_G^*(\lambda^A) - \mu_G$	$F_G^*(\lambda^B) - \mu_G$	$G^*(\lambda^A)$	$G^*(\lambda^B)$	$G/G^*(\lambda^A)$	$G/G^*(\lambda^B)$
1960	1.29	2.10	−0.0093	−0.268	16859	17611	0.780	0.747
1961	1.41	2.26	−0.0263	−0.246	18191	18827	0.788	0.761
1962	1.33	2.23	−0.0109	−0.266	19621	20387	0.809	0.778
1963	1.39	2.32	−0.0209	−0.257	21726	22502	0.822	0.794
1964	1.38	2.37	−0.0174	−0.266	23687	24500	0.840	0.813
1965	1.40	2.43	−0.0149	−0.258	26307	27161	0.855	0.828
1966	1.45	2.53	−0.0213	−0.250	29372	30226	0.868	0.843
1967	1.47	2.59	−0.0219	−0.249	32839	33737	0.882	0.858
1968	1.45	2.65	−0.0137	−0.248	36695	37648	0.896	0.874
1969	1.46	2.71	−0.0099	−0.239	40734	41729	0.907	0.885
1970	1.41	2.75	0.0039	−0.232	45294	46386	0.918	0.896
1971	1.41	2.81	0.0073	−0.226	51153	52307	0.928	0.908
1972	1.48	2.90	−0.0026	−0.219	58349	59516	0.937	0.919
1973	1.46	2.96	0.0020	−0.223	65048	66242	0.945	0.928
1974	1.23	2.94	0.0521	−0.244	70860	72271	0.954	0.936
1975	1.23	3.00	0.0549	−0.221	77253	78666	0.959	0.941
1976	1.28	3.02	0.0402	−0.229	83546	85059	0.962	0.945
1977	1.34	3.07	0.0272	−0.221	91196	92716	0.965	0.950
1978	1.50	3.13	−0.0002	−0.209	99971	101412	0.968	0.954
1979	1.50	3.16	−0.0041	−0.229	108276	109702	0.972	0.959
1980	1.25	3.17	0.0444	−0.253	115664	117202	0.978	0.965
1981	1.29	3.19	0.0345	−0.255	123234	124798	0.980	0.968
1982	1.33	3.21	0.0235	−0.255	130868	132438	0.981	0.970

a) One billion yen at 1980 prices

whole period. Thus, $G^*(\lambda^A)$ has positive marginal productivity, implying that our results do not contradict the assumption of nonnegative marginal productivity of optimal public capital.

The ratios of actual to optimal public capital are reported in the seventh and eighth columns in Table 5, and the range between the upper and lower boundaries of those ratios in time profile is designated by the hatched area in Figure 1. The ratio rose from 0.75–0.78 in 1960 to 0.97–0.98 in 1982. Compared with the corresponding results in Table 4, it is evident that in 1960s, the differences between $G^*(\lambda^A)$ and $G^*(\lambda^B)$ were rather narrower than those between $G^*(\lambda^a)$ and $G^*(\lambda^b)$. A premised value of interest elasticity of consumption can be used to improve the precision of the boundary estimates of optimal public capital.

6. Concluding remarks

This paper has assessed the optimality of public capital in Japan using a discount rate framework for public investment. To do this, we present a procedure for implementing the public discount rate formula. This procedure allows us to measure the upper and lower boundaries of optimal public capital without estimating a utility function.

We find that actual levels of public capital during the fiscal period 1960–1982 were less than the optimal levels based on the Burgess discount rate. However, public capital accumulated at a rate higher than the growth rate of the optimal levels. Public capital thereby diminished the gap between actual and optimal levels over time. In 1982, the ratio of actual to optimal levels was at least more than 0.96. In this study, we also provided a procedure to improve the precision of the boundary estimates using a premised value of interest elasticity of consumption. An application of this to Japanese public capital results in a reasonable assessment.

Our evidence for a deficiency of public capital supports the prevailing wisdom of an insufficient supply of public capital before the mid-1970s. However, that deficiency almost disappeared in the early 1980s. Due to data limitations, we confined our analysis to the fiscal period 1960–1982. Therefore, it still remains to be seen whether or not the Japanese economy was free from a deficiency of public capital after 1982. Additional research on more recent time periods will be necessary in order to augment the results of the present study.

Appendix A. Dual transformations from profit function (7) to production function (11)

We use the following formulas to retrieve production function parameters, γ_0, γ_i and δ_{ij} $(i, j = L, K, G, T)$, from profit function parameters, α_0, α_i and β_{ij} $(i,j = K, L, G, T)$:

$$\gamma_0 = \alpha_0 - \tfrac{1}{2}\alpha'_P B_{PP}^{-1}\alpha_P,$$

$$(\gamma_L, \gamma_K) = -\alpha'_P B_{PP}^{-1}, \quad (\gamma_G, \gamma_T) = \alpha'_Z - \alpha'_P B_{PP}^{-1} B_{ZP},$$

$$\begin{pmatrix} \delta_{LL} & \delta_{LK} \\ \delta_{LK} & \delta_{KK} \end{pmatrix} = -B_{PP}^{-1}, \quad \begin{pmatrix} \delta_{LG} & \delta_{LT} \\ \delta_{KG} & \delta_{KT} \end{pmatrix} = -B_{PP}^{-1} B_{ZP},$$

and

$$\begin{pmatrix} \delta_{GG} & \delta_{GT} \\ \delta_{GT} & \delta_{TT} \end{pmatrix} = B_{ZZ} - B'_{ZP} B_{PP}^{-1} B_{ZP},$$

where

$$\alpha'_P \equiv (\alpha_L, \alpha_K), \quad \alpha'_Z \equiv (\alpha_G, \alpha_T), \quad B_{PP} \equiv \begin{pmatrix} \beta_{LL} & \beta_{LK} \\ \beta_{LK} & \beta_{KK} \end{pmatrix},$$

$$B_{ZP} \equiv \begin{pmatrix} \beta_{LG} & \beta_{LT} \\ \beta_{KG} & \beta_{KT} \end{pmatrix}, \quad \text{and} \quad B_{ZZ} \equiv \begin{pmatrix} \beta_{GG} & \beta_{GT} \\ \beta_{GT} & \beta_{TT} \end{pmatrix}.$$

In the main text, α_0 and γ_0 are not estimated because profit function is estimated in the first-difference form.

Appendix B. Proof of equation (17)

A comparative statics analysis on the private sector's behavior is conducted in two steps. First, one performs a comparative statics analysis on eqs. (3) and (4) to obtain the demand for labor and capital as $L(w, r, G)$ and $K(w, r, G)$, respectively. The intertemporal budget constraint is then supposed to be

$$C_2 = (1 - t)[F(L(w, r, G), K(w, r, G), G) - wL(w, r, G)] + wS$$

$$+ (1 + r)(V - C_1 - K(w, r, G)) + (1 - \mu_K) + (1 - \mu_G) + a,$$

where V denotes initial endowment and S the exogenous supply of labor. The wage rate is assumed to be determined so that $L = S$. Second, one performs a comparative statics analysis on (2) and the intertemporal budget constraint above. Differentiating the intertemporal budget constraint with respect to C_1, C_2 and a, we obtain

$$(1 + r)dC_1 + dC_2 = da \tag{B1}$$

On the other hand, differentiating (2) with respect to C_1 and C_2, we obtain

$$[U_{11} - (1 + r)U_{12}]dC_1 + [U_{12} - (1 + r)U_{22}]dC_2 = 0. \tag{B2}$$

Solving (B1) and (B2) yields $(\partial C_1 / \partial a) = -H_1/H$ and $(\partial C_2 / \partial a) = H_2/H$ where

$$H_1 = U_{12} - (1 + r)U_{22}, \quad H_2 = U_{11} - (1 + r)U_{22} \quad \text{and}$$

$$H = -(1 + r)H_1 + H_2.$$

We thus have

$$G\frac{\partial C_1}{\partial a} = -G\frac{H_1}{H} = \left(\frac{G}{1 + r}\right)\left(\frac{H_1}{H_1 - H_2/(1 + r)}\right). \tag{B3}$$

Notice that $H < 0$ is required by a second order condition for the private sector's maximization problem. Note also that $(\partial C_1 / \partial a) \geq 0$ and $(\partial C_2 / \partial a) \geq 0$ because C_1 and C_2 are assumed to be normal goods. We then have $H_1 \geq 0$ and $H_2 \leq 0$. As a result, $G(\partial C_1 / \partial a) \geq 0$ and $G(\partial C_1 / \partial a) \leq G/(1 + r)$ follow from (B3), thus proving eq. (17).

Appendix C. Data constructions and sources

We now provide a summary of data constructions and sources. In the following, all data are taken from *Annual Report on National Accounts* (Economic Planning Agency), unless otherwise noted.

Output (Y) is measured by real GDP. Labor (L) is measured by the number of employees times the index of total hours worked. The index of total hours worked is taken from *Year Book of Labor Statistics* (Ministry of

Labor). The real wage rate (p_L) is defined as w/p where w is calculated by (total labor compensation)$/L$, and p is the GDP deflator. The real unit user's cost of capital (p_K) is calculated according to the formula $(p_I/p)(r + \mu_K)/(1 - t)$, where p_I is the deflator of private capital formation, t is the corporate income tax rate taken from *Annual Statistical Bulletin* (National Tax Administration Agency), r is the average interest rate on loans and discounts taken from *Economic Statistics Monthly* (Bank of Japan). The depreciation rate of private capital, μ_K, is calculated by (fixed capital consumption)$/(p_I K)$. Here, private capital stock (K) is obtained from *Gross Capital Stock of Private Enterprises* (Economic Research Institute, Economic Planning Agency). Profit (Π) is then calculated as $Y - p_L L - p_K K$.

Public capital (G) is taken from the Planning Bureau of the Economic Planning Agency (1986). The public capital stock used in this paper is defined as the sum of government owned assets including roads, seaports, airports, railroads, telecommunications, posts, water supply for industrial use, forestry, agriculture and fisheries. The depreciation rate of public capital, μ_G, is calculated as follows: Let A denote the volume of a depreciable asset and m denote its duration period. The total depreciation expenses are then $A\{1 - (1 - \mu)^m\}$, where μ is a fixed rate of depreciation. Assuming a scrap value as 10 percent of A, we have $\mu = 1 - 0.1^{1/m}$ by solving $A\{1 - (1 - \mu)^m\} = 0.9A$. In this paper, the duration period for public capital is set at 28.2 years, which is obtained by taking the harmonic mean of the duration period for the 10 types of public capital listed above. The volumes of the 10 types of public capital are taken as weights. The duration period for each type of public capital is available from the Planning Bureau of the Economic Planning Agency (1986).

References

Aschauer DA (1989) Is public expenditure productive? Journal of Monetary Economics 23:177–200

Baltagi BH, Pinnoi N (1995) Public capital stock and state productivity growth: Further evidence from an error components model. Empirical Economics 20:351–359

Berndt ER, Hansson B (1991) Measuring the contribution of public infrastructure capital in Sweden. NBER Working Paper No. 3842

Burgess DF (1988) Complementarity and the discount rate for public investment. Quarterly Journal of Economics 102:527–541

Dalamagas B (1995) A Reconsideration of the public sector's contribution to growth. Empirical Economics 20:385–414

Databank Bureau of Nihon Keizai Shimbun (1988) Economic analysis of the anti-wealth effect by Nikkei macro-econometric model. A paper presented at the 19th Macro Econometric Model Conference, Osaka, in Japanese

Econometric Committee of Economic Council (1984) Multisectoral econometric model for mid- and long-run analysis. Printing Bureau of Ministry of Finance, in Japanese

Evans P, Karras G (1994) Are government activities productive? Evidence from a panel of U. S. states. Review of Economics and Statistics 76:1–11

Holtz-Eakin D (1994) Public-sector capital and the productivity puzzle. Review of Economics and Statistics 76:12–21

Ito T (1992) The Japanese economy. The MIT Press

Lau LJ (1978) Applications of profit functions. In: Fuss M, McFadden D (eds.) Production economics: A dual approach to theory and applications, Volume 1, North-Holland, Amsterdam, pp. 133–216

Lynde C, Richmond J (1993) Public capital and total factor productivity. International Economic Review 34:401–414

Lynde C, Richmond J (1992) The role of public capital in Production. Review of Economics and Statistics 74:37–44

Nadiri MI, Mamuneas TP (1994) The effects of public infrastructure and R&D capital on the cost structure and performance of U.S. manufacturing industries. Review of Economics and Statistics 76:22–37

Ogura S, Yohe G (1977) The complementarity of public and private capital and the optimal rate of return to government investment. Quarterly Journal of Economics 91:651–662

Ornelas FS, Shumway CR, Ozuna T (1994) Using the quadratic Box-Cox flexible functional form selection and unconditional variance computation. Empirical Economics 19:639–645

Planning Bureau of Economic Planning Agency (1986) Social capital stock in Japan. Gyousei, Tokyo, in Japanese

Sandmo A, Drèze JH (1971) Discount rate for public investment in closed and open economies. Economica 38:395–412

Shah A (1992) Dynamics of public infrastructure, industrial productivity and profitability. Review of Economics and Statistics 74:28–36

On the long run effect of public capital on aggregate output: Estimation and sensitivity analysis*

Raymond G. Batina

Department of Economics, Washington State University, Pullman, WA 99164-4741, USA
(e-mail: rbatina@pullman.com)

First version received: January 1998/final version received: June 1999

Abstract. We undertake a sensitivity analysis of the productivity of public capital under the aggregate production function approach. Several proxies are used for the private inputs and for public capital, several dummy variables are included to adjust for energy price shocks, newly revised data is studied, and Stock and Watson's dynamic OLS estimator is used. Our main results are that the productivity of public capital depends critically on the proxies used, the effects are typically smaller than the early estimates, and omitting the oil price shocks introduces significant upward bias in the measured productivity of public capital.

Key words: Public capital, sensitivity analysis, DOLS

JEL classifications: H54, H41, E23, E25, C32

1. Introduction

The purpose of this paper is to undertake a sensitivity analysis of the estimation of the long run effect of public capital on output under the aggregate production function approach of Aschauer (1989). We use recently revised annual data on private and public capital for the United States to estimate the long run cointegrating relationship between output, labor, private capital, and public capital. (See Munnell (1992) and Gramlich (1994) for surveys.)

This paper differs from the earlier literature in a number of ways. We use different proxies for labor and private capital. Second, we disaggregate public

* The author is indebted to Dan Hamilton, Hiro Ihori, Steve Perez, two anonymous referees, and the editor for their helpful comments on earlier versions of this paper. Of course, the usual disclaimer applies.

capital by level of government into total state and local public capital and by function into highway and street public capital. Third, we include several dummy variables to account for oil price shocks, following Perron (1989), Tatom (1991), Smyth (1994), and Hamilton (1996). Fourth, we use Stock and Watson's (1993) dynamic OLS (DOLS) estimator to account for serial correlation and the possible endogeneity of some of the regressors in the cointegrating regression (See Batina (1998)).[1,2] Finally, we use newly revised data on capital and a longer span of data than previous researchers.

We find the impact of public capital on output is highly sensitive to the proxies used, whether the oil price shocks are included, and whether public capital is disaggregated, and is smaller in magnitude than obtained by Aschauer. There is an upward bias in the productivity of public capital when the energy price shocks are omitted. Finally, the productivity of the private inputs is also affected by the proxies used and the oil price shocks.

2. The data and our methodology

The data is taken from standard sources and consists of annual observations from 1948 to 1993 for the U.S. The proxy used for output is an index of output maintained by the Bureau of Labor Statistics (BLS) and published in the *Monthly Labor Review*.

We used two proxies for labor, aggregate labor hours (L1) and aggregate employment (L2), which were taken from the DRI McGraw-Hill database. Most researchers studying aggregate data have used labor hours as the proxy for labor, while researchers working with state and local data have used employment instead.

Two proxies were used for private capital. K1 is an index of capital services calculated by the BLS and published in the *Monthly Labor Review*. It measures the flow of services from the stock of private capital and can be taken as a direct proxy for "private capital services." The second proxy for private capital is taken from the BEA and has just been recently revised. It is the non-residential, real, net stock of fixed private capital including equipment and structures denominated in chained 1992 dollars and was taken from Katz and Herman (1997a, 1997b). We multiplied this stock by the capacity utilization rate for manufacturing taken from the DRI McGraw-Hill database to obtain our second measure of "capital services," K2. Most researchers working with aggregate data have used K2, although, Aschauer and Munnell (1990) both used K1 in their landmark studies instead.

TG represents a chain-type quantity index of the total net stock of non-

---

[1] Aschauer (1989) recognized the simultaneity problem and used TSLS with the lagged value of public capital variable as an instrument. His estimate of the productivity of public capital was not affected by this refinement. However, TSLS only removes one of the bias terms in the limiting distribution of the OLS estimator in this case and is not preferred to DOLS in general as a result. See the discussion in Stock and Watson (1993) and Hamilton (1994) chapter 19.

[2] Tatom (1991) used DOLS near the end of his paper in estimating the production function but included energy prices as a variable in the estimated equation. This makes it somewhat difficult to interpret his coefficients. See the discussion in Gramlich (1994) on this issue. Hamilton (1996) used the FM-OLS method in estimating the production function. FM-OLS is asymptotically equivalent to DOLS, however, DOLS may have superior properties in finite samples. See Stock and Watson (1993).

defense federal, state, and local public capital including equipment and structures and is taken from the newly revised BEA estimates by Katz and Herman
(1997a, 1997b). SLG represents a chain-type quantity index of total state and
local public capital. And SLHWY represents a chain-type quantity index of
the net stock of state and local highway and street capital. Following the literature, we multiplied each public capital variable by the capacity utilization
rate to proxy for "public capital services."

The evidence on the stationarity of the different series is somewhat mixed.
The unit root tests indicated that it is difficult to reject the unit root hypothesis
for all of the series except capacity utilization. However, it is also well known
that unit root tests tend to have low power so that it is difficult to reject the
null hypothesis of a unit root in the presence of an actual near-unit root.[3] Interestingly enough, the autocorrelation functions typically exhibited gradual
decay and the partial autocorrelation functions tended to indicate a spike in
the first lag for each series suggesting the series were best captured by an AR
process. However, the magnitude of the spike tended to be somewhat small,
usually around 0.93 or less, which is smaller than one would expect if the unit
root hypothesis were correct. We will proceed on the basis that each series is
integrated of order one, i.e., $I(1)$.

Finally, we must take into account the energy price shocks. Data on the
energy price component of the CPI revealed there were strong price shocks in
1974, 1979, 1986, and 1991. Energy prices increased dramatically in 1974 and
again in 1979 because of actions taken by OPEC. Then energy prices fell
almost as dramatically in 1986 because of the Iran – Iraq war and because
other OPEC members like Nigeria were producing above their allotted quo-
tas. Finally, prices rose once again in 1991 due to the Gulf War. The rate of
growth in energy prices over time also appears to have increased after 1974
relative to the 1950's and 1960's.

To capture the effect of this activity on the trend in output, we constructed
the following dummy variables,

SPIKE = 1 for $t = 1974$ and   SPIKE = 0 otherwise,

SLOPE = 0 for $t < 1974$,   and   SLOPE = $(t - 1974)$ for $t \geq 1974$,

OIL = 0 for $t < 1974$ and $1986 < t < 1991$,

OIL = 1 for $1974 \leq t \leq 1986$,   and $t \geq 1991$.

SPIKE allows for a single change in the intercept of the time trend function
and captures the idea that the price increase in 1974 signaled a new era in
energy pricing that private agents had to respond to. SLOPE alters the slope
of the time trend function after 1974 to reflect the higher growth rate in oil
prices after 1974. The variable OIL allows for a shift in the intercept of the
trend function to occur for the periods 1974–1985 and 1991–1993 when oil
prices were especially high during our sample period. We expect each dummy
variable to exert a negative effect on output.

We also included a ratchet variable designed to capture the impact of

---

[3] Some researchers have recently questioned the importance of unit root testing. See Perron
(1989), DeJong and Whiteman (1992), and Hamilton (1994).

rapidly rising energy prices. $\text{RATCHET}(t) = P(t) - P(t-1)$ if $P(t)$ is the highest energy price to date and $\text{RATCHET}(t) = 0$ otherwise, where $P(t)$ is the producer price index for crude oil and products, taken from the DRI McGraw-Hill database, following Smyth (1994) and Hamilton (1996). The idea is that rapidly increasing oil prices have a negative impact on the economy while a drop in oil prices has little or no effect. This suggests the ratchet effect should be negative.

3. The main results

Our results are displayed in Table 1. A blank in the table indicates the variable was either not statistically significant at conventional levels, e.g., OIL in (1.1), or was not included in the regression equation, K2 in (1.1). Equations (1.1)–(1.4) involve TG, (2.1) and (2.2) involve SLG, and (3.1) and (3.2) involve SLHWY. We focus on use of K2 in (2) and (3) since most researchers using aggregate data have used versions of K2 instead of K1.

The DOLS technique allows us to measure the coefficients of the technology very precisely; all of the estimated coefficients presented in Table 1 are highly significant, most with p-values less than 1%. Second, the DOLS technique eliminated any serial correlation that was initially present. The Ljung-Box q statistics indicate that serial correlation is not a problem in each case. We also conducted the Breusch – Godfrey LM test for serial correlation and could not reject the hypothesis that the residuals are not serially correlated. Third, the residuals also appeared to be white noise; the Jarque-Bera test for normality indicated the residuals were normally distributed with a mean of zero. Finally, the coefficients all have the expected sign with one exception, RATCHET in (1.2), and are of reasonable magnitude.

There are a number of important conclusions to be drawn. First, equation (1.1) can shed light on the disparity in results between Aschauer (1989) and Tatom (1991). The two analysts reached opposite conclusions using similar data primarily on the basis of controlling for the energy price shocks. Equation (1.1) involves data proxies similar to those used by Aschauer and Tatom. The estimated coefficient for public capital is approximately equal to the effect estimated by Aschauer (0.39), even though we have controlled for the energy price shocks. On the other hand, Tatom's point about the importance of the energy price shocks also appears to be correct since the coefficients for two of the oil price shock variables are highly significant. Notice that the SLOPE coefficient reduces trend growth from 0.45% to 0.41%, a 9% reduction.

Second, the productivity of public capital depends critically on which proxies are used for the private inputs. Use of employment rather than labor hours as the proxy for labor tends to raise the productivity of public capital. To see this, compare row five where $G = TG$ in (1.1) with (1.2), row five in (1.3) with (1.4), row 6 in (2.1) with (2.2), and row 7 in (3.1) with (3.2). In each case use of employment instead of labor hours leads to a larger coefficient for the public capital variable except in one case ($G = \text{SLHWY}$) where the coefficients are virtually the same. This is of interest since most researchers using aggregate data have used labor hours as the proxy for labor, rather than employment.

Next, notice that use of K2 instead of K1 causes the productivity of total public capital (TG) to fall dramatically. To see this compare row 5 in equa-

Table 1. Results for TG, SLG, SLHWY
(dependent variable: index of industrial production)

	1.1	1.2	1.3	1.4	2.1	2.2	3.1	3.1
L1	0.4		0.42		0.36		0.31	
L2		0.24		0.42		0.25		0.19
K1	0.362	0.38						
K2			0.35	0.28	0.402	0.35	0.45	0.47
G = TG	0.375	0.4	0.14	0.24				
G = SLG					0.134	0.20		
G = SLHWY							0.088	0.087
CONSTANT	−4.1	−3.9	−5.3	−6.7	−5.28	−5.11	−5.1	−4.97
TREND	0.0045	0.0035	0.0144	0.011	0.012	0.01	0.013	0.0134
SPIKE	−0.015	−0.0176	−0.0134	−0.0081	−0.011		−0.017	−0.0131
SLOPE	−0.004		−0.0068	−0.0027	−0.0049		−0.005	−0.0027
OIL				−0.0036	−0.0056	−.0087	−0.0067	−0.0082
RATCHET		0.068	−0.041		−0.034			
AIC	−271	−264	−275	−272	−271	−271	−273	−268
SC	−250	−243	−254	−245	−247	−252	−251	−245
DW	1.98	1.94	2.04	2.2	2.08	2.05	1.97	1.9
Q(1)	0.22	0.004	0.1	1.2	0.15	0.19	0.0	0.075
p-value	64%	95%	74%	28%	70%	89%	99%	78%
Q(10)	4.7	10.02	10.03	8.2	5.7	5.1	3.3	2.9
p-value	90%	44%	44%	60%	84%	88%	97%	98%
CRS(L, K)	no	no	no	no	no	no	no	no
CRS(L, K, G)	no	no	no	yes	no	no	no	no
K = G	yes	yes	no	yes	no	no	no	no
G (w/o shocks)	0.45	0.4	0.28	0.34	0.264	0.194	0.19	0.16

All variables listed are significant at the 1% significance level. AIC = Aikaike Information Criterion, SC = Schwartz Criterion, DW = Durbin Watson Statistic, $Q(j)$ = Ljung-Box q-stat for j lags, p-value = significance level of the q-stat. CRS(X) = hypothesis test of constant returns in the vector X; $K = G$ for $G =$ TG, SLG, and SLHWY tests the hypothesis that private capital and public capital have the same effect on output; and G (w/o shocks) is the effect of $G =$ TG, SLG, SLHWY on output when the oil price shock variables are omitted from the equation, ceteris paribus.

tion (1.1) with (1.3) and row 5 in equation (1.2) with (1.4). Notice that
0.14 < 0.375 and 0.24 < 0.40. Public capital has the smallest effect when labor
hours and the BEA's index of private capital are used as the proxies for the
private inputs.

Fourth, most researchers have discovered that public capital has less of an
effect when state and local public capital or highway capital is used as the
proxy for public capital. This is also borne out in Table 1. Both SLG and
SLHWY exert a smaller effect than TG. Indeed, highway capital has a much
smaller impact than total public capital.

Fifth, the productivity of the private inputs typically depends on which
proxies are used for the private inputs and which proxy is used for public
capital. Labor productivity is typically lower when SLG or SLHWY is used
for public capital instead of TG, while private capital's productivity is higher,
ceteris paribus. Second, labor productivity is not affected by using K2 instead
of K1 for private capital when TG is used for public capital and labor hours is
used to proxy for labor but is much higher when K2 is used and employment
proxies for labor instead; 0.42 in (1.4) is larger than 0.24 in (1.2). Third, the
coefficient for K1 increases significantly in magnitude when employment is
used rather than labor hours and TG proxies for public capital. However, the
coefficient for K2 *decreases* significantly when employment is used instead of
labor hours and TG proxies for public capital.

Sixth, it is also clear that Tatom's point about the importance of controlling for the energy price shocks also holds up fairly well across equations. The
coefficients for the variables SPIKE, SLOPE, and OIL are always negative in
sign when they are statistically significant. The productivity of public capital is
the same or higher in every equation in Table 1 when the energy price shocks
are omitted from the regression equation. Also, the slope dummy variable
designed to capture the increased growth rate in energy prices since 1974 reduces the trend growth rate in the dependent variable, industrial production,
by a significant amount in each of the three cases where the trend variable was
significant. For example, in the last case trend growth is reduced from 1.1% to
0.29%, a significant reduction.

The results involving the ratchet effect are somewhat mixed. It is statistically significant and negative in two of the eight cases considered, (1.3) and
(2.1), however, it is positive in (1.2), which is counterintuitive. Interestingly
enough, switching from labor hours to employment reduces the magnitude of
the ratchet effect to zero when K2 proxies for private capital, ceteris paribus.
To see this, compare (1.3) with (1.4) and (2.1) with (2.2).

Finally, we tested three hypotheses. First, we can reject constant returns to
scale in private inputs in all eight cases. Second, we can reject constant returns
to scale in all inputs in seven of the eight cases. Third, we can reject the hypothesis that private capital and public capital have the same productivity at
the margin in five of the eight cases. Private capital is at least as productive as
public capital and typically much more so in most of the cases considered.

4. Conclusion

We have undertaken a sensitivity analysis of the production function
approach to measuring the productivity of public capital. Different proxies
were used for the private inputs, several proxies were used for the public cap-

ital input, and several dummy variables were included to control for the oil price shocks of recent history. The DOLS estimation procedure was used to control for serial correlation and the possible endogeneity of the right hand side regressors.

A key conclusion of this paper is that the productivity of public capital depends on which proxies are used for the private inputs and which proxy is used for the public input. Another finding is that the productivity of the private inputs depends on which proxies are used for the inputs. Finally, controlling for the oil price shocks is of some importance. Public capital tends to have a smaller measured productivity when the oil price shocks are included in the model.

References

Aschauer D (1989) Is public expenditure productive? Journal of Monetary Economics 23:177–200

Batina RG (1998) On the long run effects of public capital and disaggregated public capital on aggregate output. International Tax and Public Finance 5:263–281

DeJong D, Whiteman C (1992) Reconsidering trends and random walks in macroeconomic time series. Journal of Monetary Economics 28:221–254

Gramlich E (1994) Infrastructure investment: A review essay. Journal of Economic Literature 32:1176–1196

Hamilton D (1996) How productive are public capital, private capital, human capital, and R&D in the US? mimeo

Hamilton J (1994) Time series analysis. Princeton University Press, Princeton New Jersey

Hamilton J (1996) This is what happened to the oil price – macroeconomy relationship. Journal of Monetary Economics 38:215–220

Katz A, Herman S (1997a) Improved estimates of fixed reproducible tangible wealth, 1929–1995. Survey of Current Business: 69–92

Katz A, Herman S (1997b) Fixed reproducible tangible wealth in the United States, Revised estimates for 1993–95 and summary estimates for 1925–96. Survey of Current Business: 37–47

Munnell A (1990) Why has productivity growth declined? Productivity and public investment. New England Economic Review: 1168–1179

Munnell A (1992) Policy watch: Infrastructure investment and economic growth. Journal of Economics Perspectives 6:189–198

Perron P (1989) The great crash, the oil price shock, and the unit root hypothesis. Econometrica 57:1361–1401

Smyth DJ (1994) Inflation and growth. Journal of Macroeconomics 16:261–270

Stock J, Watson M (1993) A simple estimator of cointegrating vectors in higher order integrated systems. Econometrica 61:783–820

Tatom J (1991) Public capital and private sector performance. Federal Reserve Bank of St. Louis Review: 3–15